CORPUS LINGUISTICS AT WORK

SCL

Studies in Corpus Linguistics

Studies in Corpus Linguistics aims to provide insights into the way a corpus can be used, the type of findings that can be obtained, the possible applications of these findings as well as the theoretical changes that corpus work can bring into linguistics and language engineering. The main concern of SCL is to present findings based on, or related to, the cumulative effect of naturally occuring language and on the interpretation of frequency and distributional data.

General Editor
Elena Tognini-Bonelli

Consulting Editor
Wolfgang Teubert

Advisory Board
Michael Barlow (*Rice University, Houston*)
Robert de Beaugrande (*UAE*)
Douglas Biber (*North Arizona University*)
Chris Butler (*University of Wales, Swansea*)
Wallace Chafe (*University of California*)
Stig Johansson (*Oslo University*)
M.A.K. Halliday (*University of Sydney*)
Graeme Kennedy (*Victoria University of Wellington*)
John Laffling (*Herriot Watt University, Edinburgh*)
Geoffrey Leech (*University of Lancaster*)
John Sinclair (*University of Birmingham*)
Piet van Sterkenburg (*Institute for Dutch Lexicology, Leiden*)
Michael Stubbs (*University of Trier*)
Jan Svartvik (*University of Lund*)
H-Z. Yang (*Jiao Tong University, Shanghai*)
Antonio Zampolli (*University of Pisa*)

Volume 6

Elena Tognini-Bonelli

Corpus Linguistics at Work

Corpus Linguistics at Work

ELENA TOGNINI-BONELLI

JOHN BENJAMINS PUBLISHING COMPANY
AMSTERDAM / PHILADELPHIA

The paper used in this publication meets the minimum requirements of American National Standard for Information Sciences — Permanence of Paper for Printed Library Materials, ANSI Z39.48-1984.

Cover design: Françoise Berserik
Cover illustration from original painting *Random Order*
by Lorenzo Pezzatini, Florence, 1996.
Typeset by Ipotesi, Montecatini Terme, Italy

Library of Congress Cataloging-in-Publication Data

Tognini-Bonelli, Elena.
   Corpus linguistics at work / Elena Tognini-Bonelli.
      p.   cm. -- (Studies in corpus linguistics, ISSN 1388-0373 ; v. 6)
   Includes bibliographical references and index.
      1. Linguistics--Methodology. 2. Computational linguistics. 3. Applied linguistics. I. Title.
II. Series.
P128.C68.T64   2001
410'1--dc21   2001025061
ISBN 90 272 2276 2 (Eur.) / 1 58811 061 3 (US) (Hb; alk. paper)

© 2001 – John Benjamins B.V.
No part of this book may be reproduced in any form, by print, photoprint, microfilm, or any other means, without written permission from the publisher.

John Benjamins Publishing Co. · P.O.Box 75577 · 1070 AN AMSTERDAM · The Netherlands
John Benjamins North America · P.O.Box 27519 · Philadelphia PA 19118-0519 · USA

For John
Giulianina
and Giovanni

Contents

Acknowledgements	xi
1. Introduction	**1**
Corpus linguistics: between theory and methodology	1
An empirical approach to the description of language use	2
Language as function in context	4
The input of the new technologies	5
Different corpora for different purposes	6
This book	9
The corpora used in this book	12
2. Language teaching	**14**
When the corpus does not prove the point: the example of *any*	15
Defining extended units of meaning: the example of *fickle* and *flexible*	18
Extended units and meaning disambiguation: the example of *all but*	25
Extended units and communicative grammar: the example of *except that*	29
Extended units of meaning - a view of synonyms as false friends: the example of *largely* vs *broadly*	33
The cumulative side of usage and syllabus design	40
Conclusion: discovery procedures, changing roles and self-access	41
3. Corpus issues	**47**
Introduction	47
The rise of corpus linguistics	50
Corpus definition	52
Issues: authenticity	55
Issues: representativeness	57
Issues: sampling	59
Conclusion	62

4. The Corpus-based approach — 65
Definition — 65
Insulation — 68
Standardisation — 71
Instantiation — 74
Discussion - the corpus-based approach — 78

5. The corpus-driven approach — 84
Introduction — 84
Definitions — 87
Word and lemma — 92
Conclusion — 98

6. Item and environment — 101
Extended units of meaning — 103
Extended units of meaning: the example of *the naked eye* — 104
Extended units of meaning: the example of *proper* — 106
Semantic prosodies — 111
Semantic prosodies: the example of *andare incontro* — 113
Delexicalisation — 116
Delexicalisation: the example of *real* — 118
Delexicalisation: the example of *bel* — 120
Ideology — 123
Conclusion — 128

7. Working with corpora across languages — 131
Introduction — 131
Progressive steps between form and function — 132
The example of *in (the) case (of)* and its Italian equivalents — 136
The example of *real* and its Italian equivalents — 144
Items and their collocates: a web of relations across languages — 150
Conclusion — 154

8. The contextual theory of meaning	**157**
9. Historical landmarks in meaning	**165**
The historical and evolutionist period	166
European structuralism: Saussure	167
The structuralist approach to meaning - Bloomfield and Zelig Harris	170
Formal grammars - Chomsky	173
10. Conclusion	**177**
Corpus-driven linguistics (CDL): position statement	177
Goals	177
Standpoint	178
Methodology	178
Categories	179
Body of knowledge	179
This book: assumptions and issues	180
Concluding remarks	184
References	**187**
Appendix 1 Concordance of *all but*	203
Appendix 2 Exercise on *all but*	205
Appendix 3 Exercise on *except that*	206
Appendix 4 Concordance of *proper*	207
Appendix 5 Concordance of *andare incontro*	209
Appendix 6 Concordance of *in the case of*	211
Appendix 7 Concordance of *nel caso di/del/della*, etc.	213
Appendix 8 Concordance of *in case of*	215
Appendix 9 Concordance of *in caso di*	217
Index	219

Acknowledgements

In attempting the task of putting together a full-length book on the uses of corpora in language work I have been greatly encouraged by several distinguished colleagues, whose gentle pressure counterbalanced more mundane demands on my discretionary time. I must particularly mention Maurizio Gotti, Rema Rossini Favretti and Carol Taylor Torsello, my mentors in Italy, and Wofgang Teubert, my collaborator in the series I edit and the journal he edits; their faith in me moved mountains and their example inspired me when I felt overburdened.

A word of thanks is due to the people who allow the availability of corpora for research and specifically when the corpora are the result of a corporate effort often involving a commercial partner; this was more the case in the early days of corpus work and less now that corpora can be assembled fairly easily. However, large holdings such as the Bank of English are still beyond the efforts of individual scholars. Now that Bank of English is available to scholars from all over the world through the web, one may forget that only a few years ago this was not so. Without the generosity of these people many of the early studies in corpus linguistics would have been severely limited. This volume, for a start, would have probably never seen the light.

Here, I would like to express my thanks specifically to Jeremy Clear, former Director of Cobuild, for support in access to the corpora of the Bank of English and Antonio Zampolli, Director of the Istituto di Linguistica Computazionale, Pisa, for access to a corpus of contemporary Italian.

The position outlined in this volume was at the basis of my proposal to Benjamins for the series "Studies in Corpus Linguistics" where the volume is published; I am very much indebted to Kees Vaes for his trust at a time when corpus linguistics was not yet fashionable and his continuing support.

In the process of compilation, several colleagues were good enough to read and comment on early versions of some of the chapters and this final version has profited a great deal from their constructive comments and encouragement. In particular I would like to thank Bengt Altenberg, Mona Baker, Geoff Barnbrook, Silvia Bernardini, Chris Butler, Sylviane Granger and Michael Stubbs.

There are copious references to the work of John Sinclair throughout this book because the theoretical framework that I have used is his; in his other role as my husband he cleared time for me and helped and supported me through the periods when I thought the book would never be finished.

1 Introduction

Corpus linguistics: between theory and methodology

The problem of defining corpus linguistics and whether as a theory or a methodology has been debated from different standpoints. It has been argued that corpus linguistics is not really a domain of research but only a methodological basis for studying language. Many linguists working with a corpus, however, tend to agree that corpus linguistics goes well beyond this purely methodological role. Halliday, for instance, points out that corpus linguistics re-unites the activities of data gathering and theorising and argues that this is leading to a qualitative change in our understanding of language (1993c:24). Other linguists point out the connection between the use of computational, and consequently algorithmic and statistical, methods on the one hand, and the qualitative change of the observations that derive from this approach on the other. What we are witnessing is the fact that corpus linguistics has become a new research enterprise and a new philosophical approach to linguistic enquiry.

In this context we take the view that although corpus linguistics belongs to the sphere of applied linguistics, it differs from other partner disciplines under the same umbrella in that it can be seen as a *pre-application methodology*. While a methodology can be defined as the use of a given set of rules or pieces of knowledge in a certain situation, by "pre-application" we mean that, unlike other applications that start by accepting certain facts as *given*, corpus linguistics is in a position to define its own sets of rules and pieces of knowledge *before* they are applied; this leads the linguist to make use of some new parameters to account for the data, and this entails a change in what can be referred as the *unit of currency* for linguistic description. corpus linguistics has, therefore, a theoretical status and because of this it is in a position to contribute specifically to other applications. Among the areas which have benefited from the input of corpus linguistics are lexicography, language teaching, translation, stylistics, grammar, gender studies, forensic linguistics, computational linguistics, to quote but a few. In this book we are just concerned with exploring the new approach brought about by corpus linguistics and relating it to the fields of language teaching and translation.

Before we go on to characterise the discipline of corpus linguistics in some detail, we should consider what we mean when we refer to a *corpus*. A corpus can be defined as a collection of texts assumed to be representative of a given language put together so that it can be used for linguistic analysis. Usually the assumption is that the language stored in a corpus is naturally-occurring, that it is gathered according to explicit design criteria, with a specific purpose in mind, and with a claim to represent larger chunks of language selected according to a specific typology. Not everybody, of course, goes along with these assumptions but in general there is consensus that a corpus deals with natural, authentic language. These issues, which are just mentioned in passing for the time being, are addressed in some detail in Chapters Three and Four.

Here, let us just characterise the approach to corpus work adopted along three lines: it is an *empirical approach* to the description of *language use*; it operates within the framework of a *contextual and functional theory of meaning*; it makes use of the *new technologies*.

An empirical approach to the description of language use

Corpus work can be seen as an *empirical approach* in that, like all types of scientific enquiry, the starting point is actual authentic data. The procedure to describe the data that makes use of a corpus is therefore *inductive* in that it is statements of a theoretical nature about the language or the culture which are arrived at from observations of the actual instances. The observation of language facts leads to the formulation of a hypothesis to account for these facts; this in turn leads to a generalisation based on the evidence of the repeated patterns in the concordance; the last step is the unification of these observations in a theoretical statement.

Given that a corpus is a collection of texts, the aim of corpus linguistics can be seen as the analysis and the description of *language use, as realised in text(s)*. Corpus linguistics starts from the same premises as text-linguistics in that text is assumed to be the main vehicle for the creation of meaning. The question that arises, however, is: can we evaluate *corpus evidence* in the same way as we evaluate a *text*? In spite of the initial starting point which they share, one has to accept that the two approaches are fundamentally and qualitatively different from several points of view (see Table 1 below).

Working within the framework of a contextual theory of meaning, we can say that a text exists in a unique communicative context as a single, unified language event mediated between two (sets of) participants; the corpus, on the other hand, brings together many different texts and therefore cannot be identified with a unique and coherent communicative event; the citations in a corpus - expandable from the KWIC format to include *n* number of words - remain fragments of text and the significant elements in a corpus are the patterns of repetition and patterns of co-selection. This difference entails a different "reading" of the two: the text is to be read horizontally, from left to right, paying attention to the boundaries between larger units such as clauses, sentences and paragraphs. A corpus, examined at first in KWIC format with the node word aligned in the centre, is read vertically, scanning for the repeated patterns present in the co-text of the node.

The text has a function which is realised in a verbal cotext, but also extends to a specific context of situation and a specific context of culture; a text is interpreted above all functionally. The corpus, on the other hand, does not have a unique function, apart the one of being a sample of the language gathered for linguistic analysis; the parameters for corpus analysis are above all formal.

The type of information one draws from a text is interpreted as meaningful in relation to both verbal and non-verbal actions in the context in which they occur and the consequences of such actions. The type of information gathered from a corpus is evaluated as meaningful in that it can be generalised to the language as a whole, but with no direct connection with a specific instance.

Using a Saussurian terminology one can conclude by saying that text is an instance of *parole* while the patterns shown up by corpus evidence yield insights into *langue*.

A TEXT	A CORPUS
read whole	read fragmented
read horizontally	read vertically
read for content	read for formal patterning
read as a unique event	read for repeated events
read as an individual act of will	read as a sample of social practice
instance of *parole*	gives insights into *langue*
coherent communicative event	not a coherent communicative event

Table 1

The series of contrasts between corpus and text outlined above have the purpose of differentiating two sources of evidence that may appear similar but that entail very different analytical steps. It is important to understand that a corpus contains text evidence and therefore, given a different methodological framework of analysis, it yields insights into the specific text as well. The corpus, in fact, is in a position to offer the analyst a privileged viewpoint on the evidence, made possible by the new possibility of accessing simultaneously the individual instance, which can be read and expanded on the horizontal axis of the concordance[1] and the social practice retrievable in the repeated patterns of co-selection on the vertical axis of the concordance. Here, frequency of occurrence is indicative of frequency of use and this gives a good basis for evaluating the profile of a specific word, structure or expression in relation to a norm. The horizontal axis also portrays, at the local level, the syntagmatic patterning, while the vertical axis yields the paradigmatic availability; that is the choice available to a speaker or a writer at a given point and within a certain language system.

Language as function in context

> Speech events have to be apprehended in their contexts, as shaped by the creative acts of speaking persons.
> (Firth 1957:193)

The approach outlined above works within the Firthian framework of a *contextual theory of meaning,* where a text is seen as an integral part of its context and the formalisation of contextual patterning of a given word or expression is assumed to be relevant to the identification of the meaning of that word or expression. The specific parameters of the Contextual Theory of Meaning are discussed in Chapter Nine. Here we will just address a few points relevant to the definition of the approach to corpus work that we are proposing.

For Firth, every utterance occurs in a culturally determined *context of situation*, involving the participants in the interaction, both in terms of their verbal and their non-verbal actions, the relevant objects and the effect of the verbal action. Perhaps the most basic assumption behind this view is that what we do and what we say are inextricably related, and that language is seen as action.

Firth, of course, developed the contextual theory of meaning in order to analyse a text, not a corpus. But, as we have seen above, a corpus contains texts and the type of parameters for the contextual analysis of meaning identified by Firth are particularly well suited to the analysis of a corpus. The relation of utterance to context is a special case of Item and Environment, and it persists when applied to smaller units of language than the sentence. When a clause, a phrase, a word or a morpheme is examined, each is found to occur in a context - and the verbal co-text is at least as important as the wider cultural context. The assumption is that every linguistic item occurs in a context, and that context is highly relevant for the determination of the meaning of the item, whether it be a word or a sentence. A small-scale linguistic item, such as a word, relates principally to its role in its verbal context, while a large-scale item such as an utterance relates principally to its role in the context of culture. The distinction, however, is not absolute. An utterance may relate intricately to the previous utterances as well as to the wider context, and a single word might contrive a direct relationship with the context of culture as well as contributing to the structure and meaning of an utterance. But the point to establish here is that there is no intrinsic difference in the relationship between item and environment, whether it is the linguistic or the cultural context.

Firth defined two related formal features in the context, *collocation* "the mere word accompaniment, the other word-material in which they are most commonly or most characteristically embedded" (in Palmer 1968:169) and *colligation* "the interrelation of grammatical categories in syntactical structure" (ibid.:183). Both these relationships between words had to be identified and analysed in order to make statements of meaning. Collocation and colligation are both formal features of a text and the alphabetised concordance lends itself remarkably well to the identification of such patterns. But it is important to note that, for Firth, a collocation, which at the verbal level can be seen as a meaningful relationship between two words in each others' environments, at the more extended level of context of situation and context of culture is the same kind of linguistic event as the relationship between a conversation and its cultural context.

The input of the new technologies

It is now generally assumed that corpus work makes use of the input of the *new technologies*. The computer, which has come to be associated with Corpus Linguistics, is usually seen as a very fast tool; as such it is used to process, in real time, a quantity of information that could hardly be envisaged by a team of informants working over decades even 50 years ago (cf. Nelson Francis 1992); as a tool, by its nature, it has affected the methodological frame of the enquiry by speeding it up, systematising it, and making it applicable in real time to ever larger amounts of data. In this respect the computer has made possible unrestricted access to the observation of language in use, and its analytic power has altered the nature of observation.

An important point related to the use of the new technologies is the ease with which, at the click of a button, the linguist can now assemble corpora *ad hoc*, selected according to specific language varieties, genres, topics, etc., and the specific function of the analysis for a given application. This, of course, is not new to linguistic enquiry, but what used to be an analytic technique for just a few researchers has suddenly been made available for most people in the language business - teachers and students, translators and lexicographers alike. Nowadays, anybody who owns a PC (and most people do) is able to assemble materials from the Web, scan electronic databases on CD-ROM or connect to one by remote access. Downloading electronic texts from distant sites is now comparable to what used to be photocopying an article or two from a journal. What this entails at a very practical level is an increasing *awareness of language variety*. This is, of course, very important for language scholars and below we discuss some of the different corpora that can be used for different purposes.

In corpus work there is certainly no shortage of data: indeed, texts are so plentiful that it becomes imperative to evaluate them according to a typology. The theoretical shift brought about by the computer here, just by enabling sheer accessibility to lots of texts, is from the focus on a notion of central grammar, core lexicon and general rules to a more decentralised notion of contextual appropriacy, geographical and social variety, restricted language, idiolect and style.

Different corpora for different purposes

The decisions made in assembling a corpus, or the choice of what type of corpus to access if one is going to be just a user, depend on what is the use to which the corpus is going to be put. In this respect it might be better to talk of *corpora* in the plural rather than imply some kind of unique type of corpus, good for all purposes. We discuss the issue of representativeness which concerns the corpus assembler in Chapter Three. Here, from the point of view of the corpus user we will just mention some corpora, distinguishing them according to the function they can have and the insights they can offer for different types of linguistic enquiry. The list is not exhaustive but it offers an indication of the possibilities offered by the use of corpora in different applications.

In the field of *multilingual resources*, translation scholars and contrastive linguists prioritise different types of corpora depending on whether they are focusing on translation as a process or as a product. When working across languages it is advisable to consider the evidence of both *translation corpora* and *comparable corpora* because they have very different things to offer.

Translation corpora are corpora of texts which stand in a translational relationship to each other, that is to say the texts can each be a translation of an absent original or one of them can be the original and the other(s) translation(s). A translation corpus can be used to shed light on the process of translation itself [2]. The most common use of a translation corpus, however, remains the access to translations as products where the translated corpora reveal cross-linguistic correspondences and differences that are impossible to discover in a monolingual corpus. Within translation corpora we should differentiate between *parallel corpora* and *free translation corpora*.

The original parallel corpora were truly parallel, for example the bilingual, quasi-legal records such as the Proceeding of the Canadian Parliament. The software for aligning them relied entirely on a close, sentence-by-sentence correspondence between the two texts. Some of the corpora contained in the TELRI CD-ROM (Erjavec et al. 1998), for example, are parallel: the corpus of Plato's *Republic* translated in seventeen languages and automatically aligned up to sentence level; similarly, the corpus containing George Orwell's novel *1984* in the original and the translation into six languages.

Before parallel corpora, pretty well all translations were free translations. Translation was a fairly mysterious human skill, and judgement was by results; the method was not normally open for investigation. The application of computers to the communication industry has put pressure on people to modify their behaviour to accommodate the machines, and as a result the strict literal translations have become a growth industry, and all sorts of tools have become available which allow a translator to see much of a text as a repetition of an earlier text with small variations (see translation memories, for example).

Because of misgivings about the representativeness of strictly parallel corpora, and the poor range of choice of material translated in such a rigorous fashion, it has been customary to build up *comparable corpora*. Comparable corpora are corpora whose components are chosen to be similar samples of their respective languages in terms of external criteria such as spoken vs. written language, register, etc. However, none of them are translations; no alignment is possible, but correspondences can be established among the main linguistic features of the corpora.

In between parallel corpora, made up of *literal* translations, with common features such as that they are in a translation relationship and are alignable, and comparable corpora which are not alignable, one can see a place for corpora of *free translations*[3] which offer insights into a more coherent type of translation lying in between the parallel and the comparable corpora (see Table 2 below):

Parallel Corpus	translation relationship	alignable
Free-translation Corpus	translation relationship	not alignable
Comparable Corpus	no translation	not alignable

Table 2: Different types of multilingual corpora

In the field of *language varieties* an important milestone is the assembly of the International Corpus of English (ICE) which began in 1990 with the primary aim of providing material for comparative studies of varieties of English throughout the world. Twenty centres around the world are now making available corpora of their own national or regional variety of English, ranging from Canada to the Caribbean, Australia, Kenya, South Africa, India, Singapore, Honk Kong, etc. Each ICE corpus consists of spoken and written material put together according to a common corpus design. So the ICE corpora can also be considered *comparable* in terms of size (they all contain 500 texts each of approximately 2,000 words for a total of one million words), date of the texts (1990 to 1996), authors and speakers (aged eighteen and over, educated through the medium of English, both males and females) and text categories (spoken, written, etc.). Each of the component corpora can stand alone as a valuable resource for the investigation of national or regional variety. Their value is enhanced, however, by their compatibility with each other.

In the field of LSP, many corpora of restricted varieties are being assembled for teaching purposes very much in line with a shift towards vocational language training where students of economics, for example, are exposed preferentially to the type of language they will be using, i.e. the language of economic texts, journals and/or spoken negotiations. Nowadays it is quite easy to gain access to a CD-ROM of a specific newspaper or magazine. A collection of these (for instance of *Il sole 24 ore* or of the *Economist*), containing all published material within a certain time reference or according to a specific topic, is a valuable resource that the individual scholar or teacher can put together with very little effort.

The identification of specific *terminology* is of paramount importance in LSP. Here, it has been proved that, as in other fields, the formalisation of contextual patterning can be of great help in the identification of meaning. For example, Pearson (1998) argues that a domain-specific corpus can offer the means of identifying semi-technical terminology by focusing on the meta-linguistic patterns that are a common feature of certain types of specialised text. These patterns can be identified formally in the context of such terms and can be of great help to the learner in the formulation of terminological definitions.

Special corpora are different in principle from a corpus that features one or other variety of normal, authentic language. A corpus of conversations is not a special corpus, nor is a corpus of newspaper text, or even one particular newspaper. There is a distinction made here between variety within the limits of reasonable expectation of the kind of language in daily use by substantial numbers of native speakers, and varieties which for one reason or another deviate from the general core. The special corpora are those which do not contribute to a description of the ordinary language, either because they contain a high proportion of unusual features, or their origins are not reliable as records of people behaving normally (EAGLES 1994)[4]. Their use has to do with the assumption that, in the framework of an approach that aims to standardise and simplify the chaotic nature of natural language (see the "corpus-based" approach discussed in Chapter Four), specialised language is going to offer a tidier, if more limited, picture of the idiosyncrasies of authentic usage. In this perspective the special corpus can be used as a training corpus for annotation where a corpus that would include a wider variety of texts might complicate the training of such tools.

Another type of corpus which is specifically focusing on the teaching process and is particularly useful for error analysis is what is referred to as a *learner corpus* (see Granger 1994, 1996, 1997). This can be used to identify characteristic patterns in student's writing. Fan et al. (1999) discuss the main benefits to be gained from compiling and exploiting a corpus of learner language. They point out that it is a useful diagnostic tool for both learners and teachers and can be used to detect characteristic errors made by an individual student engaged in a specific activity. It offers the possibility of identifying the text type and/or subject discipline where errors occur most frequently, enabling the teacher to pre-teach and so pre-empt common errors. It encourages and enhances a shift towards learner autonomy, and, when proper guidance is given, it enables the language learner to become language researcher and to develop the skills required to identify, explain and rectify recurrent errors. A learner corpus can become a source of learning materials and activities. With the possibility of access to large corpora, newspaper collections, etc. students can compare across corpora and discover similarities and differences in native speaker and non-native speaker usage.

In this respect it is important to remember that corpus work should always be comparative and evidence from a specific-domain corpus should be compared with evidence from a general purpose corpus, whether the focus is on LSP, translation, the learning process itself or something else. This is particularly important in the context of language teaching where the corpus can offer students an approximation to first-hand language experience. Of course, this also poses the problem of assembling *general purpose corpora* which can be taken as representative of the language as a whole. The problem of corpus representativeness is central to corpus linguistics (cf. Biber 1990, 1994) and issues such as defining a target population and sampling become very important when assembling a corpus; these are discussed in some detail in Chapter Three. Most of these general corpora are very large indeed (300 million words) and are becoming even larger, so they are beyond the undertaking of a single individual. However they are usually made available by remote access (see the Bank of English and the BNC) or on CD-ROM.

This book

The chapters of this book address the issues discussed above and in particular consider the double role we have outlined for Corpus Linguistics as a discipline that has affected the methodological basis of several applications and at the same time has changed the linguistic object that is being applied.
With this purpose in mind the chapters take a view of corpus work as alternating between three perspectives:

1. They address some of the main issues raised by corpus work in specific linguistic applications. Here the two areas of language teaching on the one hand, and contrastive linguistics and translation on the other, are discussed.

2. They consider the positions of different schools of linguistics that make use of a corpus and discuss them in relation to their chosen stance towards corpus evidence and the way this is allowed to affect the theoretical framework of the enquiry.

3. They evaluate the insights that can be gained from corpus work and define an approach that takes full advantage of corpus evidence. The methodological steps necessary to evaluate this evidence are exemplified; the issues raised are discussed. Some important positions concerning the central notion of meaning are reviewed in order to define the theoretical framework of the approach.

Chapter Two, after this *Introduction*, plunges directly into an application where the corpus can be put to work in the context of language teaching. The chapter starts from the discussion of an example where traditional reference texts commonly used in teaching do not provide much help in terms of guidance to the student. The fact that very often the rule does not reflect the evidence of language use is a problem in language teaching and this is where the corpus can help. This is an example where corpus linguistics, in the field of language teaching, changes both the object to be taught and the way it is taught. So, this chapter exemplifies first the change in the object, what is referred to as the *change in the unit of currency*, and then illustrates a way of defining 'extended units of meaning' by identifying formal elements in the co-text of a word or expression and relating them to their function; this chapter illustrates how this approach can help the student in disambiguating between the meaning of two words, in learning grammar 'communicatively', in not misjudging synonyms as interchangeable. The chapter then goes on to briefly address the issue of syllabus design centred on frequent words and their most frequent uses. The methodological issues are then addressed and a discussion on discovery procedures, changing roles and self-access concludes the chapter.

Chapter Three moves to a more theoretical perspective and addresses the main issues related to corpus work in general. After a brief section on the way a corpus has been defined it considers the theoretical stances behind the definitions presented. In particular, the issues of the *authenticity* of the texts included in the corpus, their *representativeness* and the *sampling criteria* used in the selection of the texts are discussed and evaluated.

Chapter Four considers what can be referred as the 'corpus-based' approach as a methodology that uses corpus evidence mainly as a repository of examples to expound, test or exemplify given theoretical statements. It is argued that,in this context, the potential of corpus evidence is not exploited fully because, in order not to threaten dramatically some existing theoretical positions, the richness of language usage is in many ways sacrificed and is not allowed to shape the descriptive and theoretical statements that should ideally account for it.

Chapter Five defines, in contrast with the 'corpus-based' approach, the 'corpus-driven' approach where the corpus is used beyond the selection of examples to support or quantify a pre-existing theoretical category. Here the theoretical statement can only be formulated in the presence of corpus evidence and is fully accountable to it. This approach, it is argued, brings about a qualitative change in the description of language and shakes some major assumptions underlying traditional linguistics. One of these, discussed in this chapter, is the distinction between 'lemma' and 'inflected forms' which are usually taken as equivalent in terms of meaning and function.

Chapter Six, along the lines set by Chapter Five, addresses another issue raised by the corpus-driven approach; this is the strict interconnection existing between an item and its environment which becomes immediately visible in the alphabetised concordance. The merging of item and environment leads the corpus-driven linguist to postulate an 'extended unit of meaning' bringing together the lexical, the grammatical, the semantic and the pragmatic levels. This is what we have referred to as the change in the unit of currency entailed by the corpus-driven approach. This chapter considers in some detail the identification of such units and exemplifies the process with some examples from English and Italian. In particular, issues such as 'semantic prosodies', 'delexicalisation' and ideology are addressed and discussed.

Chapter Seven considers the multilingual perspective and proposes a methodology to work with corpora across languages. The applications here can be in the field of language teaching, contrastive language study or translation; the method illustrated goes through a series of progressive steps in generalisation and de-generalisation and identifies comparable units of meaning in two languages. The first moves towards the identification of a web of relations between L1 and L2 are presented and proposed as the way forward to build up a semi-automatic translation bench. The examples discussed to illustrate this methodology come from both English and Italian.

Chapter Eight explores the Contextual Theory of Meaning, proposed by J.R. Firth. This theory is used in this volume as the central frame for corpus-driven work and the chapter revisits the main points made by Firth and relates them to the methodological and theoretical issues raised by corpus work. Notions such as 'collocation' and 'colligation', which are central to the corpus-driven approach are explored as they were first proposed by Firth. Other assumptions, such as the fact that the focus of linguistic enquiry should be on language events which are 'typical, recurrent and repeatedly observable' are discussed and related specifically to the approach advocated in this book.

Chapter Nine traces the changing attitudes to meaning over the last century or so, concentrating on those which are seen as relevant to understanding the theoretical premises of corpus-driven work. The focus is twofold; on the one hand, the chapter explores different stances towards the notion of meaning which is taken as central to corpus-driven enquiry; on the other, it considers different perspectives on the assumption that linguistic statements can and should be derived from observable data. Neither of these two assumptions - the centrality of meaning in linguistics and the need for language study to be "data-oriented" - should be taken for granted and the aim of this chapter is to demonstrate that they have had a chequered carreer in the theories of modern linguistics.

Chapter Ten, the conclusion, argues explicitly for the setting up of Corpus-Driven Linguistics (CDL) as a discipline of its own on the grounds that it has a distinctive set of goals, a specific philosophical standpoint, a unique methodology, a set of theoretical and descriptive categories for articulating the body of the research and an accumulating body of knowledge which is particular to this domain of enquiry. The chapter then goes on to sum up some of the main issues and assumptions of the corpus-driven approach presented in this volume.

The corpora used in this book

One of the primary concerns of this book is to offer the reader a set of sample analyses that can give a taste of the insights one can derive from observing corpus evidence. The sample analyses are used as starting points for a discussion of the wider issues raised by corpus work, the underlying theoretical framework and the methodological steps necessary to analyse corpus data. There is no attempt to present an integrated view of a language or a subset of a language, and the corpora are chosen for reasons primarily of expediency.

The individual corpora used here, apart from the Italian one, are or were components of the Bank of English, which at the time of writing contains over 415 million words. What we refer to as the *Birmingham corpus* is a balanced selection of written and spoken contemporary English, mainly written. Originally called the *Birmingham Collection of English Text*, it contains 19.49 million words and was used as the basis of the first edition of the Cobuild dictionary. The *BBC corpus* contains 20.54 million words and, although it is ultimately spoken, it includes a lot of material of the type "written to be spoken". The *Economist* corpus is made up of articles exclusively from the journal; it contains 13.81 million words. The *Wall Street Journal* corpus is also made up of articles from the homonymous journal and contains 6.36 million words. The Bank of English now has a broader component "Usnews" to cover this and other sources. The Italian corpus contains written texts of contemporary Italian ranging from modern novels to articles from daily newspapers and weekly magazines, coming to 4.46 million words.

The software that has been used in retrieving data from the corpora and refining the results further is of a type which is now familiar in corpus linguistics. The fundamental operation is the preparation of a "KWIC" - Key Word In Context - concordance, where all the occurrences of a designated word or phrase are retrieved along with a standard amount of *co-text* - surrounding text - and presented as lines on the screen, with the chosen word or phrase aligned vertically and highlighted. This format dates back to the earliest non-numerical computing and has proved to be congenial to investigators and amenable to flexible post-processing. There are many implementations of KWIC now available but the two that have been mainly used here are LOOKUP and CUE. The first of these is restricted to The Bank of English, but CUE is available from *clg.bham.ac.uk*; their functionality is very similar.

Once a KWIC concordance has been made, the lines can be sorted in various ways and selections can be made according to a number of objective criteria, duplicate lines can be removed, etc. The concordance as a whole can also be processed to identify collocates, and again there are now several implementations available of essentially the same process. The co-text is specified as *n* words on the left and *m* words to the right of the *node* word, the original query word, now central in the concordance. The usual default figure is five words on either side, but this can normally be adjusted according to the needs of the investigator. The computer compiles a frequency list of all the words in the co-text and then either outputs this list (with a suitable cut-off figure, because many words will only occur once) or subjects it to one of several statistical measures. An overview of the normally used measures can be found in Clear (1993) and Stubbs (1996); essentially, the frequency of each word in the co-texts is compared with the expectation of its frequency in the corpus as a whole - if it is considerably more frequent than expected, then it may be a significant collocate of the node, and this hypothesis is tested. The collocational profile is then presented as a word list, with the frequency of each word and its score on the significance test, usually in order of significance scores. There are many other tools for refining corpus evidence, but these are the two basic ones, and all the evidence in this book is the result of one or other of them.

Notes

1. It is also likely that a corpus, especially if large like the Bank of English or the BNC, will give information on the text from which the citation is taken. So there may be some information on speaker/writer, gender, date of publication, etc. all relating to a specific text, as individual communicative event.
2. See, for instance, Baker 1993, 1996 and 1998.
3. *East meets West - A compendium of Multilingual Resources* ed. by Erjavec et al.
4. See: *http://www/ilc/pi/cnr.it/EAGLES96/corpustyp/* for a discussion on different types of corpora.

2 Language teaching

When we bring corpus evidence into the classroom it is important to understand the double role of corpus linguistics, entailing a methodological innovation and a theoretical one, because together they will account for a new way of teaching. On the one hand, at the theoretical level, the explanation of observable language facts will lead to the definition of a new unit of meaning that could not be identified and observed in detail with traditional descriptive categories. From a methodological point of view, the definition and the evaluation of such unit(s) in language, when made the focus of classroom activities, add a truly communicative angle to the teaching process and the task of discovering the rules of language usage becomes real both for the student and the teacher.

It is argued here that the theoretical starting point, in the classroom as in language study in general, can be seen in the Firthian framework and this will be discussed in some detail in Chapter Nine. Here, we will just note that the way a contextual theory of meaning finds its place in corpus work applied to the classroom is in an upward-moving model, where the student starts by examining small units and their contexts. Important collocates are identified because of their frequent presence, and they are then classified on one or more parameters - grammatical position, word class, semantic similarity, etc. The classification leads in turn to generalisations that summarise the features of the repeated language events, and from this evidence it is usually possible to form a hypothesis to account for the behaviour. This hypothesis is in effect an attribution of meaning, including functional meaning, to the formal patterns. It is expected that each distinct meaning of a word or a phrase will be associated with a unique pattern of words and phrases in its environment. By searching for unique patterns, the student is simultaneously identifying meanings.

In the context of the classroom, the methodology of corpus linguistics is congenial for students of all levels because it is a "bottom-up" study of the language requiring very little learned expertise to start with. Even the students that come to linguistic enquiry without a theoretical apparatus learn very quickly to advance their hypotheses on the basis of their observations rather than received knowledge, and test them against the evidence provided by the corpus. Of course, standard reference categories of linguistic description will be called in, explored and evaluated, but the starting point will be the direct observation of language use, rather than a theoretical category that may end up being rather remote. The domain of language teaching is a field which has traditionally brought together theory, description and methodology and has, consequently, been the first to identify, in the light of classroom performance, the actual mismatches between what is taught and what is expected from the student. In this chapter we will consider the role of corpus evidence in relation to *what* is to be taught and *how* this is best achieved. The section below will start by discussing an example that clearly shows up a typical clash between theory and description.

When the corpus does not prove the point: the example of *any*

Pedagogic grammars are often criticised for misrepresenting linguistic facts. This is often reflected in the frustration that most students experience when they are taught some rule, but when they have to produce language themselves the rule, even if applied literally, is not sufficient to guarantee a good linguistic production. What has gone wrong? Berry (1999) argues that this mismatch cannot be attributed to the process of pedagogic simplification, but to wrong input. Discussing 'the seven sins' of pedagogic grammar, one of the main points he makes is that quite often pedagogic grammars "get their facts wrong".

An example in point is the way *any* is introduced to learners and here we will consider what the students are usually taught and what corpus evidence shows. *Any* is usually presented in contrast to *some* and with reference to three types of structure (cf. Thomson and Martinet 1984:24):

- negative sentences, as in *I haven't any matches and Tom hasn't any either;* or when introduced by *hardly, barely, scarcely*
- questions, as in *Have you any money? Did you see any eagles?*
- after *if/whether*, and in expressions of doubt.

The evidence from the corpus, while indeed supporting some of the statements from the pedagogic grammar, shows a far wider degree of variation with respect to the prescribed structures. Indeed, if our teaching were to be informed by this evidence there would be no justification for the prescriptive profile of *any* discussed above. Let us consider now the concordance of *any* reported in Table 1 below.

The concordance[1] can easily be scanned for the traditional grammatical categories mentioned above. Negatives of a grammatical type are present in the co-text of *any* in citations n. 2, 9, 14, 15, 19, 20, 21, 25 and in a more extended co-text (which is not printed below) also in n. 5 and 30, coming to a total of ten instances.

1.	Today there is very little, if	**any**,	scurvy or pellagra in the South,
2.	his computer print-out, is not due to	**any**	further physical development of
3.	can play with food colours in almost	**any**	way it likes. Another ancient
5.	in the evidence to show that there was	**any**	unhappiness or that there'd been
6.	would be in any way effective, have	**any**	bearing on stopping this abuse?
7.	in doing so they intended to preclude	**any**	possibility of retreat, for they
8.	them to brush up their French - or	**any**	other language for which it was
9.	If, no guarantee that they would have	**any**	taste in common, but he always
10.	red or maybe it was white, but in	**any**	event they had seen enough to
11.	his just a cosy cul-de-sac? What, if	**any**	are your chances of promotion? How
12.	of cans may fall about our ears	**any**	day. Let me end with the best
13.	Haldane?", and offered $100 to	**any**	reader who could relate what Bal
14.	bread made without yeast. Do not eat	**any**	of it raw or boiled, but eat it
15.	not to let her be on her own at	**any**	time. She was never out of the
16.	"Yes." "Did you ever have	**any**	Jewish religion? But of course
17.	of the case, as it would have done to	**any**	of us had we been in their shoes,
18.	dog and, although one could inject	**any**	amount of serum above the snake
19.	can…" "There's no need for	**any**	of that other stuff," said Flint,
20.	protested that I never brought home	**any**	of my friends. I explained, quite
21.	sport. It's clean, we don't have	**any**	bloody jockeys in this game, thank
22.	enough, it could begin to pour at	**any**	moment. If he had had a sister
23.	low taxation, they could hardly, by	**any**	feat of self-deception, beget a
24.	guarding herself against revealing	**any**	emotion, "I'm sorry". Inside,
25.	is that you don't mean very much to	**any**	of them. A Gallup poll in February
26.	be the shape of the dialogue - or at	**any**	rate these were the words I noted
27.	going to emigrate with the twins to	**any**	old fascist dictatorship in any
28.	image of the perfect housewife.	**Any**	group-living situation brings
29.	cost even more time and money to have	**any**	influence. Max Nicholson in his
30.	out, the way it was now doing, in	**any**	way painful for him. And then she
31.	are going into hospital. The amount of	**any**	extra pension you are getting for
32.	especially thick steaks. Remove	**any**	steaks for grilling from the
33.	boat. Because the island has hardly	**any**	roads, there are very few cars -
34.	injury, and reduce the development of	**any**	scar tissue. If this information
35.	by air and during storage. Is there	**any**	truth in the fisherman's claim

Table 1: concordance to *any* from the Birmingham Corpus

We can add to those two instances of "semi-negatives" realised by the adverb *hardly* (n. 23 and 33) and, in an attempt to "stretch" the boundaries of this group, two instances of what we could call "lexicalised negatives" realised by verbs such as *preclude* and *guard against* (n.7 and 24 respectively). The total number between grammatical negatives, semi-negatives and lexical negatives is fourteen out of a total thirty-five instances.

Considering now the interrogatives, we only find a total of three instances which include the question mark in the KWIC line (n. 6, 11 and 16). Of course there may be others which need a wider context to be interpreted, but it does not look as if this pattern is very frequent. The conditionals structures seem even more rare: *if* appears in citation n. 1 and is also present in a more extended co-text in n. 27.

This brings us to a remaining set of sixteen instances of clear uses of *any* with positive structures, leaving us with the unsettling feeling that 46% of actual and recurrent patterns of usage can be simply left unaccounted for in most pedagogic grammars. Other studies (see Willis:1990 and Mindt:1997) using corpus evidence have come up with similar findings[2] (Willis finds 42% positives, while Mindt 51%) and illustrate well how easy it is for pedagogic grammars, if not to get their facts drastically wrong, then at least to leave some common patterns drastically unaccounted for.

The type of findings shown by the concordance of *any* can illustrate well the difference between the *corpus-based* and the *corpus-driven* approaches (Tognini Bonelli 1996) which will be discussed in detail in the chapters that follow. The corpus-based approach would start with a set of explicit rules - the fact that *any* is used with negative, interrogative and conditional structures - and would validate and quantify these statements using corpus data. Corpus data in itself does not prove these statements wrong but, given the chance to speak for itself, it also shows a very different picture. The corpus-driven approach builds up the theory step by step *in the presence of* the evidence. The observation of certain patterns leads to a hypothesis, which in turn leads to the generalisation in terms of rules of usage and finally finds unification in a theoretical statement.

Several studies which make use of corpus evidence point out the mismatch between prescriptive statements and linguistic facts in language teaching. For example, Kennedy (1991) considers the prepositional and the adverbial uses of *between* and *through* and argues that they are not always easy to distinguish in grammatical terms because "various meanings of the words sometimes overlap regardless of whether they function as prepositions or adverbs" (ibid.: 97). He suggests that the major grammatical distinction between the two words lies in the word class they each most frequently associate with: nouns before *between* and verbs before *through*. Other studies lead to the same type of conclusion and shed some serious doubts on the way certain grammatical structures are generally taught. Mindt (1997:45-46), for example, considers *will* and *would* and concludes that, given their very different meaning distribution (*will* is mainly associated with certainty and prediction, while *would* is mainly associated with possibility and high probability), they should be treated separately not only in a grammar for teaching purposes but also in teaching materials. Berry (1994) explores the traditional equation of *unless* with *if not* in the light of corpus evidence and finds it quite simply wrong.

This type of finding points to the fact that a lot of the mismatch between traditional descriptions and actual language usage stems from the fact that the strict interconnection between an item and its environment is more or less ignored. As Kennedy himself noted (ibid.), the traditional emphasis on the grammatical paradigm has to be revisited in favour of a more syntagmatic approach to use in context.

If our starting point is going to be the evidence from the corpus, we have to come to terms with the fact that, at the best of times, this does not fully corroborate the findings of traditional descriptions. In the context of language teaching this means that the teacher is either faced with a very heavy editing job, that is if (s)he wants to bring corpus evidence into the classroom and make it "fit" pre-established categories, or a totally new approach is needed to examine and evaluate concordances as evidence of language usage. The methodological steps which need to be mastered in order to read and draw some insights from a corpus were outlined in contrast to the ones for a text in Chapter One. The fact that the concordance will be read vertically, looking for the patterns of co-selection entertained by the node with its context, shifts the focus from a model which is primarily paradigmatic and emphasises the freedom of choice to one where the syntagmatic units established in the light of repetition on the vertical axis of the concordance take precedence. The paradigm still exists but a unit becomes a possible choice only when its boundaries are defined at the syntagmatic level.

As a consequence of this change of emphasis, the traditional units of description have to be revisited. The regularities, both lexical and grammatical, that can be identified in the context of the node define the boundaries a *new unit of currency* in linguistic description. This change might be bad news for linguists who base their descriptive statements on largely unattested evidence because it certainly points to the cracks in a theory that does not account for the data. However, in the classroom, where the need for reconciliation between language rules and language facts is more genuinely felt, this is a welcome change. Below we will discuss some examples that show this new type of unit at work in the specific context of language teaching.

Defining extended units of meaning:
the example of *fickle* and *flexible*

The work of Sinclair on the redefinition of units of meaning in the light of corpus evidence (1991, 1996c, 1998b and ff.) can be seen as the theoretical framework for his innovations in the field of lexicography (1987d, 1991 and ff.). The Cobuild series of dictionaries for learners of English is the primary result of a way of identifying and defining the meaning of words which takes into account on the one hand their contextual associations and on the other their pragmatic function. It is particularly important that it should do so because it is primarily used by learners and it is vital for them to have access to reliable information on usage. In this section we will consider the methodological steps that lie behind this way of defining meaning and examine the type of information that can be gathered directly from corpus evidence. Our aim in doing so is to exemplify a method for the analysis of meaning that can be applied to other spheres of classroom activities.

The steps proposed by Sinclair to identify units of meaning starting from a node word or phrase are the following:

1. identify collocational profile (lexical realisations)
2. identify colligational patterns (lexicogrammatical realisations)
3. consider common semantic field (semantic preference)
4. consider pragmatic realisations (semantic prosody)
(adapted from Sinclair 1996c)

The units thus described are "extended units of meaning" (ibid.) because, having started with a node as a core, they have incorporated other words in the co-text that appeared to be co-selected with it and form a regular pattern. They are, therefore, multi-word units in that they are defined by the strict correlation existing between a node and its context. They involve both lexical and grammatical realisations. These units represent a shift towards idiomaticity and phraseology in that they are chosen as single units. Only when they have reached their pragmatic function (cf. *semantic prosody* above) can they be seen as 'functionally complete' (Tognini Bonelli 1996b).

In order to exemplify the definition of these units, we will consider in turn two adjectives, *fickle* and *flexible*. We will examine first their relative concordance, then the input of a program for the statistical measure of significance which evaluates the collocational patterning (see Clear 1993)[3], then the definitions as reported by the Cobuild dictionary. We will now consider the concordance to *fickle* in the original Birmingham corpus and note a few points. The concordance was reduced every n[th] occurrence from a total of 657 instances, and is reported in Table 2 below.

The lexicogrammatical patterning of this adjective is quite clear. The nouns associated with it on the concordance - usually in subject position - realise well what Sinclair (1996c) calls "semantic preference"; there are people, whether women (*she, Marianne, mistress*), unreliable men/people (*foreigners, young men, new-found friends*), or masses (*the mass favour, voters, opinion polls, public approbation, fans*); things that have to do with fortune and luck (*National Lottery, fortunes, appetites*); the world of *fashion* and *pop* music; and the *weather*. Associated with them in collocation we find adjectives (*faddy, impatient*) and adverbs (*notoriously*) which have a definite semantic prosody (Louw 1993, Sinclair 1996c) and carry a negative pragmatic load.

in Hong Kong; and foreigners are	**fickle**.	A year or so ago many of them
Will Marianne fall for it, and be	**fickle**	# again? <p> <c> PHOTO WITH CAPTION
melodramatic and less stoic, more	**fickle**	and impatient, less abiding. And we
Africa. <p> Yet the mass favour is	**fickle**	and if questions had been on the
voters are notorily--notoriously	**fickle**,	and normally you'd say, `Oh, well,
of managers. But today fashion is so	**fickle**	and markets so quicksilver that
for. More likely to have faddy and	**fickle**	appetites and have a taste for
We all know fashion is	**fickle**,	but no one who snapped up the
have learned to live without the	**fickle**	favour of the opinion polls. <p>
me that public approbation is	**fickle**.	Favourites come and go and it is
and BBC2's Weird Night to the	**fickle**	finger of the National Lottery
beds, there to contemplate the	**fickle**	fortunes of mankind, and the joys
daring to come too close. she can be	**fickle**	in her choice of nest site; one day hold.
The group has been notoriously	**fickle**	in the past, fraught with false
is that of 1990, and pop, being a	**fickle**	mistress, is dancing to a different
emotionally safer. Young men are	**fickle**,	more so I believe, than in the
be forgiven for wondering just how	**fickle**	these new-found friends may prove -
berth themselves after Melbourne's	**fickle**	weather played havoc with England's
he could be ostracised. Fans can be	**fickle**.	Who wants a leper for an idol # If James
Roberts <p> FASHION is a	**fickle**	world where few garments rank as

Table 2: concordance to *fickle* from the Birmingham Corpus

We can conclude that to be defined as *fickle* is a criticism in the English language. Certain ideological implications can be clearly seen in operation: mass opinion is seen as a wilful and capricious force, associated - on the vertical axis of the concordance - with women (mistresses), foreigners, young men and generally unreliable people and things (in the English context, the weather, of course!).

This patterning, which is apparent in the limited number of citations above, needs to be validated in the light of a statistical measure of collocational significance which can access and evaluate the whole corpus. The collocational profile reported below (see Table 3)[4] relates to the evidence from the Birmingham corpus and is ordered by *t-score*.

In the table the first column of figures gives the frequency of occurrence of the collocate in the concordance, while the second just gives the *t-score* as the measure of significance. In it we identify fully lexical collocates which realise the semantic preference: we note the world of *fashion* and *pop* music with its *fans*, the political world with its *voters*, the *weather* and the *wind*. The adverb *notoriously* figures very prominently in the collocation profile, as in the concordance, and exemplifies the very negative semantic prosody associated with *fickle*.

is	122	6.680726
are	70	5.638230
fashion	30	5.413508

as	76	5.304710
world	32	4.832816
finger	23	4.766472
notoriously	22	4.685009
and	182	4.371409
pop	19	4.282559
can	36	4.238593
nature	18	4.105562
weather	7	4.040076
fame	16	3.968368
market	18	3.816678
public	18	3.698066
how	22	3.646457
fate	13	3.563284
business	15	3.356951
of	176	3.131655
but	46	3.130169
wind	10	3.066585
be	49	3.043708
fans	10	3.039159
voters	9	2.913951

Table 3: Collocates for *fickle* ordered by t-score

The definition from the Cobuild Dictionary embodies very clearly the choice to give weight to the contextual and pragmatic implications of this use and fully reflects the evidence from the corpus. The examples are chosen to show the contextual patterning observed in the corpus: hence the presence of the adverb *notoriously* which was a prominent collocate of *fickle*. The semantic prosody is referred to explicitly in the definition ("you disapprove ..") and in the examples (*notoriously*):

> **fickle. 1** If you describe someone as **fickle**, you disapprove of them because they keep changing their mind about what they like or want. EG *The group has been notoriously fickle in the past.......She was extremely fickle.* **2** If you say that something is **fickle**, you mean that it often change and is unreliable. *Orta's weather can be fickle.*

We will consider now the adjective *flexible* which is semantically close to *fickle*. Of course, it will prove very different from a contextual and functional point of view. Let us consider first the concordance reported in Table 4 below:

as to be both systematized and	**flexible,**	able to adapt to any
ideally suited to the increasingly	**flexible**	and diverse travel demands of
keeping future options as	**flexible**	as possible. BOOKS, magazines
bedrooms? Style of house? How	**flexible**	are you prepared to be about

negotiable and marketing costs	**flexible**	but more indispensable than
time working and other forms of	**flexible**	employment. <p> FINANCE # LAW
life-style is well organized, yet	**flexible**	enough to be able to deal with
are simplified and made more	**flexible**.	However, the NAHT warns that
network would enable us to be more	**flexible**	in how we built the system
urged the UNITA rebels to be more	**flexible**	in their conditions for a
macroeconomic policies and more	**flexible**	labour markets remain the best
in, easy out syndrome. With more	**flexible**	labour markets, it surprised
like robots and so-called FMS	**flexible**	manufacturing system)technology
<h> Private heads urged to be	**"flexible"**	on pupil drug use </h> <b> By
is still common. In contrast to the	**flexible,**	open boundaries of first-stage
Committee has stressed the need for	**flexible**	planning decisions which
of robots and other automated,	**flexible**-production	equipment. But each
spare. Rowell's plan to develop a	**flexible**	style suited to all conditions
called PEP Mortgages - The New	**Flexible**	Way To Buy Your Home. <p> A PEP
before 1940. The relatively	**flexible**	and open prewar process,

Table 4: concordance to *flexible* from the Birmingham Corpus

First of all we should note that *flexible* is very frequent compared to *fickle*: it had a total of 5,500 instances in the corpus, while *fickle* had only 657. The concordance above shows immediately a very different profile from the one for *fickle*. If there is a semantic common denominator between *fickle* and *flexible*, in that they both describe an ability to change depending on a certain situation, their contextual patterning is very different. While *fickle* qualifies people, public opinions and behaviours, *flexible* qualifies mainly abstract notions like *labour markets, employment, systems, style, ways, options, planning decisions*. At the colligational (lexicogrammatical level) it is interesting to correlate the attributive function of the adjective *flexible* with the type of abstract collocates reported above. In the very few instances where *flexible* has a human subject then it is used as a predicative adjective:

How **flexible**	**are you** prepared to be about ...
would enable us **to be more flexible**	in how we built the system ...
urged the UNITA rebels **to be more flexible**	in their conditions ...
private heads urged **to be 'flexible'**	on pupil drug use ...

We should note here that this is where the contribution of corpus-driven work is felt most positively; so many rules, such as this type of correlation between a lexical pattern and a grammatical structure, exist and are ratified by use in natural language, and yet no grammar seems to pay attention to this type of interdependence. Although mother tongue intuition guides a native speaker to use a pattern appropriately, there is no guidance when one wants to pass on this type of information to learners because this is an area of usage that is perceived only at a very subliminal level.

At the level of semantic prosodies, *flexible* does not share the negativeness of *fickle*. On the contrary, several expressions in its co-text contribute to give a very positive evaluation of flexibility, consider for example: *able to adapt.., ideally suited.., as flexible as possible.., flexible enough to be able to deal with.., simplified and made more flexible.., would enable us to be more flexible in how.., urged to be `flexible.., the need for flexible planning decisions..*, etc. The cumulative effect of such expressions builds up a very positive picture in the verbal context of this adjective[5]. If we consider now the collocational profile, reported in Table 5 below, we can see that most of the patterns identified in our limited concordance are borne out by the evidence of the corpus as a whole.

more	1304	33.485466
be	940	23.097713
and	1889	19.766361
a	1502	13.926324
is	757	12.845419
are	465	12.702035
working	169	12.164025
to	1561	11.840391
enough	163	11.628228
response	137	11.364084
labour	148	11.338164
hours	142	11.126519
approach	125	10.782257
system	126	10.032375
very	166	9.366814
less	114	9.232502
can	226	9.148192
market	103	8.658206
than	183	8.592825
strategy	60	7.423553
allow	60	7.141146
arrangements	52	7.029457
markets	56	7.021388
as	387	7.010497

Table 5: Collocates for *flexible* ordered by t-score

We had not explicitly remarked on the fact that *flexible* is a graded adjective although there were several instances of *more*, for example, preceding the node in the concordance. This pattern is confirmed in the collocational profile, where *more* is at the top in terms of significance. Other adverbs and conjunctions indicating degree confirm this: *enough, very, less, as*. The fully lexical collocates give a picture of the semantic preference associated with *flexible*, very much in the field of *labour, working (hours), market, system, approach, strategy, arrangements*. The preference for abstract notions is confirmed.

When it comes to identifying the semantic prosody, the collocational profile is not much help, unless there is a specific word which is very frequent and carries a definite prosody, as in the case of *notoriously*, discussed above. With *flexible* we find that the positive evaluation is realised in a variety of ways which are not picked up by a computer program that focuses on the recurrent coselection of individual words. A collocational profile is best read as a confirmation of observations in the concordance, after the analyst has familiarised him/herself with the repeated patterns.

Coming now to consider the Cobuild definition that is based on this evidence we read:

> **flexible. 1** A flexible object or material can be bent easily without breaking. EG *The tube is flexible but tough.* **2** Something or someone that is **flexible** is able to change easily and adapt to different conditions and circumstances as they occur; used showing approval. EG *We need a more flexible decision-making system...This is a flexible arrangement... flexible working hours...People today must be far more flexible...*

Most dictionaries give priority to the more concrete meaning in a definition, in spite of the frequency that might indicate otherwise. This dictionary makes no exception, so we find that both the evidence from our concordance and the collocational tree above exemplify mainly meaning 2 of the definition. The examples quoted well reflect the evidence from the corpus, both in terms of abstract nouns and in the predicative use associated with human subjects. The semantic prosody shown by the concordance has been built into both the definition - "used showing approval" - and the examples - *We need.. must be.. .*

To conclude this section, what we have exemplified here is a way of defining meaning as 'function in context'. This approach can be applied to lexical and grammatical words and, whether the initial node is of one type or the other, what is consistently shown by corpus work is the strict correlation between lexical and grammatical choices which extends the boundaries of the initial unit. We will come back to this point in Chapter Six where the merging of item and environment emphasised by the corpus-driven approach will be discussed in detail.

A way of defining meaning that tries to account for the interwoven choices of lexical and grammatical patterning, relating them to semantic and pragmatic weight, will give great help to language learners, particularly in the process of encoding which is usually overlooked by dictionaries and reference grammars alike. The Cobuild dictionary certainly represents a major step in the right direction and, although not fully consistent with its intentions throughout, it has opened the way to a new way of defining and disambiguating meaning.

Extended units and meaning disambiguation: the example of *all but*

We will discuss here the example of *all but* in relation to meaning disambiguation and show that the theoretical stance on the definition of extended units of meaning can help learners to identify and distinguish between particular meanings which may be neither reported in reference dictionaries nor explained with reference to grammatical structures. The example treated here came up with an English language class taught by the present writer[6]. A student asked whether *all but* is the same as *except* and the answer was positive. "So - he said - 'all but impossible' means 'all except impossible', therefore 'very possible, very likely'". This, as one can imagine, gave rise to some perplexity, because, in spite of being a fluent speaker of the language, one had never thought that the two meanings of *all but* were so completely the opposite of one another: on the one hand *all but* does mean 'except', on the other it also means 'almost completely'. What guidance could be given to the learner? Practically none. A project was made out of the initial enquiry and some reference grammars and dictionaries of usage were consulted for a description of the different function of this phrase. Quirk et al. (1985) give two different definitions in two separate chapters:

> One class of **adverbials** is that of **intensifier subjuncts** which "are broadly concerned with the semantic category of degree (..) It useful to distinguish two subsets of intensifiers (..) amplifiers (..) and **downtoners**". (8.104). (..) As a downtoner *all but* comes under the sub-category of "approximators", eg. *She all but kissed us* (8.111)
>
> One class of **prepositional meaning** is that of "exception and addition" (9.58*) (..) "the noun phrase with *but*-modification must contain a determiner or indefinite pronoun of absolute meaning (..) *no, all, any..*": eg. *All but the captain were rescued...*

The Cobuild English Usage (1992) reported:

> Used to mean 'except'. **But** is also used after 'all' and after words beginning with 'every-' or 'any-'. When **but** is used after one of these words, it means 'except': eg. *Thomas Hardy spent all but a few years in his native Dorset .. He ate everything but the beetroot..*

Other grammars reported no references to *all but* (Thomson & Martinet 1980, Huddleston 1984, Swan and Walter 1997, Cobuild English Grammar 1990). As we can see, even when a description of the two grammatical functions of *all but* was given (as in Quirk et al.) no guidance as to how, and when and in what context the two meanings were used was offered to the learner wishing to disambiguate between two opposed meanings. Recourse to corpus evidence was the obvious way forward; Appendix 1 reports the concordance for *all but* from the *Economist* corpus and the *Wall Street Journal* corpus together[7].

From a rapid scan of the concordance it was immediately visible that when *all but* was associated with certain numerals and small quantities it introduced an exception and distinguished it from the general statement; the meaning here was that of "except":

to their lowest level since August. In **all but one** of the previous 13 days the
has lasted longer than most. She beats **all but five** of her predecessors since
Yegor Gaidar, who lifted controls on **all but a few** goods a year ago. Peace
of terminology have been known to defeat **all but the most intrepid** amateur

Corpus evidence disambiguates very clearly the two meanings: Table 6 below classifies the evidence from the concordance according to the model set up in Sinclair (1996) and illustrates the first meaning, where *all but* is the same as "except".

Before we go on to consider another function of *all but* we should note one point. The evidence from the corpus brings us to notice again the interconnections between lexis and grammar and relate them to a specific function. *All but*, here, is associated with a semantic preference for small quantities which, at the grammatical level is realised by numerals and superlatives. At the lexical level, the numerals are joined by words like *a handful*, *a few* which also relate to small quantities. Superlatives come with other nouns which, although not sharing the same grammatical function, are also associated with small quantities and extreme cases because of the selection process (e.g. *the initiated, the racially pure*).

This ability to observe grammatical and lexical patterning at the same time is an important asset for the linguist and something that has not been available before. If traditionally linguists have been able to isolate and study individual lexical or grammatical patterns, it is with the advent of computerised corpora that these two types of observation can be related and evaluated as realisations of the same function. This is extremely important from the point of view of applications such as language teaching and translation where the correlations and the interconnections between lexis and grammar are at the basis of proficient linguistic production and can be immediately verified looking at the outcomes.

COLLOCATION (N + 1)	COLLIGATION	SEMANTIC PREFERENCE	SEMANTIC PROSODY
— *a handful,* *a few,*	indefinite numerals	• low numbers • small quantities	1. States exception 2. Distinguishes it from general statement
— *1,2,3,5 ..* *24.8%*	numerals, percentages	• low numbers • small quantities	1. States exception 2. Distinguishes it from general statement
— *the most intrepid* *the boldest,* *the most recent* *the narrowest,* *the wealthiest,*	superlatives	• extreme cases • low numbers • small quantities	1. States exception 2. Distinguishes it from general statement
— *the initiated,* *the racially pure*	nouns	• extreme cases because of selection process • low numbers • small quantities	1. States exception 2. Distinguishes it from general statement

Table 6: *all but* with the meaning of 'except'

On the other hand, in connection with verbs (usually in the past participle) and adjectives, in other words when *all but* has the role of an adverb, the meaning is "almost", "practically"; the function is still that of introducing an exception, but this is incorporated into the general statement. Consider some examples:

the insurance market has made insurance **all but impossible** for small employers
After the new-issue market for junk bonds **all but shut down** in 1990, American
the finance ministry off. Investors had **all but given up** hope that the government

Table 7 below illustrates the formal and functional realisations of this meaning.

COLLOCATION (N + 1)	COLLIGATION	SEMANTIC PREFERENCE	SEMANTIC PROSODY
-- *achieved* *agreed* *bound* *broken down* (2) *chased* *collapsed* *come to a halt* *declare* *destroyed* *died* *disappeared* *evaporated* *forgotten* *founded* *given up* *killed* *processed* *shut down* *slain* *stopped* *suffocated*	verbs (usu. past participles)	• break down, • removal, • nullification, • getting rid of things	1. States exception 2. Evaluates it, usu. negatively 3. Incorporates it in general statement
-- *empty* *impossible* (2) *impregnable* *inevitable* *invisible* *ungovernable*	adjectives (usu. negative prefix)	• impossibility	1. States exception 2. Evaluates it usu. negatively 3. Incorporates it in the general statement

Table 7: *all but* with the meaning of 'almost', 'practically'

As we can see, if we start from the evidence in the corpus, not only are the two meanings very clearly disambiguated by specific contextual parameters, but the semantic preferences associated with them become very tangible. The visible presence of adjectives with a negative prefix in Table 7, for example, is something that it would be impossible to postulate without access to the corpus. Again we note how the semantic common denominator can be realised in a variety of ways at the grammatical and the lexical levels: with the meaning of 'almost', 'practically', the semantic preference for impossibility and nullification is realised by a grammatical feature at the level of the adjective (the negative prefix) and by a variety of lexical items at the level of the verb.

From the point of view of language teaching, corpus evidence offers an invaluable resource because the formalisation of repeated events and the matching with the functional component allows the formulation of a clear set of correspondences. It is usual, in the type of teaching that attempts to be communicative, to start with one formal realisation of a function and to match it to a functional element. It is often difficult to teach, in practical terms and with authentic examples, the fact that one function can have a series of formal realisations both of a grammatical and a lexical type. Corpus evidence reflects very clearly the variety of natural language and it offers the data needed by the teacher to focus on a specific function and examine with the students the different realisations of this function. For example, using the concordance of *all but*, the teacher, rather than teaching a class on numerals, could decide now to teach numerals (1, 2, 3..) together with indefinite numerals (*a few, a handful*) and the superlatives (grammatical and lexical ones) as the realisations of the semantic preference for "small quantities". Exercises in meaning disambiguation can offer a valuable input because they focus the attention of the activity on the function and by asking the student to identify the formal realisations of this function the teacher is giving a good guide in the process of encoding.

The level of the semantic prosody is, according to Sinclair (1996), "the functional choice which links meaning to purpose" and it is here that the initial selection of a phrase or structure is made. The very different semantic prosodies in the two meanings of *all but* can also be brought into the classroom and distinguished according to their different lexicogrammatical realisations. Exercises can be assembled easily to familiarise the students with the use of one or another function. An example could be, for instance, splitting the citations into two parts just after *all but*, jumbling the second parts around and making them available under a different heading. The task would require the students to choose a certain number of citations to recreate one meaning and then the other. Appendix 2 reports a possible exercise familiarising the students with the grammatical and communicative functions of *all but* using corpus data.

Extended units and communicative grammar: the example of *except that*

The issue discussed in this section addresses further the possible use of corpus evidence in helping the students to approach grammar communicatively. The phrase we are taking into consideration is *except that* which, whether as a conjunction or as a preposition, is usually taken to introduce exceptions. Our aim here is to see whether corpus evidence can help to identify the communicative function of exceptions, i.e. why do we state exceptions in communication.

Having started by exploring what the grammar(s) have to offer in terms of guidance for the student, the methodological steps we will follow are:

a) move from grammar to lexical grammar
b) address an extended unit of meaning that takes in the communicative function
c) prioritise the pragmatic dimension of *why* we state exceptions

The move from grammar to lexical grammar (see Hunston and Francis 2000) is brought about by the fact that corpus evidence invariably shows the interdependency of lexical and grammatical patterning. But let us first consider how the phrase *except that* is dealt with in standard grammars.

Quirk et al. (1985:15.44), for instance, identify two grammatical roles for this phrase:

> *except that* as a **conjunction**, introduces subordinate, adverbial clauses with the semantic role of exception. Clauses of exception are introduced by several subordinators, such as: *except (that), but that...*
> e.g.: I would pay you now, *except I don't have any money on me.*
> Nothing would satisfy the child *but that I place her on my lap.*
>
> *except* as a **preposition**
> e.g. everyone passed except Richard (9.58*)

The Cobuild English Grammar (1990) mentions *except that* in connection to concessive clauses:

> Sometimes you want to make two statements, one of which contrasts with the other or makes it seem surprising. You can put both statements into one sentence by using a **concessive clause**. (...) If you want to mention an **exception** to a statement that you have just made, you use 'except that' (8.69),
> e.g. she treats her daughter the same as her younger boy *except that she takes her several times a week to a special clinic.*

Other grammars (Thomson & Martinet 1984, Huddleston 1984, Swan and Walter 1997) make no reference to *except that*. We note that neither Quirk et al. nor the Cobuild grammar seem to address the function of the phrase beyond that of introducing an exception. In this context, perhaps the most sobering input can be given by the popular saying "the exception confirms the rule". This seems to imply that at least some exceptions confirm the rule while others do not, and this provides a framework within which we can discuss the function of *except that*. Just saying that the phrase introduces an exception does not help to elucidate its meaning. The concordance we will consider to clarify this point comes from the *Economist* corpus, and no claim is made that our findings will reflect the language as a whole. Since the context needed often goes beyond the limited scope of the KWIC span, here we will report the extended context of a few indicative examples to illustrate the argument.

The case where *except that* introduces an exception that confirms the rule is well illustrated by the following example:

> (1) Pluto also has its own moon, Charon, of which hardly anything is known **except that** it is anomalously large, weighing a sixth as much as Pluto itself.

Here, if we consider the general statement (hardly anything is known of Charon) and the exception (we know only one thing: it is anomalously large) we can see that the exception does not invalidate the rule, it is still incorporated in the truth of the general statement. On the other hand, if we consider:

> (2) ... say that to trust Mr Hussein is to put their heads in a crocodile's jaws. They are right - **except that** the crocodile in question is largely defanged, with its tail locked in a trap.

In this second instance the exception, the fact that the crocodile is defanged and with its tail locked in a trap, upturns the metaphorical validity of the statement: if trusting Mr. Hussein was deemed to be dangerous to say the least, now we are told that it is not. The exception here does not confirm - and actually invalidates - the general statement. These are two examples that seem to make use of the same grammatical structure in order to convey a communicatively opposite meaning. The questions that we will try to answer are: does the exception always prove the rule? And if so, when? In what context? How do you indicate the importance of an exception? How do you teach students to deploy the strategies of exception? What kind of exercises can be built up from corpus data?

Although the structure operates, as we can see, at clause level and therefore within a wider context, the concordance shows quite clearly that a certain pattern can be associated with one function or another. When the clause preceding the exception contains an evaluative statement, as in "they are right" in the instance above, we find that the exception does not confirm the rule and the general statement is upturned as a result. Consider these examples:

> (3) It is an internal Yugoslav affair. **Nobody else needs to worry. Except that** they should. True, the Yugomess is off-puttingly complicated, a morass of unpronounceable...

(4) **That is all fine** by the Bundesbank. **Except that** the matter is now out of its hands.

(5) British political culture **could almost have been designed to hamper** British influence in the EC - **except that** so little in Westminster has been designed.

(6) Reading these mixed signals, the government promises another year of austerity. **Fine, except that** it is directed at the wrong people..

(7) an aid to understanding. **All that's fine, except that** the models have taken over. You don't use them, they use you.

(8) inviting the Dublin party to sit down with the Unionists when he thinks fit. **A fine idea, except that** the Irish first proposed it last summer, and the Unionists have alternately rejected ..

(9) **An unremarkable initiative perhaps - except that** immediately opposite the proposer were sitting half-a-dozen members of Sinn Fein, ..

Quite noticeable in these instances is the presence of the adverb *fine*, an informal use connected perhaps more with the spoken language than the written one. Other evaluative patterns are also present and in every case they are upturned by the "exception" that follows them. Here the semantic prosody, which is actually the ultimate function of the utterance, performs the invalidating of the rule. This co-exists with a general semantic preference for the field of argumentation and discourse.

If we consider other instances, though, we find that to a different formal patterning there corresponds a different overall function. In the following examples, a statement of similarity *(same, identical, similar)* precedes the exception:

(10) Compare that with cell number three, where everything is **the same except that** the exchange rate is fixed.

(11) Their copies should then be **identical** to yours **except that**, thanks to SCMS, they cannot themselves be used to make further copies.

(12) It came up with the nuclear microscope. The nuclear microscope is **similar** to EPMA, **except that** it uses a beam of protons instead of electrons to produce the tell-tale X-rays.

(13) Today would be **no different, except that** the economy might worsen because, with the cold war over, the generals could not count

As we can see, here the general statement holds in that the statement of overall similarity is still valid; the fact that there is an exception does not invalidate the statement that precedes it. The exception, therefore, is incorporated into the rule. The phrase *except that* is relatively rare: only 70 instances in the *Economist* corpus. And, of course, we would need to verify these statements with a larger corpus, especially concerning other patterns which need to be examined in the light of repeated events.

What this initial examination shows is that, by extending the outer boundaries of the unit of meaning, the full function of the unit is brought into light, and this is correlated consistently enough with the formal patterns of a lexical and/or grammatical type in the co-text. The identification of specific contextual features allows us to recognise the pragmatic function of a unit of meaning.

If we take into account these insights, our teaching of grammar will have to change completely. Traditional grammar seems to be deeply rooted in abstraction and there is still the belief that to exemplify a structure we do not need to engage with the intricacies of authentic language. Corpus-driven grammar, on the other hand, shows very clearly that any grammatical structure restricts the lexis that occurs in it (cf. Stubbs 1993, Francis 1993, Hunston & Francis 2000). This was shown, for example, by the frequent occurrence of *fine* in the clause preceding the invalidating exception, and on the other hand by the presence of the adjectives of similarity in the clause preceding the confirming exception. Native speakers have no reliable intuitions about these patterns of co-selection that exist between grammatical structures and lexical items. And yet these are what determine and shape a functionally complete unit of meaning: without the possibility of identifying these patterns it would be impossible to come to some reliable function attribution. The teacher cannot rely on traditional grammars which give no guidance about these patterns. Again, the only way forward in the classroom is to get the students to engage with the data, which means supplying it, controlling it and building it into the teaching process.

One type of exercise proposed as an example to familiarise the students with this type of evidence is reported in Appendix 5. The emphasis of the teaching will be, of course, on a communicative type of activity: getting the students to manipulate the data in order to recreate the chosen function.

Extended units of meaning - a view of synonyms as false friends: the example of *largely* vs *broadly*

We will address now an issue that is as relevant to the teaching of vocabulary in the classroom as to the lexicographer who writes the dictionary that will finally be used in the classroom. This concerns the practice of identifying the meaning of an item by giving a synonym of it. This is very common practice in dictionaries where quite often the definitions end up showing a certain circularity due to this fact. So consider, for example, these definitions of the adjectives *actual* and *real*:

> **actual 1** You use **actual** to emphasise that you are referring to something real or genuine. *The segments are filmed using either local actors or the actual people involved... Officials admit the actual number of AIDS victims is much higher than statistics reflect... The difference between their final figures and the actual result was 1.4%.*

The synonyms for this entry of *actual* in the Cobuild dictionary are *genuine* and *real*. If we consider now the entry for *real*:

> **real 1** Something that is **real** actually exists and is not imagined, invented, or theoretical. *No, it wasn't a dream. It was real...Legends grew up around a great many figures, both real and fictitious.*

The synonym given for this entry of *real* is again *genuine*. So, both *actual* and *real* are defined as synonyms of *genuine*, while *real* is also quoted as a synonym of *actual*. A lot of the way meanings are explained to learners is through offering synonyms. It is argued here that this is a potential trap for the learner because, in practice, it emphasises the denotational meaning of words, and not their usage. In a study on the different functions of the adjectives *actual* and *real* (Tognini Bonelli 1993a and 1993b) the very different uses of these two adjectives have been illustrated in the light of corpus data. What has been demonstrated is that there is no such thing as a synonym (see also Partington 1998) and, by the mere fact that two words exist, their meaning(s) tend to restrict themselves to specific areas of usage, operating in specialised contexts, with a specific collocational profile and acquiring specific pragmatic functions within the text that surrounds them.

In this section we will consider two adverbs which are often given as having a synonymous meaning, *largely* and *broadly*. We will explore their use in the light of concordance data and identify specific functions linked to specific contextual patterns; we will consider their collocational profiles based on data from the whole of the corpus. On this basis the two adverbs will be differentiated in terms of their specific use. The types of insight yielded by corpus evidence in this area are certainly very new to the classroom, but it is argued that access to this data would offer the student an invaluable input, especially in the activity of writing in the foreign language.

The corpus we are using here is the *Economist* and *Wall Street Journal* corpus. The total instances found were 2136 for *largely* and 368 for *broadly*. It is interesting to note that if we compare these frequencies with the ones in the Birmingham corpus (general English), which is a similar size, we find 1084 for *largely* and 174 for *broadly*, showing that these two adverbs are more favoured in the language of economics.

We will start by considering the adverb *largely*. The most frequent function is associated with words such as *because, thanks* (these two collocates figure at the very top of the collocational profile) and, along the same lines, we find other prominent collocates: *responsible* and *result*. Consider:

four times that of America. This **is**	**largely**	**a result of** Britain's much greate
technologies - and hit back hard.	**Largely**	**as a result,** American competitors
to the anti-nausea drug Bendectin.	**Largely**	**as a result,** Litigation Sciences
ralised government on West Germany,	**largely**	**because** they believed it would
80 to under 20% this year, that was	**largely**	**because** state spending rose so
of the Liberal Democrats. This is	**largely**	**because of** the continued backing
solution to the transfer-tax problem	**largely**	**because** it is far less costly
in some poorer areas, but that is	**largely**	**because** the health of the local
$ 2.7 billion from $ 8.6 billion,	**largely**	**because** Japanese investors were
doubtful, but hard to measure, it is	**largely**	**because of** prevention: less
mer prices rose only 0.2 % in July,	**largely**	**because of** falling energy prices
ty markets have not fallen by more,	**largely**	**because** American mutual funds
exclusivity. This strategy flopped,	**largely**	**because** the first version of the
project, for instance, collapsed	**largely**	**because** it was repeatedly
on from $333.9 million a year ago.	**Largely**	**because of** cut-rate vehicle
ker for the first time in 15 years,	**largely**	**because of** a shift of production
inflation over the past 30 years was	**largely**	**due to** monetary policy. At least,
Benhachinou, the economics minister	**largely**	**responsible for** the reforms, and
Italy, France and Britain. That is	**largely**	**thanks to** its purchase, since
than 4%. This spectacular success **is**	**largely**	**the result of** the country's
irst six months of the fiscal year,	**largely**	**the result of** woes on Wall
ter. Misguided industrial policy **is**	**largely**	**to blame for** the difficulties of
ted the state to begin its inquiry.	**Largely**	**through the efforts of** Mr. Carter

Table 8: *largely* introducing cause and reason

It is interesting to note here that, for instance, the word *result* is encoded in different phrases: something is *largely the result of... is largely a result of...* or it can be used as an initial disjunct: *Largely as a result,...* This variety can be explored in the classroom and the fact that it can be matched to a common function makes the learning of vocabulary really communicative.

The other area which is associated with *largely* is the field of basis and relation. The collocates that come with this function are all verbs such as *confined to, dependent on, consists ... of, rests ... on, based ... on, depends ... on, reflect(s), rely ... on* (see Table 9 below). We should note here that the two instances of *reflect* occur both with *largely* in position N-1. This is an interesting pattern which needs to be validated in the light of more evidence. A search of *reflect** in connection with the word *largely* can be done using most concordance programs and may confirm an initial hypothesis that this particular verb (or set of verbs) tends to affect the position of the adverb (or set of adverbs). There is no place here for such detailed inquiry, but this is just a pointer to how an hypothesis is formulated in the light of the evidence, to be further validated in the light of more evidence. Consider:

<pre>
      xperts hoped that the spill would be largely confined to Prince William Sound
    lephone exchanges, but they are also   largely dependent on European Community
    ental mutual - funds market consists   largely of reassuring bonds (see chart)
              as a killer, though, still rests largely on those unfortunate rodents.
           the charts had hitherto been based largely on oral reports - immediately
              In France, citizenship depends largely on the first, in Germany on the
                the polls. The outcome will depend largely on the alliances forged by the
         £ 400,000 per name. The estimates largely reflect extra reserves against
    are keeping the average down. That   largely reflects tight public - sector
        that the EC' s finances will rely largely upon payments from members for
</pre>

Table 9: *largely* **in the field of basis and relation**

The third group of instances associated with *largely* (see Table 10 below) is a set of morphological and semantic negatives such as verbs like *dismisses, dried up, eliminated*, etc. and adjectives like *extinct, illiterate, unconcerned*.

<pre>
           by chance that the super-rich are largely absent from the list of devastated
              nd training. Labour, by contrast, largely dismisses the government's supply
         single source of income. These have largely dried up in the wake of corruptio
          with more than 325 locations, has   largely eliminated windmills and barn
       rs. The streetcar companies now are   largely extinct, but the anti-jitney laws
       ercial banks, and - though this was   largely overlooked - urged further flows
              there is one aspect of his model, largely ignored by others, that might be
             gated for so long, blacks were left largely illiterate and without non -
    Gary Condit from California. Having   largely shunned the group, the Democratic
         Kong have had enough. Legco, the   largely toothless legislature, has vowed
    previous regime doled out large and   largely unaudited sums to homeland admin
         industries. "The government seems   largely unconcerned about such complaints
          The war caused one spectacular but largely unforeseen calamity: the mass
   majority in the country, defeating a   largely unknown Republican opponent.
                 the 'hyenas of capital' will go largely unread. Management Focus: Just de
              The dollar was slightly higher, largely unruffled by the release of the
                 rural - based Zulu party, will be largely untested: no poll will be held in
</pre>

Table 10: *largely* **in the field of morphological and semantic negatives**

These patterns are not usually very prominent on the collocation profile, because the computer identifies individual collocates, which differ in spite of the initial prefix *un**. Once this pattern has been identified in the alphabetised concordance, though, it is possible to search for *largely* in connection with the prefix and then identify the set of collocates. Here we will just note the visible presence of such negative adjectives and *-ed* forms, supported by some verbs which are morphologically (*eliminated*) or semantically (*dried up*) negative.

As a brief parenthesis we note that it is important to make the students aware of the special effects that can be generated by sheer deviation from a well established norm. Louw (1993) gives us an interesting example of the diagnostic potential of semantic prosodies applied to literary criticism. The example he uses is the adverb *utterly*, which even more regularly than largely, is associated with a set of negative collocates (*arid, blackened, confused, stupid, terrified, etc.*). Louw shows how, when such a regular semantic prosody is indicated by corpus evidence, even if an instance shows deviation from the norm it acquires the bad prosody by default. We will come back to discuss semantic prosodies in Chapter Six.

If we now consider *broadly*, we can start by saying that there is a total absence of the negatives illustrated for *largely* above. On the contrary, we find a noticeable group of instances that support the positive idea of similarity and agreement:

nd visible breaks; and these breaks	**broadly**	**coincide**. They do so partly
Soviet Air Forces now had aircraft of	**broadly**	**comparable** performance to their
their fathers' footsteps and enter	**broadly**	**comparable** occupations.
work of political activists working	**broadly**	**in unison** or at least with
is that branch committee members are	**broadly**	**representative** of their
with inter-union disputes now seem	**broadly**	**satisfactory**. But the Government
industrial societies they surveyed had	**broadly**	**similar** rates of total vertical
all English-speaking countries have	**broadly**	**similar** tenure patterns with
st Marxist-Leninism has emerged in a	**broadly**	**similar** pattern - in Europe,
eat. In nutritional terms, fish is	**broadly**	**similar** to meat. Whether you
variation of format synthesis ,and	**broadly**	**the same** as the "parcor" method
Scandinavian countries, which have	**broadly**	**the same** political and economic
and superior class. All have shared	**broadly**	**the same** school education, there

Table 11: *broadly* **in connection with similarity and agreeent**

This semantic prosody for general agreement is reinstated by the discourse role that *broadly* has as a sentence adverbial; then it either introduces a new element in the argumentation as going along with what has been said before - to a large extent and on matters that are important - or it defines what one is saying as generally true, in spite of a few exceptions. The function it has here is at a wider level and it prefaces larger chunks of text. Consider Table 12 below.

>   in the section on borrowing, but, **broadly,** they operate separately from
>   and your boy is active. **Speaking broadly,** truancy means that the school
>   fairly logical and self-explanatory. **Broadly,** if you keep to your left, you
>   ping and exploring elsewhere. But, **broadly,** my attitude to certain elements
>   ulptural and conceptual activities. **Broadly,** I agree with your estimate of
>   of the gross national product, and **broadly,** a scatter diagram of the size
>   lways welcome a well-crafted film but, **broadly,** I'm with the ``reaching out'
>   igher education as far too limited. **Broadly** speaking, the debate is between
>   se is Nigeria, where British rule, **broadly** speaking, consolidated the
>   their requirements, of course, but **broadly** speaking, there are two ways to
>   inches and some further apart, but **broadly** speaking it does n't matter that
>   political debate over this issue. **Broadly** speaking, the issue has resolved
>   to which research findings are put. **Broadly** speaking, in the Communist world
>   lds in Great Britain include a pet. **Broadly** speaking, the nutritional needs
>   exible section of any organization. **Broadly** speaking those men who have
>   situation - occupation is a third. **Broadly,** there are two types of

Table 12: *broadly* and discourse role

The other function of *broadly*, which is easily identified in the concordance, concerns the basis of something as the central and very important part or feature of it. Collocates shown up by the collocational profile are the past participles *based* and *defined*, very prominently, followed by *construed*, *spread*, and words such as *range, global, groups*. Let us consider the evidence from the concordance:

>   running a one-acre holding will also **broadly apply** to larger acreages. The
>   grapher so that I should become more **broadly based** in my career. But finding
>   campaign for Press Freedom (CPF), a **broadly based** pressure group sponsored
>   determined that the company should be **broadly based** to withstand such an
>   ngly difficult to arrive at any such **broadly based** agreement. Nevertheless,
>   PA's only two purposes and they are **broadly defined**. But quite clearly the
>   ress. For instance, what "may be **broadly defined** as the radical press was
>   the early Italian Renaissance was not **broadly enough based**. The few had gone
>   second in the new polytechnics. **Broadly it consists of** the aspirations
>   your relations with management that **broadly means** taking the initiative,

Table 13: *broadly* in the field of basis and relation

Considering the examples above, it is interesting to note that although both *largely* and *broadly* have a role in argumentation and at discourse level, this is clearly different: while *largely* qualifies specific causes and reasons in argumentation, never as sentence initial, *broadly* acts at a wider level, either as a discourse adjunct (as sentence initial), or parenthetically, qualifying a certain statement. Another point to note is that again, although they are both associated with basis and relation, *broadly* tends to co-occur specifically with *ed*-forms, thus becoming part of an adjectival compound. Moreover, the contrast between the morphological and semantic negatives, very prominent with *largely*, and the positive prosody for similarity and agreement associated with *broadly*, seal two very different usages. Table 14 below illustrates the differences between these two adverbs:

	LARGELY	BROADLY
Discourse Disjunct and Argumentation	n.a.	*more broadly ..,* *Broadly speaking ..,* *Broadly ..*
Cause and Reason	*because* (v. frequent), *thanks, due – to*	n.a.
Basis and Relation	-- *based on, relying on, depends/ed, dependent on, concentrating on*	-- *based,* -- *defined,* -- *construed*
Morphological and Semantic Negatives	*in*: illusory* *un*: unaware, unchanged, underdeveloped unpredictable, unregulated, etc.*	n.a.
Similarity and Agreement	n.a.	-- *the same, similar, in line with, popular, backing, supported, agree with, agreed*, etc.

Table 14: different functions for *largely* and *broadly*

To conclude this section, we can say that although, at an initial glance, *largely* and *broadly* may appear as synonymous, they are differentiated very clearly by the patterns of co-selection apparent in the concordance and their respective collocational profiles. The correlation between formal patterns, such as collocation, and function can be identified systematically by the students, given a minimum guidance on the part of the teacher, and it lends itself very well to different types of communicative tasks in the classroom context. The different form-function links observed in Table 14 above, for example, allow the teacher to explore with the students different levels, from the morphological to the discourse one giving, at the same time, access to a wealth of lexical variety which can be very enriching in the teaching process.

The cumulative side of usage and syllabus design

The statistical dimension reflecting the routine nature of language usage has traditionally been ignored in language teaching. Concerning, for example, the selection of the texts for language study, many observers have noted that while invented examples offer an over-tidy picture of the system because they are usually made up *ad hoc* in order to exemplify a paradigm, texts that are brought into the classroom "without an awareness of how typically they represent salient features of the language can present a chaotic picture of the language" (Kennedy 1992:366).

With respect to the teaching of vocabulary, the language of ELT textbooks falls very short indeed in terms of representing natural usage. The shortcomings in this area of teaching are pointed out in an interesting study by Ljung (1990) who looks at TEFL vocabulary as shown in fifty widely used texts. He shows a major mismatch between pedagogical materials and the most frequent items in the corpus compiled for the Cobuild project. The TEFL texts are found to contain an unusually high proportion of simple concrete words and a smaller than expected number of more abstract words.

The content and the sequencing of the curriculum and the weight given to different items in classroom activities can benefit from drawing their insights from corpus evidence. Kennedy (ibid.:336), among others, points to the need to concentrate initial teaching on high frequency items and to grade vocabulary and structures accordingly.

Considering syllabus design, Sinclair and Renouf (1988:148) propose what they call a *lexical syllabus* centred around:

a) the commonest word forms in the language;
b) their central patterns of usage;
c) the combinations which they typically form.

In this respect, perhaps the most threatening implication of corpus work for the teaching profession is that experienced authors of popular text-books might not after all be able to replicate the rules of usage for the benefit of their audience of students. Quite simply, corpus evidence shows that there is a kind of evidence that goes unnoticed when even an experienced native speaker tries to render it explicitly as a rule of the language. Sinclair and Renouf (ibid.) argue this point:

> The human being, contrary to popular belief, is not well organised for isolating consciously what is central and typical in the language; anything unusual is sharply perceived, but the humdrum of everyday events are appreciated subliminally. (ibid.:151)

The type of syllabus they propose[8], therefore, would include "the essential patterns of distribution and combination" in the language (ibid.:154), thus highlighting the most common uses of the most common words. Considering the fact that words are co-selected at the lexical and grammatical levels, the initial focus on frequent words would entail an emphasis on the most characteristic patterns they engage in, and, as the authors point out, "prominent among those are devices, signals, and strategies in discourse, both spoken and written". Also, even though the starting point for the selection and the gradation of the syllabus is lexical, grammatical structures are not by any means excluded, and they will find their place in association with the most common words and their uses.

Conclusion: discovery procedures, changing roles and self-access

What we have exemplified in the sections above shows that the kind of insight that the student can derive from corpus work is qualitatively different from the descriptive statements found in traditional pedagogic grammars and reference texts. The ability to identify the function of an item and, within the same page of concordance, match it with its formal realisations, has become suddenly very easy for linguists, teachers and students alike. The new units of meaning, made of the strict interconnection of lexical and grammatical patterns, can be seen as the new currency for linguistic description. If we want to teach the student to communicate this new perspective on language usage must be brought into the classroom.

It has been pointed out that one of the failings of language teaching is the lack of correlation between *form* and *meaning*[9] (Berry 1999); here the corpus can help because it provides the ideal resource for the re-unification between formal and functional parameters: their strict interconnection becomes obvious and can be easily observed scanning the vertical and the horizontal axis of the concordance.

Of course, when it comes to teaching with corpus data, there is a new methodology to teach: going back to the parameters differentiating the reading of a text from that of a corpus (cf. Chapter One), we can say that the students have to be taught to *read vertically*, to *read fragmentarily* and to *focus on repeated events*. It is this third element which may be more difficult to master, perhaps because traditional teaching is based on texts, and the students learn from a very early stage to focus on the individual instance of language rather than on the repetition of similar linguistic patterns.

When we bring the corpus into the classroom, we have to teach the student to focus on three different types of repetition. First, there is the most visible repetition of words that collocate with the node. This becomes obvious when the concordance is alphabetised: N-1, N-2, N-3, etc. on the left co-text of the node, N+1, N+2, N+3, etc. on the right co-text of the node. Second, within this initial level of co-selection at word level, we have to teach the students to query the patterns further in the light of grammatical categories. The example of *flexible* found in attributive position when qualifying abstract notions, and in predicative position when qualifying a human subject, is a case in point. This interconnection between the grammatical and the lexical inputs is not obvious, because most teaching and, indeed, linguistic description, separates drastically between the two types of observation. In the classroom it is still not unusual in some places to find a grammar class and a vocabulary class well separated, both physically (different days of the week) and theoretically.

The fact that we are still focusing on repeated events must be kept in mind at all times. It is not sufficient to find one instance; the pattern has to be validated in the light of more evidence, different corpora, etc. At this stage a program such as the collocate program used here, which gives a measure of the significance of co-selection, is very important. The student will immediately be captured by the frequency of certain items, but this may not be remarkable at all if the item in question is a frequent one and it might not be telling us much about that specific instance of co-selection.

The third type of repetition is at the semantic and functional levels. It is a further stage in abstraction compared with the collocational and colligational levels, so it is not necessarily realised at the level of repetition of individual words. It requires the identification of a common functional core between different lexicogrammatical realisations. Sometimes the frequent collocation of certain words may help the students to identify this core; at others there is a lot of variation that has to be evaluated functionally. This is where the identification of the semantic preference and the semantic prosody takes place and where the definition of the functionally complete unit of meaning is made. It is, in other words, the most important stage and the most useful in classroom activities: it is the final step bringing together the other two stages. In itself, practice in the identification of this third category of repeated events is very useful in familiarising the students with the communicative use of language. A lot of materials can be assembled using the concordances and asking the students to evaluate them in terms of formal parameters (collocation and colligation) and regroup them according to certain functional tasks.

In terms of classroom methodology, some observations on the change brought about by corpus work into the classroom have to be made. For instance, *formulating a rule* is something that traditionally was left to theoretically minded linguists; it certainly did not belong to the teaching. The student was happy to find the "rules" in the grammar, perhaps less happy to learn them. The usual problem was that the rule seemed always somewhat remote from normal usage. The mismatch soon became evident in classroom activities and end-of-term tests. The type of activity based on corpus evidence, on the other hand, requires the student to formulate the rule in the presence of the evidence. Reference works will be used and consulted, but corpus evidence will invariably lead both students and teachers to evaluate them critically in the light of the patterns observable in the concordance. A positive outcome of this process will indeed be the development of a critical approach to evaluating the patterns of usage and the way these can be adequately described into rules of usage.

Another positive point concerning the use of corpus evidence in the classroom is the exposure students get to *variation*. This is, of course, part of natural, authentic language production. Quite often variation has been seen as a problem in the classroom: the student should first master his/her rule, then get exposure to the different lexical and grammatical patterns that could come under the same umbrella. With corpus work variation is in at the very beginning; it has to be identified in the framework of repetition and accounted for. The 'rule', as a reflection of the linguistic norm, has to be formulated in its presence. To learn how to cope with variation, it is argued, is a very healthy process for the student and it is similar to the process of first language acquisition. In corpus work, one can conclude, there is the initial requirement to learn to identify repeated patterns and separate them from "casual acquaintances". The famous statement of Firth comes to mind:

> We must separate from the mush of general goings-on those features of repeated events which appear to be parts of a patterned process, and handle them systematically by stating them by the spectrum of linguistic techniques. (Firth, in Palmer 1968:187)

In order to classify the new type of evidence, and to formulate a statement that explains it, teacher and students will have to become co-workers, research collaborators, and the difference in status endemically present in the activities of teaching and learning levels out. The teacher's experience, of course, will give him/her a lead role, but as a facilitator rather than a despatcher of truths. One of the results brought about by access to corpus evidence in the classroom is therefore a *change in the roles* in language teaching. Traditionally the teacher is invested with the authority to reconcile rules and actual usage and to fill the gap between the textbook and the communicative activity as best as (s)he can. Exposure to corpus evidence can, however, do more, and by actually encouraging the students to work on their own and formulating their own hypotheses, it can make them into more active participants in the learning process.

The corpus-driven approach advocated here, therefore, when applied to teaching, can be seen as going along with a "bottom-up" methodology: the computer is used as a special type of informant and the students are led through a process of self-discovery: they learn to formulate their questions and they ask the computer to provide the evidence. Tim Johns, the father figure of *data-driven learning*, explains that "the task of the learner is to *discover* the foreign language, and [...] the task of the language teacher is to provide a context in which the learner can develop strategies for discovery - strategies through which he can learn how to learn" (Johns 1991a:1). It is felt, pedagogically speaking, that it is a more valuable experience for the learner if the hypotheses are personal - induced and not learned, perhaps closer to the experience of learning a first language.

The traditional and well established assumption about language teaching is, of course, that the methodology for bringing the language facts into the classroom should be deductive and explicit (Berry 1999:37): language facts are stated and then exemplified. When it comes to evaluating such an input with corpus evidence we may enter into some difficulties. The demand for explicitness requires the grammatical statements to be articulated proficiently at a theoretical level. Here we have the problem that, at the best of times, our students may not have an adequate training in linguistic analysis and may therefore find it difficult to interpret a rule adequately. The deductive methodology is also called into question in that the general rule is not always in accord with authentic examples. As we have seen when discussing the examples in the preceding sessions (see also Tognini Bonelli 2000), the general statements issued by the grammar or the dictionary do not always respond to the realities of language usage and the input of corpus evidence may indeed not support the theoretical statements which students will find in their textbooks.

In contrast with these more or less explicit assumptions, the corpus-driven approach can be seen as primarily *inductive* because it does not start with an openly stated rule but derives it by generalising from particular language facts. It is also a methodology that relies on implicit teaching in that the students, once the initial methodological steps are mastered, can handle the data more or less on their own, without an explicit previous knowledge of the rules[10]. Traditional descriptions will indeed be called into action because they will be needed as a reference and as a terminological input to describe the evidence. The example of *all but* above illustrates well this point: the two different functions, one related to the meaning of "except" and the other to the meaning of "almost, practically", are connected to the grammatical functions of preposition and adverb respectively. This explicit grammatical statement, though, the differentiation between an adverb and a preposition, does not need to be explicitly formulated beforehand by the student: the functional attribution of meaning based on the evidence can take place before the explicit input of the grammatical description, and the student can learn a lot from it. It is argued that this approach *creates the need* for a theoretical descriptive statement, and perhaps the comparison between several of them, and this is communicatively very positive.

There is one last point worth mentioning in connection with the corpus-driven approach applied to language teaching. The fact that it takes an inductive stance on teaching and that it progressively builds the theoretical statements from the concordance data can be put to work in a very positive way in the field of *self-access*. Nowadays, with student numbers going up, and more and more demands being made on schools and University Centres to provide adequate language teaching support and training, inevitably a lot of the teaching will have to be organised as self-access. The language centres in particular will have a very important role to play (see Sinclair 1999d) and access to different kinds of corpora on line can be seen as an invaluable resource that students can consult in their own time. In the writer's own experience, not much prompting is needed because the students, once they become familiar with "reading" the concordances, usually become so enthusiastic about the insights they gain - and that they can feel proud ownership of - that the problem is stopping them, rather than spurring them on.

Notes

1. The source of the concordance is the original Birmingham Corpus; 35 instances were selected out of a total 21636, and reduced every n[th] citation.
2. Using formal parameters Mindt considers negation and the semantics of *any* and shows that the traditional description (non-assertive meaning with a syntactic environment which is basically marked by negation) is true for less than 50 per cent of the occurrences and that the majority of cases of *any* occur in a syntactic environment which is affirmative (1997:194). Mindt's findings confirm a similar analysis done by Willis who clearly states: "Far from being an aberration, the use of *any* in an affirmative sentence is in fact much commoner than its use in interrogatives. In this particular instance the information given to learners by some coursebooks and grammars is simply wrong" (1990:49).
3. Clear (1993) describes t-score as one of the two measures of significance (the other being MI value) to select and evaluate significant collocations. T-score measures the strength of association between two items, and in particular the *confidence* with which we can claim that there is some association (ibid.:281). It is important, when we evaluate collocational patterning that we should focus on patterns which co-occur significantly often in order to rule out the possibility that it might be a freak of chance. In general, Clear notes, the collocates highlighted by the t-score statistic will be frequently recurring items (often grammatical words such as prepositions, personal pronouns, determiners and particles) along with those fully lexical words which are clearly associated with the node word (ibid.:281).
4. The collocational profiles that are presented follow the Bank of English convention.
5. Here we can cast a glance at an ideological perspective, because Fairclough (1999) points out that although *flexible*, *flexibility* etc. may be used positively by employers and economic theorists, as a concept it is bad news for employees because it leads to insecurity in jobs and homes.

6. This work was done within a first year university class for students of Economics.
7. It is important to note here that there may be a difference between the patterns shown by the limited concordance and what is shown as frequent and significant in the collocation profile. The concordance in question has been reduced every n[th] from the original 2136 instances; of course a lot of individual patterns are sieved away when the reduction takes place.
8. The lexical syllabus proposed by Sinclair and Renouf (1988) has been elaborated by Willis (1990).
9. It is now generally accepted that a pedagogic grammar must link the formal and semantic-functional aspects of a language, regardless of which of the two it takes as basic. This principle is explored by Higgs (1985) and Berry (1999) among others. In teaching terms it amounts to the tenet of specifying the formal characteristics of grammatical items in terms of their communicative functions. Unfortunately, the lack of systematic correlation between form and meaning is still one of the major failings in most of present day language teaching.
10. In line with a more implicit and inductive methodology, it is worth recalling the work of Rutherford & Sharwood Smith (1985) who take a view of teaching as "consciousness-raising" including "the deliberate exposure of the learner to an artificially large number of instances of some target structure" (ibid.:275).

3 Corpus Issues

Introduction

In the previous chapter we plunged into the middle of the new discipline of corpus linguistics with only the minimum of introduction. Having demonstrated one important way in which we can make use of this new means of studying language, it is now necessary to provide an explanation of how this arose, what its origins are and how it relates to established positions in linguistics. Such a discussion is necessary, because while the relation of corpus linguistics to other activities in linguistics can be seen as very simple indeed, it is ultimately rather complex.

Most linguistic research demands evidence of language in use, and a corpus provides such evidence. The need for the input of authentic language, as we have seen, was particularly felt in the field of an application such as language teaching because in the classroom the emphasis on verification and immediate testing makes it indispensable to reconcile the descriptive statement and communicative tasks. A notable exception is the particular position of generative linguistics to which we will come back at a later point (see Chapter Four). Linguists investigating unfamiliar languages developed techniques for noting utterances and gathered large collections; those describing more accessible languages nevertheless referred much of what they said to extensive quotations from suitable sources. For many years a corpus was thought of as a natural extension of these traditions, where the computer stored and ordered the evidence and presented extracts on instructions from the researcher; the computer was seen essentially as a very fast tool.

We can see three stages in the penetration of the computer corpus in linguistic work. In the first stage it is seen simply as a tool; it was used to process, in real time, a quantity of information that could hardly be envisaged a few years ago. This is still the most impressive contribution of corpora to language research.

But in changing the dimensions of evidence, the corpus reached a second stage of penetration into linguistic work; not only was it providing an abundance of new evidence, it was by its nature affecting the methodological frame of the enquiry by speeding it up, systematising it, and making it applicable in real time to ever larger amounts of data. So Leech in 1992 (p.105) saw that there was now a distinctive methodology associated with corpus work; while a corpus was little more than a big collection of evidence, one approached it in a different way from the perusal of separate texts. The means of retrieving information was getting more and more sophisticated, and the results required more and more skilled interpretation.

Leech (ibid.) drew a clear distinction between corpus linguistics and such varieties as sociolinguistics and psycholinguistics, which although manifestly hybrid are regarded as disciplines in their own right; the corpus advanced the methodology but did not change the categorial map drawn by linguistic theory. For many linguists, that is the limit of the changes brought about by the addition of corpora to the computational toolkit. The computer as a tool was not expected to upturn the theoretical assumptions behind the original enquiries themselves, and so no such effect was expected. It was not even felt necessary to look out for such fundamental changes.

However, we can now show that a further development has taken place in the nineties, a third stage of penetration; what had started as a methodological enhancement but included a quantitative explosion (we are referring here to the quantity of data processed thanks to the aid of the computer) has turned out to be a theoretical and qualitative revolution in that it has offered insights into the language that have shaken the underlying assumptions behind many well established theoretical positions in the field.

Writing a little after Leech, Halliday foresaw the signs of a qualitative change in the results of the quantitative studies opened up by corpus research. Of all current theoreticians he remains the closest to the data, and saw that corpora were gradually moving theory and data together. He warned that not only language, but semiotic systems in general would be affected by this new proximity of theory and data (Halliday 1993c:24). This is clearly a stage beyond methodology.

Others expressed similar points of view around this time; one theme concerned the effect of increasing the arithmetic power under the command of the linguist. Clear (1993:274) pointed out the connection between the use of computational, and consequently algorithmic and statistical, methods on the one hand and the qualitative change in the observations; not only could the language researcher speed up the process of analysis, he or she could carry out procedures which were just not feasible before computers became available; the difference of scale led to a qualitative difference. Leech himself (ibid.:106) envisaged the computer as doing much more than acting as a research tool; it was going to open up new ways of thinking about language. It is strange to imagine that just more data and better counting can trigger philosophical repositionings, but that is what these writers felt, and that indeed is what has happened.

Saussure's famous words, "c'est le point de vue qui crée l'objet", can be reinterpreted in this turn of events; if the dimensions of the viewpoint change, or the granularity of the research results, the object created is substantially different from before. We could say that it is our chosen methodological standpoint which determines both the object and the aim of our enquiry. In other words it is, in this instance, the methodology that defines the domain. Thus, it is argued in this study that corpus linguistics is much more than "the methodological basis" for the enquiry, that it carries with it and becomes inseparable from the actual consequences of this stance; in this way it becomes a discipline in its own right and acquires its own domain.

Given these premises, we should note a few points. Linguistic data is now available in such large quantities that patterns emerge that could not be seen before; this is what a scholar like Sinclair observed (1991:1) and much of his theoretical work on the definition of units of meaning as well as on lexicography amply proves this point. Some examples of the change in the quality of evidence that we can now observe were given in the previous chapter. Linguistic evidence of this type has to be reckoned with and observations about instances of language use, if not dismissed as secondary with respect to insights derived from intuition, are bound to affect statements about the language system in general. The problem for the linguist, therefore, is to elaborate a methodology that can allow him/her to describe and take into account this type of unprecedented evidence.

Halliday's point about the converging paths of theory and data raises question marks around some of the most familiar dichotomies of modern linguistics, in particular *langue* and *parole*, 'competence' and 'performance'. What they seem to have in common is the effect of basically separating the linguistic theory from linguistic evidence, creating a tidy world where the one does not really have to be accountable to the other. Although theoretically motivated, they are certainly methodologically convenient, and they cut right across the descriptive framework which is necessary for deriving linguistic information from corpora. Whereas in "pre-corpus" linguistics such buffers were needed because no way could be envisaged of accounting directly for all the evidence, corpus work offers no reason or motivation for selecting some evidence and ignoring the rest. The corpus provides all the evidence and demands adequate explanations. The theoretical statement derived from corpus evidence, therefore, will have to start from new presuppositions.

We must consider what kind of theory can reconcile the evidence and the statement, the instance and the system; in what way might frequency of occurrence reflect meaning, and indeed in what way should it be allowed to shape the categories and affect the system. Many authorities, coming from widely separated positions, are suspicious of even the simplest statistical evidence in relation to language. Is it wise to put our faith in numbers?

There is, however, no escape route - corpus evidence has to be both quantified and evaluated, and part of its value lies in the quantity; the famous linguistic dichotomies have to be reviewed in the light of the data, and reconciled if possible. Statements about the system must be more directly accountable to statements about the instances. This is the stance that is taken in this study.

This point of view is diametrically opposed to theoretical stances which do not regard data gathering as a necessary step towards theorizing, and which view the evidence of language use as marginal for determining speaker-hearer competence. As always, in between these poles we will find a number of intermediate positions, and the different stances with respect to the appropriate data for the linguist reflect alternative traditions which will be considered in more detail in Chapter Four. In the meantime we can mark the extremities of this continuum by juxtaposing some quotes, (the first set following Stubbs 1993:3), one set by Chomsky and the other by Sinclair, which well summarise two opposed positions. The quotes speak for themselves, and they are further discussed below.

Like most facts of interest and importance (..) information about the speaker-hearer's competence (..) is neither presented for direct observation nor extractable from data by inductive procedures of any known sort. (Chomsky 1965:18)	The ability to examine large text corpora in a systematic manner allows access to a quality of evidence that has not been available before. (Sinclair 1991:4)
Corpus linguistics does not exist. (Chomsky, in an interview to Bas Aarts, 1999[1])	Corpus Concordance Collocation (Sinclair 1991)

One of the main themes in this book is setting out the basic tenets of the new discipline of corpus linguistics. It is argued that this has its roots in the combination and the merging of certain theoretical stands from earlier in the twentieth century, and it has begun to blossom with the advent of the computer age, where instantaneous access to, and automatic processing of large amounts of data is taken for granted. So we will begin with a brief glance at the recent origins of this discipline.

The rise of corpus linguistics

Although the discipline of corpus linguistics as such is relatively new, the practice of it - and by this is meant the use of a corpus of language as the basis for language description - is as old as linguistic enquiry. In this section we will go back over the development of modern linguistic enquiry in general and of corpus linguistics in particular; later on, in Chapters Eight and Nine, we will put this in the more general context of the debate around the notion of meaning and the emergence of modern linguistics.

So here we will be focusing more specifically on the issue of observable data, the starting point of corpus linguistics, and how it has been handled in different periods and across different theoretical schools.

Of necessity, historical linguistics has always been corpus-based; by far the principal evidence of language change and evolution is to be found in collections of texts of different periods and locations (Johansson 1995:22). It is therefore to the historical tradition that we should turn to observe the beginnings of the practice of corpus linguistics. A century ago, for example in the work of Bréal, the study of language was simply equated with the *observation of data*; the laws that governed the historical development of meaning could only be discovered by looking at specific and observable phenomena.

Since modern linguistics owes its impetus to the lively work of the historical linguists of the nineteenth century, it is interesting that in a relatively short space of time it should shift its focus to an approach based on intuition and introspection from the data-based approach, as Biber and Finegan (1991:205) notice. In spite of its data-based origins, modern linguistics after the historical-evolutionist period, shifted away from the observation of data and, starting with Saussure, the object of linguistics is defined as the system, abstract par excellence, and non-identifiable in single tokens. Rules are no longer directly linked to specific phenomena.

Saussure had little early impact in the United States, which produced its own theoretical framework starting with Bloomfield. Under the influence of the positivist and behaviourist trend, post-Bloomfieldian linguistics in the USA became concerned to account for the observable data, and there was little room for abstract speculation. While introspection was not ruled out it was seen as secondary; if sufficient naturally-occurring data could be assembled there would be no need to look elsewhere. Leech (1991:8) points this out with reference to Z. Harris and A. Hill in the 1950s, and Harris at that time, looks with hindsight, like a corpus linguist who unfortunately lacked a computer.

With Chomsky, though, the pendulum swung back towards a refusal of observable data as the basis for linguistic statements; this was clear in the quotation that ends the previous section. The corpus, seen as a large body of language in use, could not be seen as relevant to linguistic enquiry, largely because it could not be relied upon as evidence of how the language faculty is organised. In another famous judgement that shaped the course of linguistics in the USA and beyond, Chomsky makes this claim:

> Any natural corpus will be skewed. Some sentences won't occur because they are obvious, others because they are false, still others because they are impolite. The corpus, if natural, will be so wildly skewed that the description would be no more than a mere list. (Chomsky 1962:159)

The contrast between this position and the theoretical assumptions of corpus linguistics are noted by Leech (1992:107) discussing the key features of corpus linguistics, each of which highlights a divergence from the Chomskian paradigm: (1) focus on linguistic performance, rather than competence; (2) focus on linguistic description, rather than linguistic universals; (3) focus on quantitative, as well as qualitative models of language; (4) focus on a more empiricist, rather than rationalist view of scientific enquiry.

For Chomsky and his followers the real source of insights into the structural nature of language is introspection. This was by no means a novel position in linguistic theory - for example Hjelmslev (1943/1961:106 and 1942:43) posited a differentiation between individual structural types that are manifested and those that are manifestable: the theoretician, of course, was only interested in the manifestable, what Hjelmsvev called 'linguistic schema'. This stance on the marginal nature of actual and observable tokens of language use is still well represented within the discipline of corpus linguistics; this may seem a contradiction in terms given that, as already mentioned, corpus linguistics by definition draws its insights from actual language usage; we will come back to this later when looking at the different issues related to corpus work in Chapter Four below.

Although corpora were very much in existence and taken as the basis for the historical analysis of languages, it is around the late 1950s and the early 1960s that the beginning of corpus linguistics proper can be located. In 1959 Randolph Quirk announced his plan to start a Survey of English Usage of both written and spoken English. The Survey corpus was not intended to be computerised because of the considerable element of spoken language it was meant to contain (50%). Shortly afterwards (1963), Nelson Francis, Henry Kucera and others at Brown University set out the principles for a computerised corpus - "a standard sample of present-day edited American English, for use with digital computers" (Francis and Kucera, 1979) - what later became known as the Brown Corpus. At around the same time at Edinburgh University the first computerised corpus of spoken language - British English - was collected by John Sinclair under the sponsorship of the Department of Scientific and Industrial Research (DSIR) of the UK government (Sinclair, Jones and Daley 1970).

Corpus Definition

The growing popularity of corpus linguistics has generated pressure to relax the criteria that, without explicit definition, guided the early corpus builders to their goals. Every few months in the *Corpora* and other relevant lists there is a query about whether or not a certain collection of language, or a means of collecting it, would constitute a corpus, and there is a wide spectrum of views elicited by these stimuli. To give a recent example, there was a lively discussion in January 2000 as to whether or not a collection of proverbs constituted a corpus. Let us review some authoritative definitions of the early nineties, when it first became necessary to be precise about a corpus was, and how it differed from other collections of language.

> a corpus is a collection of texts assumed to be representative of a given language, dialect, or other subset of a language to be used for linguistic analysis. (N. Francis, 1992:17 quoting Francis 1982:7)

> a corpus is a collection of naturally-occurring language text, chosen to characterize a state or variety of a language. (Sinclair, 1991:171)

> [a corpus is] a subset of an ETL (Electronic Text Library) built according to explicit design criteria for a specific purpose (Atkins, Clear and Osler, 1992:1)

> a corpus is understood to be a collection of samples of running text. The texts may be in spoken, written or intermediate forms, and the samples may be of any length. (Jan Aarts, 1991:45)

> A corpus is a collection of pieces of language that are selected and ordered according to explicit linguistic criteria in order to be used as a sample of the language. (EAGLES 1994:2.1)

We can see that they all agree that a corpus is a collection of language text, though not necessarily texts. Aarts talks of samples, and EAGLES of pieces of language. Francis alone talks of texts, and Atkins et al. appear also to see a corpus as restricted to a collection of whole texts (though most corpora, including Francis' Brown Corpus, are not). Aarts adds the important word "running", which would exclude a collection of proverbs falling under his definition.

The word "samples" implies a design and a purpose, and the definitions are united in this, some more explicitly than others. Francis uses the word "representative", which remains a contentious term because it challenges Chomsky's position head-on; Sinclair talks of "characterising the language", and Atkins et al. more generally demand a "purpose" - not necessarily a linguistic one. The design criteria must be explicit for Atkins et al. and for EAGLES, and we return to this point below.

So whereas to many people a corpus must seem like "a helluva lot of text, stored on a computer", as pointed out in the jocular definition by Leech (1992:106), there are a number of important issues that corpus builders are alerted to, not all of which are by any means likely to be settled in the near future. But there is a reasonable consensus that a corpus will not just yield insights into itself, i.e. its contents, but also that the results of these investigations will be claimed or assumed to be typical of the language from which the corpus was selected.

In the sections that follow we will outline several points which are implicitly raised by these definitions and some major theoretical stances that underlie them. The points we will address are:

- the authenticity of the texts included in the corpus
- the representativeness of language included in the corpus
- the sampling criteria used in the selection of texts.

Before going on to discuss in some detail the above issues, we should make a point still relevant to the definition of a corpus; this concerns *the function of the corpus*. Nelson Francis, in his definition reported above, qualifies the function of a corpus as that "to be used for linguistic analysis"; the definitions given by Sinclair (1991) and EAGLES (1994) invoke similar criteria: that the corpus should be selected "to characterize a state or variety of a language", "according to explicit linguistic criteria in order to be used as a sample of the language". This point is quite important since, as N. Francis explains (1992:17), there can be large collections of text whose purpose is other than linguistic; a typical example is the case of anthologies, whose purpose is literary, or the Corpus Juris Civilis instigated by the Emperor Justinian in the sixth century, whose purpose was legal. Other collections, such as the citation collection behind the Oxford English Dictionary, for example, cannot be called corpora in the modern sense as they are "inevitably skewed in the direction of the unusual and interesting constructions that the readers encounter" (Francis 1992:28) - nor are they running text.

This is obviously a point where we are waiting for a consensus to settle on the matter. It is now so fashionable to use a "corpus" in any empirical language project that some data collections bear the name without respecting the criteria that are emerging. So, for instance, McEnery et al.(2000:46) refer to their "Lancaster corpus of abuse" (LCA) as a "problem-oriented corpus based upon data extracted from the BNC and the BOE, containing examples of swearing from transcribed spoken language" and they they state that:

> in deciding which words to include within the corpus, we have partly been guided by claims within the literature, partly by our own intuition and partly by words we encountered within the corpus. (ibid.:46)

It seems as if these scholars have gathered a file of extracts from corpora, chosen according to criteria which differ substantially from those advocated by the writers quoted above. The file will probably be very useful in the research proposed, but is it a corpus, or is it not closer to a set of concordances to selected words and phrases?

For most linguists, then, a corpus cannot be equated with just a large collection of texts or citations, but needs to be justified in linguistic terms. The definition of Atkins et al. is seen as too broad, since any purpose whatever is sufficient for them. The issue of what is the function of a corpus also underlies the chosen methodology with respect to sampling. We will come back to this point below.

To summarise the discussion, in the context of this study a corpus is taken to be a computerised collection of authentic texts, amenable to automatic or semi-automatic processing or analysis. The texts are selected according to explicit criteria in order to capture the regularities of a language, a language variety or a sub-language.

There is another important point to note here, though it falls short of being part of the definition. It is that the texts contained in a corpus are held in a common format, and so are as accessible as if they formed a single character string; but they do not lose their textual identity and in most retrieval systems the original source of a given stretch of language is accessible to the analyst on demand. This makes it fairly easy to study text typology and register, for instance.

Issues: authenticity

The obvious starting point of linguistic enquiry within the scope of corpus work will be the data itself and corpus linguistics, by definition, will deal with language in use (Aarts, 1991:45; Johansson 1995:19). All the material included in a corpus, whether spoken, written or gathered along any intermediate dimension (Biber 1988), is assumed to be taken from genuine communications of people going about their normal business.

That is what we must assume if we are going to use corpora as reservoirs of evidence. If it is not so, and there is some special restriction on the choice of texts, then we expect that this fact will be very clearly stated in the documentation. So, if it is a corpus of bible translations or lyric poetry or interviews with psychiatric patients this should be made clear, and even more critically if the language has been elicited in an artificial or experimental setting. Most corpora can be loosely described as "general-purpose" (Leech 1991) or "reference" (EAGLES 1994) corpora, and so users are likely to see this as a default, leaving the responsibility of labelling the specialised corpus to the originator.

If we accept that our corpus is a reasonable sample of the language under study, we must now consider what sort of evidence it provides. This is a rather controversial matter, especially for scholars working within the Chomskian framework. The simplest position would be to assume that any word, phrase or sentence that occurs in the corpus is representative of the language under study, but that is oversimplified. Aarts, for example, having pointed out that corpus linguistics, by definition, deals with language use, is caught in the dilemma of what should be accepted as "language use". For him "to maintain that an utterance, if it occurs in a corpus, is by definition acceptable and should therefore be incorporated into a grammar of language use" (Aarts ibid:52) is an unattractive stance for several reasons. In the first place, writers and speakers sometimes deliberately break the normal conventions of an encounter or a document to illustrate a mistake, or for stylistic or dramatic effect, or for a number of other everday reasons. The computer selecting an example at random would eventually hit on one of these aberrant forms, and the user would find it unsatisfactory.

More seriously, Aarts argues that if we try to write a fully comprehensive grammar for a corpus - one that accounts precisely for all the sentences, phrases and words in it - we are likely to lose generality; the grammar may not be able to analyse further sentences from the same language except by chance.

If this predicament is understandable in the light of what we know of the general theoretical stance behind it, it is perhaps sobering to remember that the centrality of language as evidence for linguistic statements has not always been recognised, even by linguists who have explicitly seen it as central to their theory. In this respect, Stubbs (1993:8-9) points out that "it is easy to forget or ignore how little data, either invented sentences or real texts, is actually analysed in the most influential literature in twentieth century linguistics" and he goes on to list several linguistic milestones where, in spite of occasional lip service being paid to the reliance on evidence to justify theoretical statements, data is hardly referred to or indeed discussed.

And even when reliance on data is explicitly behind major initiatives such as the "Survey of English Usage" in the 60s, used as evidence for *A Comprehensive Grammar of the English Language* (Quirk et al. 1985), Stubbs notes, "the relation between corpus, example sentences and description is not discussed (..) and the accountability to data of description and theory is therefore undefined" (Stubbs 1993:9, see also Francis 1993:138).

The reason behind this lack of systematic correlation between data, description and theoretical statement in most theories not informed by corpus evidence may well be that the evidence from the corpus - if untampered with and respected in its integrity - is distinctly likely to challenge existing linguistic theories with unprecedented insights into the language, obliging the profession to reconsider every aspect of theory and description. We are not here talking about occasional gaffes or deliberate mistakes, but about the core organisation of the language.

Some examples of this problem were discussed in Chapter Two, in connection with language teaching. If corpus evidence was allowed to be the basis for grammatical statements, many pedagogical grammars would have to revise their prescriptive rules quite drastically.

Issues: Representativeness

The second issue mentioned above is closely related to the one of authenticity, and it is the vexed question of the *representativeness* of the language included in a corpus. According to Leech (1991:27) a corpus is representative when "the findings based on its contents can be generalized to a larger hypothetical corpus"[2]. With regard to this Biber (1994:377) points out that most of the uses of a corpus in language work rest on the reliability of the corpus as representative of the language - grammars, dictionaries and analytical software all make such assumptions.

Biber here argues the case for general-purpose tools and descriptions; the point is relevant also for more specific applications requiring special types of languages or sub-languages; it would be difficult to see the reason for choosing an "unrepresentative" corpus. Thus there seems to be general agreement among scholars who choose to work on a corpus that this should be representative of a certain population and that the statements derived from the analysis of the corpus will be largely applicable to a larger sample or to the language as a whole.

Having invoked, one way or another, the representativeness of a corpus, one word of caution is now in line. We should always bear in mind that the assumption of representativeness "must be regarded largely as an act of faith" (Leech 1991:27), as at present we have no means of ensuring it, or even evaluating it objectively (see also Sinclair 1991:9). For example, with regard to size, how can we ever know that a corpus is not large enough for our purposes? Fillmore (1992:38) points out very perceptively that a native speaker would only come to this conclusion if he or she failed to find some things that were intuitively expected.

Presence or absence is one thing, but frequency is another. It is perhaps worth looking more closely at the extent to which the representativeness of a sample - a corpus - is allowed to affect the parameters of the theoretical framework within which the linguist is operating. In other words, having accepted the need for a frequency-based model in order to account for the cumulative effect of data, we should see whether the typicality of patterns observed in the corpus will be equated with representativeness in terms of the linguistic system involved.

Let us consider for a moment the theoretical stand behind this issue. The assumption of representativeness is a natural correlate of the model upheld by Firth, Halliday and Sinclair. These three scholars, among others, share the belief that each single act of communication shows the language system in operation.

Moreover, the Firthian notion of "repeated events" is taken as crucial in the formulation of generalisations about language, be it in the specification of a paradigmatic model of grammar (Halliday 1993c:3)[3] or, in the field of lexis, the introduction of information about the frequency of headwords in a dictionary for example (Cobuild 2nd ed., 1995).

We shall see later in this section that there is a delicate relationship between the representative status of the corpus and the feedback that comes from working with it. A prima facie assumption of representativeness must be made before work can start, but the results may be two-edged, suggesting amendments to the structure of the corpus itself. Although, ideally, a corpus should be unassailably representative, in practice it is something of a fait accompli and at a later stage, when the results of the data analysis are evaluated, the linguist may sometimes come to question the parameters according to which the corpus has been created or the typology of the texts included[4].

Such direct correlation between corpus evidence and theoretical statement has been severely criticised by neo-Chomskian scholars. The predicament of Aarts discussed above is a case in point: for him language use, however backed by frequency of occurrence, cannot quite justify generalisability; however representative the corpus may be, sole evidence of occurrence cannot justify inclusion in the Grammar. We will come back to Aarts' position, namely to his proposal of merging "intuition-based" and "observation-based" grammars in Chapter Four.

In parallel with this neo-Chomskian orthodox position, in recent years there have been expressions of interest, even within the Chomskian framework, for deriving statements about the language from corpus evidence and taking into account the frequency of occurrence. The work of Bod (1992, 1995,1998) is a good example of this approach and of the general trend and we will briefly discuss it below.

Bod (1995) starts by positing the well-known distinction between a linguistic *competence* model and a linguistic *performance* model; while the former is taken to characterise the set of grammatical sentences together with their analyses, the latter aims to describe how sentences are actually produced and perceived in specific situations. He proposes a statistical approach to linguistic description. However, since a frequency-based model derives statements from observable and quantifiable linguistic phenomena rather than from intuitions about an internalised grammar, the obvious conclusion is that the insights yielded by his model cannot in any way contribute to the competence side of language. Frequency of occurrence thus firmly belongs to performance and, as such, it will only relate to what happens when people use language in natural situations. Where Bod finds the counting useful is in disambiguation, and the statistical performance model he proposes purports to account for the process by which, out of the many possible analyses, comprehenders actually assign one to their input sentences[5]. Corpus evidence thus comes to be accepted as representative of the "input-output properties of human language perception" (ibid.:12)[6], but it is still considered as irrelevant to statements concerning the underlying system, that of competence.

Issues: sampling

Assuming that a corpus has to be representative in order to be used as the basis for generalisations about the language, the most important issue in corpus design is to define the target population the corpus aims to represent (Biber 1994:378). The criteria used in this "definition" will provide the rationale for the collection and the classification of the corpus; issues such as what kind of texts are to be selected, the number of texts, the selection of particular texts, the selection of text samples from within texts and the length of text samples will have to be addressed and, as Biber again points out, these are all sampling decisions (ibid.:377).

It is important to note at this point that these decisions involve very clearly a theoretical stance on the part of the corpus builder and they will have a direct effect on the insights yielded by the corpus. This is why the criteria, according to which the corpus is assembled should always be made explicit and accessible to the corpus users: even though users normally cannot alter the contents of a corpus (beyond selecting components of it where this facility is provided) they should always be in a position to evaluate the corpus using the criteria and relate the statements they derive from the analysis of the corpus to the typology of the texts included in it[7]. Biber, in his article (1994) about *Representativeness in Corpus Design*, defines representativeness as "the extent to which a sample includes the full range of variability in a population" (ibid.:378) and proposes that this variability should be considered both from situational and linguistic perspectives. *Genre* or *register* are "situationally defined text categories" (for example fiction, sports broadcasts, psychology articles) while *text types* are "linguistically defined text categories" (ibid.:380)[8]. Biber goes on to propose a framework of situational parameters listed as hierarchical sampling strata.

He begins by offering three varieties of "primary channel" - written, spoken or scripted speech. When he wrote, electronic communication was not so widespread, and so e-mails, chat-lines and web pages are not included, though they might be in a similar framework today. Next there is the question of whether the language is published or not, with various formats within the category "published". Biber makes a distinction between institutional and other settings, and offers several parameters of classification of the presumed addressee - how many, whether present or absent, how much interaction there is and how much presumption of shared knowledge. The writer or speaker is then classified according to the usual variables of sex, age, occupation, etc., and whether performing as an individual or on behalf of an institution. Then the text is classified under "factuality", on a continuum between factual-informational and imaginative, under "purpose", which offers a list of activities like persuading, explaining, expressing various attitudes, opinions or emotions, and finally "topic".

In contrast to register and genre, as situationally defined parameters, text types concern the different linguistic distributions that are to be found within texts, between one text and another, and within and between groupings of texts into text types. So texts that share a number of linguistic features may be grouped into a text type, and other texts are excluded; they group themselves into other types, and the classification aims to bring out the maximum discrimination between types and the maximum similarity among members of the same type. Biber uses the distribution of linguistic features within texts as a basis for addressing the issue of optimal text length, in particular the number of contiguous words required in text samples. He compares pairs of 1,000-word samples taken from single texts in the LOB and London-Lund corpora using a set of linguistic features to see how similar and how different they are from one another. He reasons that if two such samples from the same text show similar choices from the feature list, while two samples from different texts show different choices, then there it is reasonable to conclude that the sample size is large enough; if the results are not as clear-cut then perhaps the sample size needs to be enlarged until it is adequate.

The linguistic features that he uses have already been used in variation studies - so independent researchers have found them indicative - and they are chosen from different functional and grammatical classes. These features are: first person pronouns, third person pronouns, contractions, past tense verbs, prepositions, passive constructions (combining by-passives and agentless passives), WH relative clauses, and conditional subordinate clauses. Biber justifies the choice:

> Pronouns and contractions are relatively interactive and colloquial in communicative function; nouns and prepositions are used for integrating information into texts; relative clauses and conditional subordination represent types of structural elaboration; and passives are characteristic of scientific or technical styles. (ibid.:389)

Situational and linguistic criteria are obviously not independent of one another; one of the principal uses of a corpus is to investigate the correlations between them. It is important to define them carefully and distinguish them from each other, because if they are confused then there is a serious risk of vicious circles arising; the fact that, for example, passive constructions are frequent in scientific English would lose its meaning if it turned out that the occurrence of the verb forms had informed the original selection of texts. Only if there is strict separation between situational and linguistic criteria can the results of investigations have any meaning.

Very often a change in register will affect linguistic parameters such as frequency distributions and co-occurrence patters, and, conversely a change in the latter is likely to reflect a change in the former (see also Mindt 1991)[9]. For many years researchers in language variety have been drawing our attention to the correlation between the provenance of a text and its internal linguistic preferences. Halliday points out (1992a:68) that these preferences may or may not be "diagnostic" - that is, sufficient to distinguish a specialised variety from the rest and from the general language. He cites the preponderance of imperatives in recipes and the simple future tense in weather forecasts as the kind of features that are at least indicative, but says that these are fairly gross observations; only corpus studies will show the "perturbations in frequency" that may eventually inform a detailed classification of registers.

Notwithstanding this interrelation between situational and linguistic criteria and the diagnostic potential of the latter, in corpus building the only safe first step is to base the initial selection of texts on situational parameters. As Biber (1994:380-81) explains, these can be identified in advance, whereas the linguistic types cannot.

To account for the differentiation between situational and linguistic criteria, Biber posits a distinction between theoretical research which defines the former and empirical research which defines the latter. He outlines a methodology for corpus design that should "proceed in a cyclical fashion" from a stage of theoretical research, which will identify external criteria without reference to specific texts, followed by a stage of empirical research, which identifies and characterises selected linguistic features of a text. Therefore, first a pilot corpus is assembled "representing a wide range of variation" in registers and texts, then the coincidence of external and internal parameters is measured. As a result, some of either type may be changed, and the process repeated until they appear to converge, with new texts being added "as they become available". Two levels of this activity are envisaged - an informal, almost continuous adjustment during research sessions, and more formal reviews and reworkings from time to time to consolidate the adjustments.

We may note at this point that, although there seems to be agreement as to the importance of internal criteria in the design of a truly representative corpus, relatively little research has been done on this. The few existing studies (e.g. Biber 1988, Nakamura 1993, Nakamura and Sinclair 1995) certainly corroborate the feeling that internal criteria are of paramount importance; however, they do not identify and quantify as yet a threshold of representativeness except in relative terms, as in Biber above.

The publication in 1999 of Biber et al.'s large grammar marks a new level of intensity of investigation, and explores hundreds of internal criteria, in this case not to improve the classification of text types, which are taken for granted, but to show how the categories of a detailed, if conventional grammar of English are distributed across four representative text types. This is close to Bod's model - the text types are "given", presumably by the theory, and the frequency of particular choices serves a descriptive purpose, in this case the characterisation of genres.

Concerning the sampling decisions taken in the assembly of a corpus, one of the most controversial issues is the size of the sample; the modest size used in early corpora stems, of course, from the technological restraints on corpus building that existed then, and we find across the spectrum of corpora available at the moment a lot of variation. The Survey of English Usage, for instance, had sample texts of 5,000 words each, while the Brown and the LOB corpora in the early 1960s consisted of 500 samples of 2,000 words each. Nowadays, however, with increased computer storage, the tendency is to go for whole texts rather than uniformly sized samples of texts (see for example the Bank of English). The policy of selecting uniform samples, though, is still popular and there is still a tendency to follow the dimensions adopted by the pioneers, if only for comparative purposes; so the ICE Corpus (International Corpus of English) (see Greenbaum, 1992:176) fixed its sample texts at 2,000 words, just as the Brown and the LOB corpora, and the FLOB and FLOWN corpora from Freiburg, are specific remakes of the earlier ones.

The issue of sampling, however, has more to do with a theoretical stand on the nature of language than with computer storage. This is pointed out by Stubbs (1993:11) who identifies as one of the principles underlying "British Traditions in Text Analysis" the fact that the unit of study must be whole texts. The reason for this is that few linguistic features of a text are distributed evenly throughout, as demonstrated by the work of Swales (1990), for example. This theoretical stand is indeed the one advocated by Sinclair (1991) who points out that "a corpus made up of whole documents is open to a wider range of linguistic studies than a collection of short samples" (ibid.:19). Thus, in the Brown corpus, for instance, "since the limitation on continuous text is 2,000 words, any study of largish text patterns is likely to be inappropriate" (ibid.:23-24).

Conclusion

These issues of authenticity, representativeness and sampling will be with us for some time; corpus linguistics is a very young subject and its assumptions and work practices will be the topic of almost continuous discussions in the coming years. There are, as this chapter has shown, a variety of opinions and approaches, and the important point is that workers in the field should be as explicit as possible, particularly about what they have done in assembling their corpus, and if possible some discussion about why they have taken these decisions. Progress will be made close to a consensus viewpoint if they are willing to explain and defend their work.

Notes

1. As quoted by Stig Johansson at Tuscan Word Centre (April 2000).
2. One could be forgiven for thinking that one thing that a corpus can not be is "hypothetical". Perhaps what Leech means here is the language as a whole as realised in the sum of individual linguistic manifestations.
3. Halliday states that "any concern with grammatical probabilities makes sense only in the context of a paradigmatic model of grammar, one that incorporates the category of *system* in its technical sense as defined by Firth" (1993c:3).
4. A corpus study of the word-forms *ascoltato* and *ascoltata*, carried out as part of a feasibility study in bilingual lexicography for the Council of Europe (Tognini-Bonelli: 1991), revealed a surprising difference in the collocational patterning of the two forms. While *ascoltato* was associated with words such as *stima, rispetto,* etc., *ascoltata* showed a consistent collocation with *confessionale*. It appeared that while a man is listened to because he is respected, women are only "listened to" in the context of confession and penance! This kind of observation, which initially seems to confirm our worse fears of a machismo inbuilt in language and society, cannot be questioned except with hindsight, when the judgement of the linguist may call into question the representativeness of the corpus.
5. The words he uses are "statistical enrichment" and "extension",which seem to indicate the ancillary character of the contribution derived from frequency of occurrence.
6. Bod motivates the statistical approach from a psychological point of view. Considering the problem of disambiguation, he points out that (1) people register frequencies and differences in frequencies, (2) people prefer analyses that have been experienced before, (3) the preference for "old before new" is influenced by the frequency of occurrences of analyses. Hence, he concludes, "a comprehender tends to perceive the most probable analysis of a new input on the basis of frequencies of previously perceived analyses" (1995:13). The implication of this is that "different linguistic experiences can yield different perceived analyses of sentences" (ibid.:13).
7. This point is subsumed quite clearly in the definitions of a corpus quoted above where we find expressions defining the criteria adopted, such as "according to explicit design criteria" (Atkins, Clear and Osler 1992), "according to explicit linguistic criteria in order to be used as a sample of the language" (EAGLES 1994), or relating to the target population the corpus is trying to "represent", such as "assumed to be representative of a given language, dialect, or other subset of a language", "chosen to characterise a state or variety of a language" (Sinclair 1991).
8. A similar distinction is posited between *external* and *internal* criteria by Sinclair (1989; 1991); Nakamura (1993), Sinclair and Nakamura (1995), as well as by Atkins, Clear and Osler (1992).
9. Mindt (1991), in his article *Syntactic Evidence for Semantic Distinction in English*, also finds evidence of the correlation between linguistic and situational criteria. He uses two corpora (one of conversations and one of contemporary plays) in a comparative study of different syntactic features and points out that specification "can be used for an operational distinction of different text types" (ibid.:186). Examining the question of whether there are systematic

dependencies between personal and non-personal subjects and constructions which express the future he concludes that "as with specification, there is systematic difference between the text types: the figures of personal subject are in each case higher in 'plays' than in 'conversations' (ibid.:187).

4 The corpus-based approach

Definition

As the discussion on the issues raised by corpus work in the previous chapters has anticipated, a corpus can be used in different ways in order to validate, exemplify or build up a language theory. Different terms are often used by different scholars, but all centre round one basic distinction. The terms that are frequently used are *corpus-based*, as against *corpus-driven*, and they will be discussed here in that order. To begin with, this chapter will define the *corpus-based* approach in general terms.

The claim of being based on a corpus can be used of all types of work that relate to and draw from a corpus; it confers some authority on the work, but since 'based' is a vague and general relationship, such claims are difficult to validate, and the relationship can be very informal and/or partial. But for the purpose of making a methodological distinction, the term *corpus-based* is used to refer to a methodology that avails itself of the corpus mainly to expound, test or exemplify theories and descriptions that were formulated before large corpora became available to inform language study. Traditionally, linguistic theories are the result of reflection by a scholar after absorbing a great deal of experience of language and languages, and testing the implications and consequences with reference to the intuition of competent or native speakers. The precise nature of the language experience is impossible to ascertain because it figures only as part of the linguist's credentials, and not as part of the methodology of research. If a corpus was to be used to evaluate one of this class of theories, the theory would have to be put into an explicit form so that those aspects of corpus patterning that it covered could be distinguished from those where the theory did not cover, or was at variance with, the evidence. Such a relationship between theory and data is the classical one in linguistics.

We have seen some of the problems arising from such a standpoint in connection with language teaching, discussed in Chapter Two. The example of *any*, for instance, showed clearly how a corpus can be used to validate a theory which is already explicitly articulated in precise statements. The concordance seemed to prove the point that *any* was indeed used for negative statements, for instance. Corpus evidence here was used to quantify existing categories. But the example of *any* also showed the potential problem associated with the corpus-based approach, in that it did not leave the methodological and theoretical space to discover that *any* is also used for a lot of other things.

We could say, therefore, that corpus-based linguists adopt a 'confident' stand with respect to the relationship between theory and data in that they bring with them models of language and descriptions which they believe to be fundamentally adequate, they perceive and analyse the corpus through these categories and sieve the data accordingly. The corpus is considered useful because, on occasions, it indicates where minor corrections and adjustments can be made to the model adopted and, of course, it can also be valuable as a source of quantitative evidence. In this case, however, corpus evidence is brought in as an extra bonus rather than as a determining factor with respect to the analysis, which is still carried out according to pre-existing categories; although it is used to refine such categories, it is never really in a position to challenge them as there is no claim made that they arise directly from the data.

Discussing different methodologies among computational linguists, Atkins, Osler and Clear (1992:14) talk of the 'self-organizing' group which they contrast with 'knowledge-based'. While the former use statistical regularities as a key to analysing and processing the language in the corpus[1], the latter "brings in the result of linguistic theory and logic as the foundation for its models of language" (ibid.). The knowledge-based linguists, therefore, seem to be very similar to what we have described above as corpus-based, and their attention to corpora is fairly recent and rather specific; they are primarily interested in how well their theories account for the data.

Atkins et al. here indirectly point to the gap between theoretical categories designed *a priori*, and corpus evidence. A 'received' theoretical statement pre-exists corpus evidence. It might be based on no textual evidence at all, or on some, but almost certainly on less comprehensive and representative evidence than that provided by a corpus. This fact may be at the root of a mismatch often observed between received categories and corpus data.

In connection with language teaching, Berry (1999) refers to the problem of "unidirectionality" as one of his "seven sins of pedagogic grammars". He argues that unidirectionality is "a problem in the relationship between language description and language pedagogy", and explains that "it occurs when descriptive studies are motivated purely by language theory, by a desire to validate one aspect of a particular theory" (ibid.: 39), so the problem occurs when the data does not fit the theory. This is the point where, in the context of language teaching, the teacher and the theoretician have to part company. The teacher is in constant contact with the class and this does not allow him/her to stray very far from the facts of language; the quality of the teaching and of the methodology adopted is evaluated in the light of regular results. The theoretician, on the other hand - especially the type that is not concerned with building his/her theory on language usage, even when consulting a corpus, chooses to retain priority of judgment. This stance on the priority of pre-existing theoretical statement is very much connected with the choice of a deductive methodology taken for granted in most teaching of grammar as well as in the field of computational linguistics where the model provides the basis for the tags and the parsing categories; but we will come back to the latter in the sections that follow.

There is, however, a problem that jeopardises the tractability of the data in terms of explicit and established categories. This is the inherent variability of naturally occurring language. One could argue that the two positions we are addressing with respect to corpus work, the corpus-based and the corpus-driven, reflect two opposed stances concerning this issue and while the corpus-based linguist attempts to insulate it, standardise it and reduce it, the corpus-driven linguist builds it into the theoretical categories (s)he derives from the data.

Aarts points out (1992:181) that the amount of variation to be found in one single corpus is far in excess of what is described in the grammars; looking forward to the completion of the ICE project, which will make available some twenty comparable corpora of different varieties of English around the world, he does not see how a grammar will ever describe them, even the large *Comprehensive Grammar* (Quirk et al. 1985). So, we could say that when the data does not fit the theory, as pointed out by Aarts above, it is often because of this inherent variability, the apparent ambiguity and the surface instability of language in general and of corpus evidence in particular. It was argued in Chapter Two that, in language teaching, exposing the students to this inherent variability in language and teaching them to identify the relevant patterns of co-selection against the background of variation was a very healthy process. This is perhaps more understandable in an application where the contact with the reality of language facts should have a sobering effect.

However, when we consider the realm of language theory, sometimes the validation of the theoretical statements with language facts is not felt as necessary, or perhaps not as vital. A problem then arises, one that has been cropping up throughout the history of linguistics: given that the data is non-negotiable, does the linguist choose to revise the theory and derive it more directly from corpus evidence, or does (s)he opt to insulate the data from the theory?[2] What is the answer of the corpus-based linguist to this predicament? Given what has been said in the paragraphs above, the answer is that the corpus-based linguist will go for the second option, feeling that a certain amount of variation that has not been accounted for is not important enough to topple a well-established theoretical position. For one thing, there is no need to suppose that simple extensions of the existing statements in grammars will not cover the remainder, and for another the matter of variation between speakers is not accorded high priority among theoretical issues.

There are three popular ways of resolving the problem of the data not fitting the theory. One is to keep the two apart so that there is never a confrontation; another is to use principles of simplification and standardisation, and 'find' a neat and tidy theory within the jungle of data; a third is to build at least some of the corpus evidence into the description as probabilities in systems of choice. Each of these will be considered in turn, first briefly and then at greater length.

The first way of coping with a corpus is to insulate the data so that it does not really affect the theoretical categories adopted; this is in effect discounting it. It must be stressed that what might be considered a dangerous manoeuvre in many lines of academic enquiry - discounting the field data - is seen in linguistics as a perfectly reasonable policy, given that the linguist, as a language user, has intuitive and introspective resources to call on. The stance of insulation will be illustrated by looking mainly at the work of Aarts and referring again to the work of Bod, and considering one of the foremost concerns of Natural Language Processing - anaphora. This kind of work falls in the category of corpus-based because, although accepting in principle the empirical foundation of linguistics and the centrality of language use as evidence for theoretical statements, the theorists and researchers do not strictly derive these from the cumulative effect of repeated events. In other words, such work still sieves the actual evidence of language use through pre-existing theoretical stands that have not themselves been formulated in the light of corpus data.

This is where the second and the third stances within the corpus-based approach come in[3]. The second is to simplify and standardise the data by reducing it to a set of orderly categories which are tractable within existing descriptive systems. Often this process is referred to as 'enriching' and the result is a manually annotated corpus; in this context we will mainly look at the position of Leech. The third is to build the data into a system of abstract possibilities, where the probabilistic dimension added by corpus evidence does not really affect the abstract paradigmatic choices available in the system at any one time. Here we will mainly consider the position of Halliday. These possibilities are not necessarily mutually exclusive, but what these three stances have in common is that the effect on the theory of the corpus experience is limited to validating existing parameters rather than perhaps - if so shown by the evidence - forcing the linguist to look for new ones. Let us discuss these three positions in the light of some examples.

Insulation

In this approach the data is relegated to a secondary position with respect to the theoretical statement proper. This typically happens when the linguist first posits a dichotomy, such as *competence-performance*, and then decides that the insights derived from the corpus only relate to one sphere and not really to the other, or that while some data can be given the stamp of acceptability under certain conditions, other data does not really fit in. The 'whether or not' is usually the product of ad hoc decisions on the part of the linguist and often causes problems when the scholar tries to test his criteria in a scientific way.

The work of the Nijmegen group of scholars and in particular of one of their major exponents, Jan Aarts (1991; Aarts and Oostdijk 1988 etc.), well exemplifies this type of approach. Aarts contrasts *intuition-based* and *observation-based* grammars and gives initial primacy to the former; the linguist first makes hypotheses about the language and expresses them in a formal grammar, with the implication that a corpus is not necessary at this stage. Then a corpus is used as a test-bed for the formal grammar, and the model is presumably extended by this 'confrontation' (Aarts, 1991:47); the result, if all goes well, is that the grammar becomes an observation-based one, and therefore accounts for the facts of language use. So both types of grammar are necessary for a successful outcome: the intuition-based grammar, reflecting competence and the adaptations that result from relating this grammar to a corpus, turning it into an observation-based grammar. The assumption here seems to be that the two grammars are actually amenable to comparison and combination: the observation-based grammar is expected to complement the intuition-based grammar. In case of a clash,it will, in any case, be the linguist's intuition, behind the theoretical model, which is primary compared with the evidence from the corpus.

As we can see, the main concern for the corpus-based grammarian is to establish to what extent the language (in this context it would be perhaps better to talk about sentences[4]) occurring in the corpus is grammatical or at least acceptable . This cannot be achieved solely with reference to the Firthian notion of 'repeated events' as typological statements. For Aarts the first criterion used to decide whether or not a particular construction found in the corpus should be accounted for in the grammar is *frequency of occurrence*, but the other is *normalcy*, that is its acceptability to a large number of users[5]. While the first criterion seems to accept the evidence provided by the corpus as determining, the latter notion cannot be assessed objectively and returns to reliance on intuition as the ultimate criterion for grammaticality. Language use, therefore, will need to be purified and decisions will have to be taken by the linguist as to whether, and in what circumstances, a sentence that occurs should be accounted for in the grammar.

It has been argued that whereas in theoretical linguistics (in the neo-Chomskian tradition) the issue of observable data has been radically excluded from linguistic enquiry, the field of computational linguistics has brought together the theoretical model without necessary excluding the statistical input (Ferrari 2000). However, even when the attempt is to integrate a theoretical and formal approach on the one hand and a statistical and quantitative one on the other, priority is retained by the initial theoretical model and is "guaranteed" by the process of mark-up and annotation which derives its tags from the original model (Ferrari 2000, Bod 1998). This can be seen as another way of insulating the theory from the evidence of the corpus.

Bod's work (1992, 1995, 1998), discussed in the context of corpus representativeness, also falls within what we have called a corpus-based approach which, it is argued, discounts the data. Bod proposes a Data-Oriented Parsing approach and uses a stochastic, corpus-derived model to account for language *performance*, but only in so far as "different perceived analyses of sentences" (1995:13) are concerned. The corpus, therefore, offers the possibility of a statistical extension to a linguistic theory but, as we have noted in Chapter Three, the theory itself remains unaffected by the data observed: the input from the corpus evidence is channelled into a separate container.

So, while for Bod corpus data firmly belongs to *performance*, never to challenge *competence*, for Aarts it has to be thoroughly sieved in order to edge its way into the intuition-based grammar, and again the linguistic categories which belong to competence remain untouched and unaffected by corpus data. In neither case, therefore, is language use really allowed to determine or affect the theoretical statement, which could only exist within the realm of competence, derived by intuition and introspection.

For a slightly different example, we turn to the vexed but central question of anaphora and its resolution. An anaphor is a linguistic entity which indicates a referential tie to some other linguistic entity in the same text. Pronouns are simple and obvious anaphors, but there are some tricky ones, like ellipsis, where the evidence for the anaphor is the absence of something. To describe text adequately each referential tie must be identified, and each anaphor must be resolved. The only way to be sure of the success of this resolution is to automate it. Hence the long and hard search for the rules of anaphora, of which the surface realisations are different in each language.

From the examination of language in use, and in particular the mass of corpus evidence, it seems that there are a number of cases of anaphors which are not resolved, and are never likely to be. Their existence is not challenged by the research community, but just put on one side, while the main research thrust continues to work on the assumption that the correct model for anaphora is the one that treats anaphors as requiring unambiguous resolution. Botley and McEnery (2000) is a state-of-the-art book on anaphor which is quite explicit about this position, while discussing anaphor using a great deal of corpus evidence. Some of that evidence might suggest an alternative model for anaphor, where resolution is one meaningful strand, but only one among several; this evidence cannot be evaluated in the book because the pre-existing definition of anaphor is not open to query.

Once again we see the characteristic corpus-based position, where corpora are extensively worked with and improvements are made to various software identification routines because of the information derived from the corpora, but where the theoretical framework is buffered from exposure to the corpus evidence.

Standardisation

The research policy that is called here 'standardisation' is another attempt to reconcile the statements of an intuitive grammar and the evidence of a corpus, but whereas the adherents of the 'insulation' policy relate essentially to a formal grammar, those who favour standardisation include linguists who adopt a more empirical approach.

The work of Leech is our focus of discussion because his work is influential, and he represents fairly typically the stance of the standardiser. His general position on grammar is recorded in his co-authorship of the *Comprehensive Grammar* (Quirk et al. 1985) as empirical and data-oriented, and in his corpus work he tries to reduce the inbuilt variability of raw data by a process of corpus annotation. The categories of annotation that he adopts reflect received grammatical categories that may or may not fit the data - but are certainly not derived from it.

In this stance the standardisers are not so different from the insulators, except that on investigating their procedure one might expect that they have a less difficult job to do; their grammars seem to be closer in principle to the patterns of the language in use. But there are still substantial problems.

Leech (1992:111), describing the paradigm of empirical research in corpus linguistics, states first of all that this will deal with observed evidence provided in the form of corpora, and secondly that this evidence will be used according to the principle of total accountability, that is exhaustively; nothing will be selected in advance and nothing will be deliberately ignored as irrelevant. Although corpora are to be treated just as large samples of the language, and not as representative of the grammatical potential of the language, there is to be no shirking of the information about the language that they contain. The emphasis is thus strongly empirical, prioritising observation over theory, and in particular demanding that the theory is tested against the "independent" data derived from a corpus.

Note that the theory pre-exists the corpus examination; Leech is quite specific about this. First devise a theory, then test it out. He points to the popularity of this kind of strategy, where the researcher uses the full armoury of intuition, experience and experiment to arrive at the theoretical position, and then adds quantitative information derived from the corpus.

Leech's position here overlaps with the one held by Bod and Aarts above in that he posits a clear distinction between "the model" on the one hand and "the quantitative values of the model" on the other. Whether we call it competence and performance, intuition-based and observation-based grammars, or simply posit a dichotomy between categories and probabilities, the effect is the separation of the theoretical statement from the evidence.

The second stage in Leech's procedure will involve the testing of the accuracy of the model, and this is done in the stiffest test of all - the automation of the annotation process. For this purpose Leech distinguishes between a "training corpus", which is carefully annotated by hand according to the categories of the input grammar, and a "test corpus", which is used in the second stage[6]. He points out that such a procedure can provide an objective measure of the quality of the input grammar, and that grammars can be compared with each other with respect to their performance over a test corpus. Also, because the empirical grammar is negotiable, and can be altered and adapted by feedback from corpus trials, the iteration of "annotate - test - revise" is a powerful method of arriving at a satisfactory grammar and annotation system (note that the corpus used in the middle step - test - is a different corpus from that of the other two).

The evaluation of performance over the test corpus is done with reference to a model of grammar which is independent of both the initial empirical grammar and the grammar implied by the annotation process. So where those disagree, the final decision could go against the corpus evidence.

There is a practical advantage to the approach of Leech, one that has led to a great deal of work in many languages; once the model has been devised and properly tested, it can be related to the data in the form of annotation tags. The data is thus "enriched" (Aarts 1992:180, Bod 1998:2, Leech 1991), enriched being the word often used to describe an annotated - usually parsed or tagged - corpus. The assumption behind the use of this word is that a raw corpus cannot yield the parameters necessary for linguistic analysis unless additional information, derived from pre-existing theoretical descriptions, is somehow built into it.

The reason for adding analytic tags to running text is because the items in the text, by themselves, do not give enough information for a reliable analysis to be made. At the word level, Leech (1991:12) points out that the differences between "*I* (personal pronoun) and *I* (Roman numeral); between *minute* (noun) and *minute* (adjective); or between *lying* (telling untruths) and *lying* (in a recumbent position)" cannot be retrieved from the word forms themselves. It is necessary to identify such distinctions by intuitive means and impose them by means of tags.

This is indeed the predicament of any grammarian facing a corpus and trying to isolate grammatical categories without reference to the specific integration with lexis; we will come back to this point when discussing the corpus-driven approach which adopts a very different position. The problems that Leech raises so clearly have absorbed scholars for more than a decade; there is no doubt that for him there is a real need for annotated corpora calling for "a division of labour between the corpus and the human mind" (1991:15). Thus the human expert will intervene first in analysing the corpus and providing the parameters for such analysis, secondly "at the crucial stage of diagnosis of errors in the corpus analysis, and the feedback of those errors into the corpus analysis" (ibid.:18)[7]. The model used for the analysis will be at first some "intuitively plausible" model, which will then be "trained" to predict future occurrences in the corpus. The result of this process is an annotated corpus, "no longer the 'raw' (or pure) corpus which was originally input to the computer but a version in which linguistic information, of particular kinds, is extensively provided" (Leech 1991:19).

The problem that ultimately lies behind the issue of annotation is that raw data does not appear to be tractable unless it is reduced to a set of systematic parameters. Annotation, therefore, is needed as a kind of interface between the chaotic, imprecise and variable side of language on the one hand, and a formalisable set of parameters on the other. Annotating a corpus, although it will no doubt demand a lot of manual labour on the part of the linguist, and some adjustment of the theoretical categories, will ensure that the data will finally fit the theory.

The good points of annotation lie in its value in applications. Those who are engaged in the language industries require simple and firm classifications; they do not want to cope with ambiguities and they have no intention of waiting while theories are refined and all problems are ironed out. Annotation makes the structures of the language manageable and it allows processing at a level of abstraction that would not otherwise be possible using current techniques, by bringing out the likeness of like events.

The other side of the coin, though, is what Sinclair (1992b:385-6) identifies as loss of information. Discussing taggers, for example, Sinclair points out that the replacement of a text by a string of tags is a reduction of information; for example, words which are different but are allocated the same word class lose this distinctiveness in favour of the recognition that they belong to the same word class.

It could be argued that in a tagged text no information is lost because the words of the text are still there and available, but the problem is that they are bypassed in the normal use of a tagged text. The actual loss of information takes place when, once the annotation of the corpus is completed and the tagsets are attached to the data, the linguist processes the tags rather than the raw data. By doing this the linguist will easily lose sight of the contextual features associated with a certain item and will accept single, uni-functional items - tags - as the primary data. What is lost, therefore, is the ability to analyse the inherent variability of language which is realised in the very tight interconnection between lexical and grammatical patterns. This is the price paid for simplification; a process that is so useful - but it is argued here that the interconnection betzeen lexis and grammar is crucial in determining the meaning and function of a given unit: any processing that loses out on this is bound to lose out in accuracy.

Linguists used tags first of all for word class tagging and then moved on to build parsers on the platform of tagged text; there is now quite a lot of variety in tagging research. But annotation schemes in general prioritise syntactic or wordclass parsing even when the aim is to build up a lexicon[8]. Ironically, therefore, it is the use of annotation advocated by Leech as "additional information" which bypasses the formal contextual features (both lexical and grammatical) which, if included in the processing, would allow the linguist to discriminate between the two uses of "I", "minute" and "lying", and all the hundreds of other homographs in a language.

Perhaps the most obvious point against annotation, though, is the fact the categories of analysis are provided by the linguist, and these categories, at the outset of a study anyway, have not themselves been derived from corpus data. True, they may be modified by confrontation with corpus evidence, but there seems to be an implication that any modification will be of a minor nature. Thus in a way a vicious circle is established: the linguist provides the tools, which in turn assume and provide pre-set solutions. Aarts recognises this relationship (1992:181) but not its viciousness, and makes it quite clear that not only are tools like taggers and parsers essential but they control and even determine the analysis. The results of this activity will no doubt be intuitively acceptable, as they reflect the initial assumptions of the linguist, but they will inevitably reflect real language use only partially.

So far our discussion of the *corpus-based* approach has shown a principal concern with assessing "the level of coverage" and the accuracy or fit of a certain model to the data. As we have seen, although the pre-existing model can be *tested* and in certain cases improved, the question as to whether it should or could be *derived* from corpus evidence does not come into the picture. We will return to this point in Chapters Five and Six which deal more specifically with the *corpus-driven* approach.

Instantiation

Still within the corpus-based approach, the third stance to be presented here is the one referred to earlier as building the data into a system of abstract possibilities, a set of paradigmatic choices available at any one point in the text. This approach is very clearly embodied in the work of Michael Halliday and the Systemic school; Halliday has always had a place for the relative frequency of choices, and in the early nineties he published several papers that make his position clear (Halliday 1991 a, b; 1992a, 1993c, Halliday and James 1993).

Halliday's approach to grammar is straightforwardly paradigmatic (*see*

Introduction to Halliday 1995); it gradually assumed that character in its development over the years. Within this framework Halliday proposes to treat the system as inherently probabilistic (1992a:65,76), and therefore amenable to a stochastic interpretation and analysis.

The basic assumption behind corpus work is, for Halliday, the equation between frequency of occurrence and probability in the paradigmatic grammar. This in turn carries an assumption of representativeness of the corpus, but it is an equation which is normally and naturally made. If a word has appeared ten times per million in a corpus of a hundred million words, there is a good chance that it will do much the same in the next hundred million if there is no major change in the corpus constituency. Halliday's analogy of the weather and the climate, the system and the instance, also apply in this case: "there is no discontinuity when we rewrite frequency as probability"(Halliday and James1993:66). The relative frequency of occurrence observed in the corpus, therefore, can be equated with the *instantiation* of probability in the grammar (ibid.). Given this first assumption, the linguist can proceed to interrogate the corpus with a view to giving a probabilistic substantiation to the parameters of a grammatical system; Halliday (1992a:67ff.) proposes seven strands of investigation which can be summarised as follows:

1. Determine the overall frequencies of the terms in a number of low delicacy grammatical systems.
2. Investigate the same grammatical systems with the frequencies broken down according to register.
3. Determine whether, and if so how far, the probability of selecting one term in a given system is affected by previous selections made within the same system (transitional probabilities).
4. Determine how far a text shows a tendency to increase in complexity.
5. Determine the degree of association between simultaneous systems (conditional probabilities).
6. Consider the insights that conditional probabilities can give into historical linguistic processes.
7. Consider the possibility of a general quantitative principle governing all kinds of "marking".

Thus, by interrogating the corpus, the terms of the system are validated and quantified both as single choices available at one point in time, that is from a purely paradigmatic point of view (cf. points 1 and 2). But they are also considered as interrelated terms in structure (cf. 3 and 5), that is at the syntagmatic level. However, the tendency in the Hallidayan framework is for the environment to remain at least partially paradigmatic, in that the "entry conditions" for a system may require the selection of terms from less delicate systems in the abstract network (Butler 1985:45). Therefore, the syntagmatic level reflects the interconnection between abstract classes, and the interconnection of specific elements (including lexical elements) in structure is not available to the grammarian.

Let us consider a bit more closely the implications of prioritising the paradigmatic point of view with respect to the syntagmatic. The issue of paradigmatic and syntagmatic relations is closely linked to another issue, the one of lexis and grammar. Halliday points out that grammar and lexis are really the same phenomenon spread along a continuum but observed from two different angles. So, at the grammatical end, we find the typical grammatical system, with a small number of terms - often binary - mutually exclusive, and very frequent. They intersect with each other but are in principle distinct. At the other end of the continuum is the lexical perspective, where the picture is almost the opposite. There is a very large number of items, loosely organised with respect to each other; the items - typically words - are each a 'bundle' of features that are not really separable one from another; the features form networks of a sort, but not the stable and regular ones that we see at the grammatical end of the continuum - the networks of lexical features are "local and transitory". Although one would ultimately pursue a unified approach to lexis and grammar, the phenomena at the two poles are qualitatively different and ultimately separable.

This is a mature position regarding the relation of grammar and lexis; Halliday, in his earlier works in the 1960s, talked in terms of "exit to lexis" (1961:266) and saw lexis as a separate component of the level of language form. Once a word has entered the lexical component, the grammatical choices that lie behind its emergence cease to be relevant. The interrelation between lexis and grammar hardly exists; the unit of lexis, the "lexical item" is a construct that is quite independent of the grammar, and does not need to map onto the grammatical structure in any consistent way (1966b:153).

Perhaps now, in the light of the new studies showing the systematic interdependencies between lexis and grammar uncovered by corpus work, he would not subscribe to the same statement any more. However, he still maintains that "it is perfectly possible to treat the whole phenomenon grammatically (..) and it is equally possible to treat the whole phenomenon lexically" (1992a:63). Therefore one could - as he does - adopt a "grammar-observer" stance and get "grammar-like answers"; or, conversely, adopt a "lexis-observer" angle and get "lexis-like answers" (ibid.:64).

Although this position has its attractions because it allows us to delimit our data under very clear headings and it goes along with well established distinctions within the discipline, one has to query it from a methodological perspective when it comes to working on a corpus. The point is brought up by Halliday when, adopting the stance of a grammar-observer, he observes that while the lexicologist's data are relatively easy to observe, "the grammarian's data are very much less accessible" (ibid.). Even the simplest classifications of a systemic grammar are too abstract to be put as retrieval targets in a corpus query language; Halliday instances clauses of mental process, marked circumstantial theme and high obligation modality. Although effortless to a grammarian, the description of these categories in such a way that they can be identified in a corpus is currently impossible. The grammarian is faced with unattractive alternatives; one is to formulate a query, the answer to which will probably include most of the phenomena that are targeted, and the other is to plod through manually and use only the arithmetical facility of the computer, not the analytic one. The first alternative is preferred, despite the manual task of clearing away what is not wanted, because the second alternative inevitably restricts the amount of language that it is possible to examine (1992:64).

Grammatical patterns represent one step in abstraction with respect to the lexical ones; as such they are not easily retrievable from the corpus unless it is annotated. We are reminded here of Firth's observation that a word in usual collocation "stares at you in the face just as it is" (in Palmer 1968:182) and therefore lexical patterns become self evident at a sheer surface scanning of a page of concordances. What Firth insisted upon, though, was that the two were closely linked and that colligation was to be identified *from within* collocational patterns.

We should conclude here that although Halliday starts from a Firthian framework, having adopted the stance of the grammar-observer, he does not really expect to find that a grammatical pattern might be systematically accompanied by, or realised in connection with, a more or less precise lexical constellation. This leads him to exclude from his analysis, from a methodological rather than from a theoretical perspective, the interconnections between lexis and grammar and to try to identify abstract grammatical categories almost in isolation. Recent work on "pattern grammar" (Hunston and Francis 2000), while largely compatible with systemics, takes a different view, and is discussed in the context of the corpus-driven approach below.

When the corpus linguist chooses to isolate and protect received grammatical categories there is no way to avoid the input of a trained human to label parts-of-speech and resolve ambiguities so as to achieve a certain tractability of the data in grammatical terms. Leech is in the same predicament because he cannot avoid recourse to the human annotator. The parsing of the evidence will inevitably be done according to accepted parameters reinforcing the traditional divisions within a discipline; ultimately, frequency will not seriously put into question existing categories either because it will be formally excluded from doing so, as we have seen with Aarts and Bod, or because statistical regularities will only superficially affect what is perceived by the linguist to be a "structural regularity" inbuilt in the system. The absence of a pattern will not be considered as significant and will not jeopardise the existence of a category even if the corpus has been assembled as a representative sample for the description of the language or the specific language variety under study.

Discussion - the corpus-based approach

So far we have seen a group of approaches to the use of a corpus as evidence for linguistic description, and we will shortly proceed to present another kind of approach - the corpus-driven approach. The theoretical assumptions behind corpus work and the issues raised by the evaluation of the findings bring to light opposed traditions with respect to the nature of linguistic evidence. Although there is agreement to the effect that the corpus *can* be used as evidence, this may mask the fact that there seems to be little agreement about *what* the corpus gives evidence *of*. This points to a problem that is not often talked about in explicit terms within the discipline of corpus linguistics; a problem, though, that is at the root of the different factions within the discipline and the different methodological stances with respect to corpus evidence. This is the problem of language use. By investigating this problem we can show the difference between the corpus-based approach which has been discussed in this chapter and the corpus-driven approach which will be introduced in the next.

In the development of linguistic theory in the last century there has been a notable reluctance to derive statements about the linguistic system from the evidence of language use, as we will see in more detail in Chapter Nine. Both within the Saussurian and the Chomskian traditions, in different ways, the theoretical statement remains unaccounted for with respect to the evidence of *parole/performance*. The Firthian tradition (which will be discussed in Chapter Eight), on the other hand, represents a totally different stance and sees the evidence of language use as central for language theory and description.

A corpus is, if nothing else, evidence of language use, and it is ironic that corpus work should now bring together scholars that have such a radically different opinion about what language use yields insights into. The problem reflects the difficulty in accepting, from a neo-Chomskian position, that there exists a relationship, and indeed a continuum, between what Hjelmslev would call the *manifested* and the *manifestable* (1943/1961:106 and 1942:43)[9]. If the theoretician is only to be concerned with the manifestable, and if statements about the manifestable cannot be derived from the manifested, then what indeed is the role of corpus evidence? The paradox seems to lie in the fact that what is actually attested - language use - entertains the possibility of being ungrammatical; as such, it is believed, it has to be sieved and purified before it is allowed to yield insights into the `possible' and be generalisable in terms of the linguistic system. A grammar of the manifested cannot, by definition coincide with a grammar of the manifestable.

In the terminology used in the field, two terms best bring out the different positions with regard to the problem of language use: these refer to the issue of *representativeness* and the issue of *generalisability*. These two terms seem to be used consistently by two opposed schools of thought and reflect two sets of opposed assumptions about language study. Generalisability is used within the neo-Chomskian framework to refer to the hypothetical projection of a sentence or a structure on to an idealised grammar; it bears no direct relevance to the frequency of occurrence, or indeed the likelihood of occurrence in a given corpus. It cannot, by definition, be the property of a "mere list", no matter how comprehensively this is analysed, and it can only be evaluated with respect to mother-tongue intuitions. A grammar that accounts for every single sentence in a corpus can never hope to achieve generalisability simply on the basis of total accountability.

On the other hand, representativeness is used within the neo-Firthian framework and assumes the possibility of a direct link between an attested population and a target population. Representativeness is assessed by comparing the range of variability of a sample with the characteristics of a target population. Although it can be measured only in relative (statistical) terms, a corpus which is taken to be representative is designed to be used as the basis for generalisations about the linguistic system. It follows that the scholars who defend representativeness must account exhaustively for the instances that appear in the corpus; they are not allowed the luxury of selection (see Sinclair 1996 and ff.).

Thus, while, within the neo-Firthian framework, the representativeness of a corpus is considered as the necessary and sufficient condition for making generalisations about language as a whole[10], in the neo-Chomskian tradition a corpus cannot be representative of a given target population, attestation can never be a sufficient condition and the application of mother-tongue intuition has to complement and ratify attested language use before this is given the stamp of acceptability. As is clear in Bod's work, among others, the notion of grammaticality is kept well separate from the notions of production and perception, the assumption being that what is indeed `produced' and `perceived', i.e. understood, may not need to be explained as `grammatical', that is ratified by the language system. Conversely, the notion of what is `grammatical' may indeed encompass a much larger field of what is manifested by language use, and the range of choices allowed by the grammar may go well beyond the `merely' attested ones (Bod 1998).

It is not then surprising that scholars in the generative tradition adopt the attitude to corpus evidence set out above, but we have seen that the position of "empirical" grammarians like Leech - possibly a majority in the language profession as a whole - is not very different when the comparison is made just on this point. The insulation of observations of language usage from statements about the language system is even found in the work of scholars who accept the centrality of language use. These scholars have relied heavily on the analysis of authentic texts, and are accustomed to argue points about the language system from a small number of individually selected examples; they are unsympathetic to the artificial 'problem-case' examples concocted in the generative school. Their method of argument would seem to accommodate, in theory, the evidence of a corpus of authentic texts, but the insights are very different from what we will see emerge from an approach to corpora that does not protect the categories set down by the theory.

The systemic grammarians also present a welcoming attitude to corpus data, and accommodate the frequency information in such a way as to strengthen the theory, not weaken it, but the examination of the corpus is conducted with analytic tools deriving from the theory and not open to much, if any, modification. So although from many quarters corpus linguistics has been heralded as a qualitative revolution, in practice it is mainly being contained, and the radical changes that the discipline can offer are not visible to most of the researchers. A lot of detailed research is needed to persuade the academic community that the findings gained from corpus work are indeed qualitatively different from the findings of pre-corpus work.

Some indication of the rather dubious middle ground between the two positions, the corpus-based and the corpus-driven, is given by Widdowson (1991) who produces a monodimensional simplification of the problem[11]. Considering how different aspects of language knowledge are to be accounted for in linguistic descriptions, Widdowson claims that between Chomsky's view, i.e. "go for the possible", and Sinclair's view, i.e. "go for the performed", the middle ground is represented by scholars such Quirk (as exemplified by Quirk et al. 1972, 1985, etc.) who apparently manage to "go for the feasible". Assuming that the starting grammar is adequate, the feasible is a subset of the possible, excluding sentences that are deemed to have almost zero likelihood of occurrence[12] and thus getting close to describing a competence that "has the implication of performance". The feasible overlaps substantially with the performed, but excludes sentences that are not sanctioned by an external arbiter of "normality".

It is highly doubtful that even a user-friendly notion such as `feasibility' will stand up to analytic examination. Francis (1993:138) for instance, outlining the parameters of a truly 'corpus-driven' grammar, discusses Quirk's work (1985) and points out:

Opening the book at random, we find sentences like:

(1) Walter played the piano more often in Chicago than his brother conducted concerts in the rest of the states. (ibid.:1132)
(2) I've never seen a dog more obviously friendly than your cat. (ibid.:1135)

These examples do not feel natural and it would be difficult to imagine a suitable context that would justify them; and yet anybody involved in language teaching knows very well that they are all too common in standard textbooks as a way to exemplify a grammar rule to learners. In this respect Francis, pointing out the artificiality of these examples, observes:

> While real corpora often provide some very odd examples indeed, their oddness rarely has this unmistakable ring of artificiality. One of the reasons for the artificiality of examples like the above is that they are given as possible variants of other sentences, in order to contrast one item, structure or system with another in terms of what is possible and what is not. (..) These two examples are not ungrammatical sentences, but they do not meet basic standards of conversational relevance: they are unnatural precisely because they point to possibilities rather than realities. The descriptive base of the grammars which accommodate them is essentially contrastive. (Francis 1993:138)

What seems to take place here is some kind of curious reversal of priority. If the grammarian had originally started with the aim of accounting for the language by explaining the system, it would seem now that the system has taken over and examples of `language use' - some of them quite implausible - are actually being made up in order to account for a system of abstract possibilities.

Going back to the corpus-based approach discussed in this chapter, what has been referred to above as insulating the data is a necessary implication of a position that does not fully accept the direct relevance of actual usage to theoretical statement. On the other hand, as emerges from the discussion, it is clear that even the greatest respect for the `feasible' does not, in fact, always produce very likely sentences and the categories derived from the feasible are not likely to fit the attested. This is where corpus evidence does not support the pre-set aims of the linguist: faced with the mismatch, and in spite of the lip service paid to the importance of corpus representativeness, many linguists still choose to retain `the last word' with respect to the patterns shown up by the corpus. Authority is still kept in the hands of the few, and remains cloaked in mystery.

To sum up, we can say that the corpus-based approach refers to a type of methodology where the commitment to the data as a whole is not ultimately very strict or systematic. Frequency distributions, or the absence of a given pattern, although noted, may not be determining in the formulation of a theoretical statement about the system. In this way, as we have seen, corpora are typically used to validate - but only to a certain extent - existing categories or to supplement the theory with a probabilistic dimension. Typically, the corpus-based approach will prioritise the information yielded by syntactic rather than lexical patterns. The systematic interrelations between the two are likely to go unnoticed and therefore are not allowed to determine the categories of the system.

Notes

1. Leech (1992:111) gives as an instance of this type of "more extreme empiricism" the trigram modeling of corpus data which is used in the development of speech recognisers. He notes that "here the model of language is that of a hidden Markov model, and its content is derived automatically from transitional word-frequency statistics in large corpora" (Leech quotes as examples Bahl, Jelinek, Mercer 1993 and Jelinek 1986). I will differentiate between this approach and the *corpus-driven* because the latter still makes use of the input of the linguist.
2. Perhaps what we are asking here is whether the linguist recognises the fact that corpus data is not just more data, it is also data of a different quality.
3. Some authoritative works such as Quirk et al's *A Comprehensive Grammar of the English Language* (1985) fall within this approach because, although they claim some reliance on corpus evidence (the Survey of English Usage), they do not derive their categories from the corpora they are using and, when it comes to exemplify these categories, often resort to idealised or invented examples. This point is illustrated very convincingly by G. Francis (1993) in her article "A Corpus-driven Approach to Grammar".
4. We are reminded at this point of the observation made by Biber and Finegan (1991:209): "while corpora comprise collections of texts, studies have most commonly exploited the corpora as collections of sentences, analysing particular lexical items, phrases or grammatical constructions within their sentential context. Such studies are significant, among other ways, in that they analyse particular constructions in naturally occurring discourse rather than in made-up sentences. But the research goals of most such studies could be met equally well by a corpus of isolated sentences. Reflecting the state of linguistic studies generally, few studies have exploited the corpora to analyse characteristics of texts rather than characteristics of sentences". Notions such as "acceptability" and "grammaticality", therefore, will tend to be applied to sentence level and ignore wider issues such as representativeness, register and naturalness".
5. Here "acceptability" is defined in terms of the "contextualizability" of a sentence (Aarts, 1991:55).
6. Bod (1995:18) refers to a similar process of testing; according to it, "a manually analyzed language corpus is randomly divided into a training set and a test set, where the analyses from the test set are kept aside. The analyses from the training set may be used to train the system, while the sentences of the test set are parsed by the system. The degree to which the most probable analyses generated by the system match with the test set analyses is a measure for the accuracy of the system".
7. This procedure is clearly explained by Leech with reference to a grammatical word-tagging system: "the human expert here - say, a grammarian or a lexicographer - proposes a set of grammatical tags to represent the set of English word categories; a lexicon and other databases are built, making use of these categories; and programs are written to assign an appropriate word tag to each of the word tokens in the corpus. The program achieves its task at a success rate of x per cent (x being typically in the region of 96-7 per cent); the errors that it makes - judged to be errors on independent linguistic grounds - are fed back to the expert, who then proposes modifications to the original set of categories, or the program, or both" (1991:15).
8. For the results of a recent "shallow-parse" project see the 1998 report of the SPARKLE project, *http://www.linglink.lu/hlt/projects/sparkle/AR/ar-98.asp*.
9. Similar dichotomies such as *langue* and *parole*, *competence* and *performance* also assume the total separability of the two entities and their unaccountability with respect to each other.
10. Although we are talking here of language as a whole or the linguistic system in general, the notion of representativeness may relate specifically to a certain language variety or sublanguage.

The point here is the relationship between the attested and the possible.
11. See de Beaugrande's discussion in "Large Corpora and Applied Linguistics", forthcoming 2000; *www.beaugrande.com.*
12. Widdowson cites *This is the malt the rat the cat the dog chased killed ate* as an example.

5 The corpus-driven approach

Introduction

The examples discussed in Chapter Two show corpus linguistics at work, but in a different mode from the corpus-based approach that has been extensively discussed in the two intervening chapters. We now turn to a closer examination of the *corpus-driven* approach to corpus linguistics, where the linguist uses a corpus beyond the selection of examples to support linguistic argument or to validate a theoretical statement.

In a corpus-driven approach the commitment of the linguist is to the integrity of the data as a whole, and descriptions aim to be comprehensive with respect to corpus evidence. The corpus, therefore, is seen as more than a repository of examples to back pre-existing theories or a probabilistic extension to an already well defined system. The theoretical statements are fully consistent with, and reflect directly, the evidence provided by the corpus. Indeed, many of the statements are of a kind that are not usually accessible by any other means than the inspection of corpus evidence. Examples are normally taken verbatim, in other words they are not adjusted in any way to fit the predefined categories of the analyst; recurrent patterns and frequency distributions are expected to form the basic evidence for linguistic categories; the absence of a pattern is considered potentially meaningful.

This approach is the one adopted in this book and, although it still is largely unexplored in terms of the qualitative revolution it brings about, every step taken in this direction seems to lead the scholar to uncover new grounds, posit new hypotheses and not always support old ones. This is where the change of attitude indirectly brought about by the computer becomes most threatening for the linguistic status quo; the evidence that comes to light has to be either rejected by argument or respected - it cannot be ignored. In contrast to the corpus-based approach, which works always within accepted frameworks, often dichotomies like competence/performance, system/instance, lexis/grammar, in this chapter we will explore whether such dichotomies as these are borne out by the corpus or whether, and if so in what way, they should be revisited in the light of the new evidence.

The position that we shall examine here, therefore, starts by accepting the evidence and sees that theoretical and descriptive statements "reflect the evidence" (Sinclair 1991:4). The theory has no independent existence from the evidence and the general methodological path is clear: observation leads to hypothesis leads to generalisation leads to unification in theoretical statement. It is important to understand here that this methodology is not mechanical, but mediated constantly by the linguist, who is still behaving as a linguist and applying his or her knowledge and experience and intelligence at every stage during this process. There is no such a thing as pure induction; we should always bear in mind Firth's statement pointing out that:

> Each scholar makes his own selection and grouping of facts determined by his attitudes and theories and by the nature of his experience of reality of which he himself is part[1] (J.R. Firth, in Palmer 1968:29)

Firth had concluded that "there are no scientific facts until they are stated", (ibid.:30)[2] and the immediate feedback that can be provided from the corpus for an emerging hypothesis makes it easy to detect inaccuracies and incompatibilities.

The freshness of this approach could not have been predicted; twenty years ago there was no awareness of the need to build up a corpus-driven approach, and the small corpora of the time yielded plenty of interesting information when interrogated with a corpus-based strategy (Johansson & Hofland 1994, Francis & Kucera 1979). It was only gradually that researchers realised how fundamentally the traditional pre-corpus descriptions of language were being implicitly questioned by the evidence of larger corpora. The Cobuild project, which reflects Sinclair's stances on language theory and descriptive methodology (Sinclair 1987d), can be seen as the very first study in corpus-driven lexicography. The series of reference materials that stemmed from it are extending the range of studies into other areas such as grammar (Cobuild English Grammar 1990, Hunston and Francis 2000), collocation (Sinclair, in preparation), language teaching (see Cobuild Guides 1991 and ff.) and have changed the way meaning is identified and defined. We have looked at examples of definition and matched them with the data they reflected (see section on *fickle* and *flexible* in Chapter Two), but it is argued that the change brought about is all pervasive, both theoretically and methodologically, and once the conceptual adjustment to the new unit of meaning proposed by Sinclair (1996c, 1998b) is made, there is no way to turn back and it is impossible to return to the old ways of thinking, of teaching, of translating.

In spite of the revolutionary nature of the change he brought about, Sinclair (1987d; 1991:2), reporting the initial aims of the Cobuild project, recalls that the project was not expected to find out new facts about English, and there was no provision in the plans or the budget for coping with restructuring the lexicography when it became clear that such a course was necessary. Sinclair has been accused of "ferocious empiricism" (Hanks 1997) and it is his determination to find methods of interpretation of what he saw that let him to formulate the methodological steps and define the theoretical framework that made them possible.

It is within this approach that Sinclair's disparaging remark about what he calls 'pre-corpus beliefs' (see also 1991:2) can be understood: the analysis of corpus evidence has truly brought about a qualitative change in the description of language. However, it is not only a question that the existing descriptive statements can be shown to be wrong or inaccurate. There might be a large number of potentially meaningful patterns that escape the attention of the traditional linguist; these will not be recorded in traditional reference works and may not even be recognised until they are forced upon the corpus analyst by the sheer visual presence of the emerging patterns in a concordance page. In this respect Kennedy, working in the field of language teaching, warns that the corpus linguist needs to have an open mind because:

> "Language description can be challenged by corpus research. It should not be assumed that the types identified in traditional descriptions should be the only things which are quantified" (1992:367).

The examples discussed so far show the type of patterning that can go unnoticed to the most trained eye and yet can be proved to be determining in the attribution of meaning. Both with *all but* and *except that,* the correlation of specific formal patterns in the concordance and their function led to very precise meaning disambiguation on the one hand and the identification of a wider pragmatic dimension on the other. In either case, the different possibilities were not just "shades" of meaning, which - it could be argued - can go unnoticed, but they were almost diametrically opposed in function; furthermore, in terms of frequency they were very common. In either case, the evidence of what descriptive statements had produced on the meaning was totally insufficient and wrong as a general guidance for the learner.

The general gist of remarks such as the one by Kennedy above (see also Sinclair 1991, 2000; Stubbs 1993), therefore, points to the unsettling nature of the findings yielded by corpus evidence on two accounts. First, so much data is now at the tip of one's fingers that patterns which have hitherto been considered inaccessible are now on the screen; *parole* is, therefore, becoming amenable to systematic observation. Second, the novelty of the first findings, the tradition of the theory and description of languages is not yet prepared for the patterns that now systematically emerge in a simple structure such as an alphabetised concordance.

The unexpectedness of the findings derived from corpus evidence leads to the conclusion that intuition is not comprehensively reliable as a source of information about language.

As Sampson points out, justifying his conversion to corpus-oriented work :

> I knew it was time for a change of intellectual direction. If intuition could get the facts of language as wrong as this[3], there seemed little purpose in continuing to pursue abstract philosophical arguments for or against the existence of innate knowledge of language. There had to be some way of engaging with the concrete empirical realities of language, without getting so bogged down in innumerable details that no analytical conclusions could ever be drawn. (Sampson 1996:25)

The corpus-driven approach will be illustrated further in a range of current scholarship in the remainder of this book. We will return to a Firthian theoretical position in tracing the assumptions behind this type of corpus-driven work and, within this framework, define the relevant terminology and illustrate the methodological steps that need to be taken. We will then examine some of the specific assumptions and the theoretical changes that this "new perspective on description" has brought about by looking at some work by Sinclair and exemplify some of the issues raised with some English and Italian examples.

Definitions

In the Introduction to this book we briefly defined the approach to corpus work adopted here as an empirical approach to the description of language use, assuming a contextual and functional theory of meaning and making use of the new technologies. This outline definition does not necessarily apply to the corpus-based approach where the relationship between an item and its context is not taken as systematic and determining in the definition of linguistic categories. The corpus-driven approach, on the other hand, fits well the definition in that it aims to derive linguistic categories systematically from the recurrent patterns and the frequency distributions that emerge from language in context. Taking this one step further, we could say that it goes along with a holistic approach to language in that the cumulative effect of repeated instances is taken to reflect the semiotic system; the text is seen as an integral part of its verbal context and, ultimately, no discontinuity is assumed between this and the wider context of situation, and the even wider context of culture.

Although this study will use the term *co-text* to refer specifically to the verbal environment that we are aiming to formalise, and the term *context* to refer to the situational and cultural parameters involved in the interaction, it is assumed here that contextual elements, such as the relevant participants or the relevant objects, will often have a correlate linguistic realisation in the co-text.

This link between co-text and cultural context becomes, of course, very important in the study of a foreign language or in the comparison of languages or varieties. Louw (1991, personal communication) provides a good example of how a collocational patterning can reflect genre and language variety and how physically observable this connection is in a set of concordances. He instances the different collocates of *wash, washing,* etc. in a corpus of British English and another of Zimbabwean English; he shows that in the first the collocates are items like *machine, powder, spin,* while in the second more likely collocates are *women, river, earth, stones.* Collocates reflect the context of situation, and the latter may include features such as genre and register. The Zimbabwean corpus had a prominent element of literary texts (for example "Waiting for the rain" by Charles Mungoshi, where women washing in the river are a recurrent theme across the novel) and this feature is easily correlated with the collocational patterning shown by the concordance. Louw's observation is a good example of how internal criteria (Biber 1994, Nakamura and Sinclair 1995) can be used to assess the representativeness of a corpus.

As we can see, when it comes to a corpus-driven approach, the issue of the representativeness of the corpus can be seen in its true importance; since the information provided by the corpus is placed centrally and accounted for exhaustively, then there is a risk of error if the corpus turns out to be unrepresentative. At present, until we know a lot more about the effect of selections on the overall picture, it is imperative to be explicit about how a corpus is constructed, and to review the relevance of a particular corpus if there is reason to query the data it provides. In practice, the corpora available today are a mixed bunch of vastly differing sizes, ages and philosophies, and it is at a later stage perhaps, when the results of the data analysis are evaluated, that the linguist sometimes comes to question the parameters according to which the corpus has been assembled or the typology of the texts included.

Because corpus linguistics is a new approach, the issue of corpus reliability is one that raises concern. It is indeed a matter that has to be continuously monitored, as Biber (1994) maintained. A corpus can never be taken for granted, and must always be able to show its credentials. Corpus evidence relates to description and theory in exactly the same way as any other scientific evidence that goes through sampling procedures; the unfamiliar feel of it for a linguist is that it adds further authority and reliability to previous ways of gathering field evidence.

Given these preliminary remarks, it is understandable that the Firthian contextual theory of meaning (see Chapter Eight) is seen to suit well the assumptions behind the corpus-driven approach. Firth advocates a view of language as the vector of "the continuity of repetitions in the social process" (1957:183), and this seems particularly well fitting for a methodology where frequency of occurrence is made tangible and quantifiable by the use of the computer. Here, again using Firth's words, we could say that the role of the linguist is to "abstract the impersonal from the personal by regarding it as typological" (ibid.:188), and this is indeed what the corpus-driven linguist does when (s)he isolates the repeated patterns on the vertical axis of the concordance and derives from them statements of meaning and insights into language. In the Firthian framework the typical cannot be severed from actual usage, and "repeated events" are the central evidence of what people do, how language functions and what language is about. The statements derived from the *formalisation of repeated events*, therefore, are taken to correlate directly with language as a semiotic system, as realised in the specific corpus.

It is therefore appropriate to set up as the minimum sufficient condition for a pattern of occurrence to merit a place in the description of the language, that it occurs at least twice, and that the occurrences appear to be independent of each other (so if the only two occurrences are from the same document, there is too much of a risk that we are recording a personal idiosyncrasy and not a regular feature of the language). Then we need to define what a pattern is, and what counts as a repetition.

Let us consider now what type of repeated event is amenable to be observed in a concordance and formalised. First of all we should note that different degrees of formalisation are allowed by the computer. Apart from frequency of occurrence of individual words or phrases, which is in itself significant, the most obvious and the most immediately identifiable pattern is *collocation*, the "recurrent co-occurrence of words" (Clear, 1993:277). Nowadays there are several simple software packages which will provide a collocational profile of a given node word with information about its list of the relevant collocates, along with such information as the co-occurrence frequencies, overall frequencies in the corpus and significance value[4]. Collocations can thus be characterised in terms of their frequency and their position as well as the variation in their composition; in other words, their idiomaticity. Specific collocational patterns can also be contextualised and examined in detail by using a search pattern like $W+W$ in a concordance package and specifying a maximum number of words intervening between the two nodes.

Another type of pattern that is amenable to automatic or semi-automatic formalisation is *colligation*, the grammatical patterning in which the node word, as member of its class, is embedded. Colligation, defined by Firth as "the interrelations of the syntactical categories" (in Palmer 1968:23), is the statement of meaning at the grammatical level and concerns therefore the relationships between word classes and sentence classes. In the light of corpus evidence, however, the concept of colligation is being extended to include the syntactic constraints, or indeed preferences, that a specific word, seen as a unique lexical item rather than as a member of its class, entertains within its environment[5].

While collocation is instantly identifiable on the vertical axis of an alphabetised concordance, colligation represents a step in abstraction and is therefore less immediately recognisable unless the text is tagged with precisely the required grammatical information. In English, small corpora of one million words with extensive tagging and parsing are available from many sources (for example the ICAME, BNC Sampler, ICE). Now that large corpora, parsed or semi-parsed, are also starting to become available for a growing number of languages (for English one hundred million words from the BNC and some four hundred million from The Bank of English), it is possible to retrieve a lot of grammatical information, and some investigations are speeded up. The Constraint Grammar (Karlsson et al. 1995) can be used to parse a corpus of any length, with minimal manual preprocessing.

Unfortunately, none of these methods gives entirely satisfactory results; because the type of annotation categories according to which the evidence is sorted are entirely grammatical, they are shown to be insufficient and only partially replicable. The "grammatical sieve" seems to leave large quantities of evidence unattended, and in the generalisation a lot of information is lost. The various examples which follow make it clear that many of the meaningful patterns would not appear if the analysis was restricted to grammar, or was required to treat grammar and lexis separately. Grammatical parsing on its own is not sufficient to account for the crucial evidence in many cases, and unless lexical constraints are built into the picture, the grammatical categories adopted will lack generalisibility and replicability. Automatic annotation will, at best, leave some questions unanswered, whereas manual or semi-manual annotation will often end up stretching the evidence to fit the categories.

This is a classic case of misplaced effort caused by theories which are not up to accounting for the evidence. Once this type of truly lexical-grammatical description becomes the standard, it will be possible to use its categories for parsing corpus data, and then the data will be truly "tractable" in colligational terms.

Collocational and colligational patterns will, together, form the basis of the formalisation of repeated events. Only a descriptive statement that identifies their interconnections will yield insights into meaning. The notion of "pattern" as the meeting point between lexis and grammar thus becomes central to corpus-driven linguistics. An example of this approach is given by Hunston and Francis (2000), for instance, who define their *Pattern Grammar* as a corpus-driven approach to the lexical grammar of English. We will report below their definition of what counts as "a pattern":

> The patterns of a word can be defined as all the words and structures which are regularly associated with the word and which contribute to its meaning. A pattern can be identified if a combination of words occurs relatively frequently, if it is dependent on a particular word choice, and if there is a clear meaning associated with it. (Hunston and Francis, 2000:37)

It is this notion that, when systematically applied to the description of language, radically affects the unit of currency for linguistic description.

Given the assumptions of corpus-driven work discussed above, let us now briefly outline the methodological steps that the corpus-driven linguist is likely to take. We will exemplify this by looking at Mindt (1991) and the way he sets out both his methodological parameters and his assumptions. Mindt considers "syntactic evidence for semantic distinctions in English" and observes that "with traditional methods it is not possible to perform analyses of language data which are large enough to permit empirically founded generalisations" (ibid:194); as a consequence, he points out, "semantic distinctions are very often arrived at intuitively and described accordingly" (ibid.:182). The assumption of Mindt's study is that "the meaning of an element is either unambiguously revealed by its form or clarified by a contextual signal" (ibid.:182). We could say, therefore, that he also works within the framework of a contextual theory of meaning, even though he does not quite goes as far as accepting the interrelations between lexis and grammar. Still, his approach leads him to uncover very basic inadequacies of traditional grammatical statements. We have discussed in Chapter Two, for example, his contribution on the semantics of *any* where he pointed out that the traditional description (non-assertive meaning with a syntactic environment which is basically marked by negation) was true for less than fifty per cent of the occurrences.

The interdependencies he uncovers between syntactic regularities and semantic distinctions suggest two points which well sum up the general approach. Firstly that now for the first time the linguist, unlike his/her predecessors, who had to rely on traditional manual procedures of linguistic analysis, can "arrive at generalizations inductively from the data rather than look for examples that confirm hypotheses based on smaller sets of data" (Mindt ibid.:195). Secondly, that the type of conclusions drawn from the data more often than not make it necessary to "redefine linguistic classes, regroup cases or reclassify items" (ibid.:194).

The position outlined above goes well beyond what Leech (1991) defined as the empirical paradigm of corpus linguistics because Mindt and others systematically derive generalisations only from tested phenomena and refuse to superimpose on the data categories which have not been derived from, and substantiated by, the corpus evidence. It also casts serious doubts on the role of intuition and introspection, consistently proven to be unreliable when it comes to representing exactly how language is really used (Sinclair 1991:39). Intuition will still be considered an essential input; it will play a big part, for instance, in selecting the phenomenon that the linguist will choose to investigate, and ultimately it will have an important role when it comes to evaluating the evidence in the corpus. The corpus can still be used as a test-bed for the linguist's hypotheses and intuitions about language but, as G. Francis points out, "only if we are ready to abandon our theories at any moment and posit something new on the basis of the evidence" (1993:139).

The research platform established by Sinclair as corpus-driven has begun to publish substantial grammatical reference works, like the Cobuild Grammar Patterns (1996, 1998) whose rationale is explained in Hunston and Francis (2000). By looking at the co-selections of nouns, verbs and adjectives they show that this brings out a semantic correlate that was obscured when the perspective was exclusively grammatical.

In the sections that follow we shall examine some of the issues that need to be revisited on the basis of this kind of evidence; we will do so looking specifically at some work by Sinclair who has set out the parameters of corpus-driven study.

Word and lemma

The fact that lemma and inflected forms are bound to share the same meaning and differ only in their grammatical profile - the lexical profile is not usually considered relevant - is one of those apparently inoffensive assumptions on which most of our reference works are based: we look up a verb in a dictionary under the base form, or an Italian adjective under the masculine singular. An association that has a certain value in terms of convenience (a dictionary entry, for example) should not be taken for granted and left totally unquestioned. We will start our investigation into the issues related to a corpus-driven approach from here, as we believe that revisiting the lemma/forms association in the light of corpus evidence makes a good starting point because of its pervasive involvement of so many aspects of language patterning.

In several detailed studies of lexical items, Sinclair (1985, 1987f, 1991, etc.) questions the traditional association between lemma and word-forms as potentially unfounded. He takes as examples words of the common vocabulary stock such as *decline* (1985, 1991:41ff) and *yield* (1988, 1991:53ff) or phrasal verbs such as those with *set* (1991:67ff) and shows that not only is each inflected form clearly associated with a specific pattern of usage, but also that different senses of a word or phrase can be correlated with a characteristic environment and pattern of choice at the lexical, the grammatical and the semantic levels.

So, for instance, in the lemma |*decline*| Sinclair observes that "the form *decline* is associated with nominal usage, *declining* with adjectival usage, and *declines*, *declined*, with verbal usage" (1991:46). Corpus evidence also invariably shows that there is no guaranteed similarity between inflected forms if we consider their frequency (Sinclair 1991:68-9) and their collocational associations.

Along the same lines, a revealing example of this is given by Stubbs (1996) who considers the lemma |*educate*|:

In 130 million words, frequencies were: *education* 27,705, *educated* 3,450, *educate* 858, *educating* 463, *educates* 29. The form *education* collocates primarily with terms denoting institutions (e.g. *further, higher, secondary, university*). The form *educate* with approximate synonyms such as *enlighten, entertain, help, inform, train.* (..) The form *educated* frequently collocates with *at* (often in the phrase *he was educated at*) and then with a range of prestigious institutional names, including *Cambridge, Charterhouse, college, Eton, Harrow, Harvard, Oxford, school, university, Yale*. The collocates of the form educated therefore provide a little list of ways in which men (much less frequently women) are classified and talked about. (Stubbs 1996:172-173)

Using Sinclair's words, we can conclude from this that:

There is a good case for arguing that each distinct form is potentially a unique lexical unit, and that forms should only be conflated into lemmas when their environments show a certain amount and type of similarity. (1991:8)

We will illustrate and support this position with two worked examples, one from English and one from Italian. The English evidence concerns the different meanings of *faced* and *facing*, with a sidelong glance at the effect of the different components of a corpus on the results - a broadly-based subcorpus differentiates the words quite well, while a more homogeneous subcorpus does not. The Italian example compares the two infinitive forms *saper* and *sapere*, which could be taken as alternative forms given specific grammatical constraints.

First, we will consider the differences between two inflected forms of the verb *to face*, that is *facing* and *faced*, looking specifically at their collocational profiles in the Birmingham corpus (general English) and the *Economist* and *Wall Street Journal (WSJ)* corpus (semi-technical language of economics). Among the various usages of the verb there are two which identify respectively:

(1) a more concrete area of meaning where things or people "are positioned opposite another thing or person or are looking in that direction"
(2) a more abstract area where "if you face something difficult or unpleasant, or if you are faced with it, it is going to affect you and you have to deal with it" (Cobuild English Language Dictionary).

We will consider these two meanings and identify them and their relative frequency by looking at the most significant collocates of our chosen inflected forms.

Let us first consider the relative frequency of these inflected forms in the two corpora which we are considering at the moment (see Table 1 below). We note the tendency here for both forms to appear more frequently in the *Economist* and *WSJ* corpus even though this is smaller than the Birmingham corpus:

FACING		FACED	
Bham Corpus (19.5 mill words)	Economist &WSJ (15.7 mill words)	Bham Corpus (19.5 mill words)	Economist &WSJ (15.7 mill words)
668	827	787	910

Table 1: relative frequencies of *facing* and *faced* across corpora

One glance at the collocational profiles set out in Table 2 below dispels any possible illusion that inflected forms are grammatical variations of a certain base form, but broadly share the same meaning of the base form and have a similar behaviour. Elements from the context in which these two forms operate are found in their verbal co-text and so we find traces of the participants in the verbal event, the verbal action, and the non-verbal events connected with it.

FACING		FACED	
Bham Corpus	Economist &WSJ	Bham Corpus	Economist &WSJ
forwards	crunch	squarely	grim
palms	toughest	spun	dilemma
stood	challenges	dilemma	obstacles
sat	reformers	alternatives	challenges
problems	dilemma	prospect	prospect
windows	tasks	task	pressures
chair	troubles	choice	competition
sitting	choices	problem	difficulties
direction	difficulties	problems	shame
river	challenge	enormous	criticism
each	charges	challenge	choice
problem	task	practical	challenge
door	biggest	possibility	threat
table	prospect	situation	task
across	tough	threat	firms
feet	makers	with	tough
serious	immediate	crisis	defeat
wall	problems		
front	competition		

Table 2: collocational profiles of *facing* and *faced*

In this table we see that the concrete meaning indicating position and direction can be disambiguated quite clearly at the collocational level. So with *facing* in the Birmingham corpus we find words such as *forwards, palms, stood, sat, windows, chair, sitting, direction, river, each, door, table, across, feet, wall, front* which are very obviously related to position. We find also words that relate to the more abstract notion which has to do with confronting problematic areas: *problems, problem, fear, serious,* but as we can see they are relatively rare compared to the first group, so we could conclude that in a corpus of general English the physical meaning of *facing*, indicating position and direction, is much more common than the abstract one. It is interesting to note that the same generalisation does not apply to the *Economist* & *WSJ* corpus where the collocates of *facing* are consistently abstract. Considering now the form *faced*, we do not find a parallel with the preference for the physical use either in the Birmingham or in the *Economist* & *WSJ* corpora: the only collocate that could refer to something physical, *squarely*, does not in fact do so, but always indicates the connection with problems and difficulties when it accompanies the verb to *face*. The two inflected forms have taken on different roles and this specialisation according to word form has also followed register boundaries between a more general purpose corpus and a more specialised corpus such as the *Economist* and *WSJ* corpus.

We should also note that a specific grammatical pattern has become associated with the word form *facing*, but not with *faced*. This is the possibility that the subject can either precede or follow the verb. In Table 3 below we see instances from the *Economist* and *WSJ* corpus where the subject is preceding the verb; this choice is represented by 40% of the instances:

1. venue of $ 1.5 billion. The company, **facing** a severe liquidity bind, sought pr
2. markets closed. U.S. chip makers are **facing** continued slack demand following a
3. with established markets. Consumers **facing** dearer petrol and heating - oil aft
4. to the FBI. Still, with individuals **facing** fines of $250,000 and prison for
5. ll of hard currency. Some hotels are **facing** hard times, though not the Palace
6. ries in rich industrial countries are **facing** more and more competition from the
7. would stop. France, for example, **facing** recession and rising unemployment,
8. it rule. Most European countries are **facing** the task of chopping two or three p
9. declared bankrupt. Mr Nadir, who is **facing** theft and false accounting charges
10. problem: The world's airlines are **facing** their biggest-ever shake-out

Table 3: subject preceding *facing*

On the other hand, in another more common, possibility, it is the object that precedes the verb (60% of the instances); Table 4 below reports this pattern.

1. Washington market. One of the problems **facing** Cadillacs in Washington is the demo
2.   Thai capital. An immediate question **facing** Mr Banharn is how to deal with two
3.   The number of hostile troops directly **facing** NATO in central Europe has thus fal
4.   supposedly the most difficult dilemma **facing** North Korea may be nothing of the
5.   ba joke about the economic challenge **facing** Poland. ``Capitalism is to commun
6.   time of troubles THE great challenge **facing** Russia is to prevent what Boris Yel
7.   ted and underreported safety problems **facing** airlines. To combat lax record-
8.   ere firms often trip up. The dilemma **facing** managers is that whereas total -
9.   ojects. The two biggest difficulties **facing** regional reformers are the local
10.   makes no bones about the danger **facing** the country: 'I am deeply convinced

Table 4: object preceding *facing*

As we have seen, the different patterns associated with *facing* and *faced*, as different forms of the same lemma *face*, have drawn a very clear dividing line between the two in terms of their use and their meanings.

The lemma/forms association is also consistently called into question when one looks at the case of a strongly inflected language such as Italian. Let us consider below a sample set of lines showing the patterns of the word-form *saper* and compare its lexico-grammatical profile with that of *sapere*. Usually grammars differentiate *saper* from *sapere* because the *-er* form is followed by an infinitive form, but the difference between the two forms is not even mentioned in a dictionary (cf. Collins Italian Dictionary, New First Edition) as they are taken to share the same meaning. The citations of *saper* reported in Table 5 below are just a sample automatically reduced from the total 184 instances present in the Italian corpus.

1.   lingua italiana. Ad esempio, occorre **saper** capire al volo se una parola che suo
2.   l'enologo: educhiamo l'olfatto. **Saper** degustare e valutare il vino non è
3.   occorre cioè, applicando la ragione, **saper** distinguere i veri dai falsi presupp
4.   campagne pubblicitarie, è importante **saper** giudicare una fotografia, scegliere
5.   era scomparsa in cucina. Non voglio **saper** niente, ne approfittò avidamente
6.   enton aveva detto subito: non voglio **saper** niente in anticipo: un autore dev'
7.   di comparse di cui non ci interessa **saper** nulla, come appunto il Giovannino
8.   erabile, deve essere paziente, deve **saper** padroneggiare la propria fisionom
9.   voro all'amore. Il segreto sta nel **saper** pianificare nel modo più razionale
10.   essere soprattutto attori: bisogna **saper** soffrire, amare, piangere. Per questo

Table 5: *saper*

A quick scanning through the citations above will suffice to identify the typical environments of *saper*. The main colligational feature associated with the node word is the infinitive immediately to the right and this confirms what we are usually told in the grammars; this pattern accounts for the majority of the instances

(82%). To the left, given that *saper* is an infinitive itself, we have in Italian a limited set of options, but it is interesting to note the distribution of different features. The patterns show a prominent usage of *saper* as a nominalised infinitive such as *nel saper pianificare* in citation 9 above (26%). When *saper* is a standard infinitive it is usually introduced by an impersonal expression such as *occorre* (n. 1, 3), *è importante* (n. 4) or *bisogna* (n. 10), or by a modal such as *voglio* (n. 5, 6) or *deve* (n. 8). Only 14% of the instances are negatives, and in this case *niente* and *nulla* (n. 5, 6, 7) usually follow the node word *saper*. Only two instances are followed by a dependent clause, but this is not confirmed by other instances.

From the collocational perspective, certain patterns emerge. Apart from the negative polarity words noted above - *niente* and *nulla* - there is a set of semantically related verbs that have to do with discernment: *capire* (n. 1), *distinguere* (n. 3), *giudicare* (n. 4). It is important to note here that this "ability to tell/judge" has a positive semantic prosody and carries with it an evaluative stance which in a way defines it as a desirable attribute. If we examine the type of action associated with *saper* further, we will indeed identify a wider set of actions which are approved of by society, are "the done thing", and are social acts rather than individual statements. The type of activity that is associated with *saper* reflects people's ability to fit into their social roles and do the right thing at the appropriate time. In this context, even *soffrire* (cf. n.10: *bisogna saper soffrire, amare, piangere* ..) is a desirable activity and it implies a desirable standard of how to go about suffering on the stage, a standard which we would wish to be respected by a good actor. Although this semantic set of approvables could only be identified with hindsight, it seems to support the pattern established at the collocational level.

Let us now consider a similar concordance of the word-form *sapere* (Table 6), again selected as a sample from the total 650 instances. We should note the very different frequencies between the two inflected forms, *sapere* being far more common than *saper*.

1.	re nulla, perché sapevo o credevo di	**sapere**	che il malore della ragazza era sta
2.	ide per la condizione di singola deve	**sapere**	che deve fronteggiare il fantasma d
3.	tua capanna tutti si preoccupano di	**sapere**	chi sia il padre di tuo figlio.
4.	scurarsi? Posso prevedere il colpo,	**sapere**	da che parte verrà, pararlo, sfuggire
5.	ando a ridere. La madre si voltò per	**sapere**	la cagione di quella risata, e la
6.	sere, cioè sull' antico oggetto del	**sapere**	metafisico. Ed è l' essere stesso
7.	ti portati sul mercato. È importante	**sapere**	quale sia l'effetto dell' approp
8.	paese circolavano strane voci. Voleva	**sapere**	se era vero che la bambina che port
9.	oggi conviene il nome di storia. Il	**sapere**	storico è esso stesso nella storia
10.	ricostruttivo. Un tal desiderio di	**sapere**	tutto quanto era avvenuto che per

Table 6: *sapere*

The first thing we notice in this concordance is that *sapere* is almost invariably followed by a dependent clause, rather than by an infinitive as was the case with *saper*. The only exceptions are the pronoun *tutto* (n. 10) and a noun, *la cagione* (in n.1)[9]. The negative polarity is also associated with *sapere*, but never in the presence of negative pronouns such as *niente* and *nulla*. Moreover, the lexico-grammatical profile of *sapere* differs from *saper* in that while the former often functions as a nominalised infinitive, this use is totally absent from the concordance of *sapere*. What appears instead is the nominal use of *sapere* (as in *del sapere metafisico* in n. 6 and *il sapere storico* in n. 9) meaning "knowledge" (rather than "the fact of knowing how to .." as in the case of *saper*).

If we compare the semantic profiles of the two forms, it is interesting to note that the positive semantic prosody brought about by the collocational patterning of *saper* is totally absent in the concordance of *sapere*.

Conclusion

To conclude this chapter, we will consider some of the theoretical points indirectly raised by our discussion of the relationship between lemma and inflected forms. The lexico-grammatical profile of the inflected forms discussed above has led us to make observations about the system starting from observations about individual instances. The shift has been one from *parole* to *langue*, and the transition has been a "smooth" one in that no major qualitative barrier has had to be overcome.

In order to illustrate this point, let us examine for a moment the properties of a concordance in general. Each line in the concordance is an example of language in use, an individual instance. Someone put this particular utterance together on a unique occasion to express something that may never need to occur again in precisely the same form. In terms of Saussure's famous distinction between *langue* and *parole*, each concordance line is clearly an instance of *parole*. When many such instances are gathered together and sorted, new patterns emerge, this time on the vertical axis; we identify the predominance of the infinitive following *saper*, and of dependent clause following *sapere*, for example. Individual instances which have no repeated elements in them do not contribute to the vertical pattern, but those instances which share formal features such as these can be associated together.

The patterns on the vertical axis are the patterns of *langue* and these are just as physical and concrete as those of *parole*, but they could not be observed until the instances were gathered together - until the advent of computer corpora. The theorists of the earlier part of last century thought that the organisation of *langue* was abstract and unobservable, but that position was an indication of the state of the technology and not the state of the language. The *langue* of Italian, as it relates to the profile of *saper* and of *sapere*, for instance, is there on the page, every bit as physically present as each of its component utterances. Our analysis has uncovered what we may call the unique lexico-grammatical profile of two words; the semantic profile of the words considered has also become apparent as inextricably linked to a specific item-environment combination[10].

Another issue that we have tacitly assumed in our discussion is that there is a direct correlation between *form* and *meaning*. Although both *facing* and *faced* on the one hand, and the two infinitive forms *saper* and *sapere* on the other, show some overlap in meaning, it is clear that specific meaning dimensions and different connotations are associated with each of them. In this respect Sinclair, like Firth and Halliday, is adamant in claiming that the distinction between form and meaning is only a methodological convenience and this leads him to posit formal observations as criteria for analysing meaning. However, he goes on to claim a stronger connection between the two than his predecessors and, reporting on the work of the eighties, he explains (my emphasis):

> Soon it was realised that form could actually be a determiner of meaning, and a causal connection was postulated, inviting arguments from form to meaning. Then a conceptual adjustment was made, with the realization that the choice of a meaning, anywhere in a text, must have a profound effect on the surrounding choices. It would be futile to imagine otherwise. *There is ultimately no distinction between form and meaning.* (Sinclair 1991:7)

Form and meaning, therefore, are seen as two aspects of the same phenomenon - language in action - and ultimately to analyse the former according to objective criteria will yield insights into the latter. This potential fusion pervades all the analyses in this book.

Notes

1. In "The Languages of Linguistics", unfinished paper 1953.
2. Along similar lines, Halliday talks of "the corpus as a theoretical construct" (1992a) and of corpus linguistics as "a highly thoretical pursuit" (1993:1).
3. Sampson is talking here about the existence of multiple central embedding.
4. For a full discussion of several measures of collocational significance see Stubbs 1995.
5. An example of this extension in the notion of colligation is the analysis of the two Italian infinitives *saper* and *sapere* below where we see that two inflected forms of the same lemma (and indeed the same infinitive) show different "colligational" features.
6. A concordance can be alphabetised at one word to the left or the right, but also at two, three, four, etc. positions to the right or to the left. I will use N-1, N-2, etc. to indicate the words preceding

the node word and their positions with respect to it, and N+1, N+2, etc. to indicate the words following the node and their positions with respect to it.
7. This was suggested by Firth when he argued that "the study of the collocations in which a word is normally used is to be completed by a statement of the interrelations of the syntactical categories within collocation" (in Palmer 1968:23). This is an early pointer to the interrelations between lexis and grammar.
8. Sinclair observes: "the problem about all kinds of introspection is that it does not give evidence about usage (..) Actual usage plays a very minor role in one's consciousness of language and one would be recording largely ideas about language rather than facts of it" (1991:39).
9. Other nouns following *sapere* in the complete concordance are *I risultati*.
10. To be precise, the relationship between the horizontal patterns and *parole* is exactly the same as the relationship between the vertical patterns and *langue*.

6 Item and Environment

Perhaps the most pervasive issue in corpus-driven work, and one that leads us to question some very basic received ideas about language, concerns the way in which word choices interact with each other in fairly close proximity. If we accept the fusion of form and meaning, which was the last notion put forward in Chapter Five, then it must follow that if adjacent choices are affected by each other, so is the meaning that they produce; hence we have to abandon the fiction that each word is some kind of independent selection, and accept that the choice patterns of words in text can create new, large and complex units of meaning.

The computer will start, by default, by assuming that the unit of meaning is the word, defined as a string of characters between two spaces. The systematic interconnections between an item and its environment which become apparent on the vertical axis of the concordance, and the realisation on the part of the linguist that the formal co-textual features surrounding a word determine its meaning and its function in a specific discourse, cast serious doubts on the idea that item and environment can be clearly separated.

The general name for this phenomenon is *co-selection* (see Sinclair 1991 and ff.)[1] which, as the term implies, involves the habitual selection of two or more items together. The tendency of the words to co-occur is so strong that they cannot retain independent meanings. The most obvious types of co-selection, and the ones that are traditionally acknowledged, are idioms and compounds, where two or more words with independent meaning combine to form a new meaning (e.g. *vacuum cleaner; it's raining cats and dogs*). What is usually not recognised, and it only becomes obvious when one starts looking at corpus evidence, is that there is a cline of co-selection ranging from words that are isolated from their environments, such as technical terms, to words that acquire a new idiomatic function by virtue of being strongly co-selected with other words. Co-selection will involve the co-occurrence of lexical items, identified in the concordance as strong collocational patterns, and the co-occurrence of grammatical patterns which will be identified in the concordance as colligational features, a mixture between the two almost inevitably bringing together lexical and grammatical patterns.

Co-selection has been referred to in different ways by different scholars[2]. Clear (1993:272), among others, refers to the same phenomenon as "stereotyping", that is when words lose their ability to combine freely. He exemplifies it with corpus examples using the word *keep*, which, he observes, "is quite frequent in any corpus of modern English, and which defies coercion into a tidy list of discrete, enumerable senses" (ibid.). Among the many examples Clear quotes, here are just a few to illustrate the point:

> The grant includes £19 for your keep during the vacations
> They keep their discoveries to themselves.
> .. she had to hurry to keep up with me.
> I ought never to have kept you up so late.
> Keep to the path.
> .. keep a look-out for him.
> How is your mother keeping?
> Private property. Keep out.
> Keep going!

Clear concludes that it is impossible to specify a single semantic unit that will cover all the normal meanings of *keep*, despite a certain homogeneity among them; he also notices that some of the co-selections have acquired individual characteristics - perhaps from being used frequently - rather particular meanings, and some syntactic constraints.

Hunston and Francis (2000:8) refer to the same phenomenon as "lexical phrases", which are units where lexis and grammar are typically co-selected, and point out that common concerns in this respect are:

- the frequency and therefore importance of lexical phrases
- the varying degrees to which lexical phrases are open to variation in wording
- the functions of lexical phrases
- the importance of lexical phrases to a model of language that gives lexis and grammar equal priority.

The consequences of co-selection could involve meaning loss or imbalance, an added connotative or ideological dimension to the unit, but often, and perhaps less obviously so, a great deal of redundancy and overlap between the meaning of words that are chosen together. This last point will be explored in the context of the section on *delexicalisation* at the end of this chapter.

From a theoretical point of view, the realisation that this phenomenon is so pervasive (see May Fan 1999) leads the linguist to posit a new theoretical stand that will account for it in the main body of the theoretical statement rather than relegate it to the "ragbag of usage". We have already used the notion of *extended units of meaning* in the discussion of several examples in the preceding chapters. In this context, let us look more closely at the work by Sinclair who first defined and exemplified the theoretical framework within which these units operate.

Extended units of meaning

If my syntagma begins with `in the nick ..' it must end with ` .. of time'.
(Lecercle 1990:30)

As Lecercle clearly illustrates in the quote above[3], the realm of extended units of meaning has traditionally been associated with idioms. And idioms are indeed where extended units of meaning are unmissable, they are easily recalled to memory and they capture the attention of the linguist and the foreign student alike. The phenomenon, though, is much more pervasive than the odd idiomatic or proverbial usage and it is again the access to large corpora that makes it possible for the linguist to describe it systematically.

By way of introduction we will recall an analogy given by Sinclair in 1996 at a conference[4] because, although half seriously, he identifies well the problem of extended units of meaning and appropriately invites the linguistic community to re-negotiate given linguistic categories in the light of the evidence from the corpus. We can paraphrase the analogy as follows:

> I could write a dictionary of English that had an entry for the letter `p'. It would have many, many senses; for example, one sense would be when it occurred in front of `in'. It would be defined as a sharp object that hurt if you sat on it. Then there would be another sense where it also meant something sharp but this time you wrote with it - this `p' is always followed by `en'. And another sense again means something sharp, but in a figurative way, to do with words - this `p' followed by `un'.

Sinclair maintains that people would not like this dictionary. They would say that, surely, the meaning was not really in the `p', but in the whole word. His point is that in so many cases a word is not enough, and we have to add in the regular environment of the word to get the unit that carries the sense. But he adds:

> We still write dictionaries as if thousands of words were ambiguous, and we pay very little attention to these crucial environments - as if my entry for `p' didn't even give you the `in', `en', `un' clues. No wonder people find them difficult.

If the analogy is given tongue-in-cheek, the work that backs it up is sound. Having established that each word develops its own unique lexico-grammatical profile, and assuming that formal criteria are capable of identifying meaning, Sinclair looks more closely at the usage patterns that become apparent in the environments of words. It soon becomes clear that the item-environment distinction is another methodological convenience and the evidence from the corpus forces the linguist to re-assess the notion of meaning both in terms of the discreteness of the units involved and their extent. In a paper on "The Search for Units of Meaning" (1996c), Sinclair argues the case for extended units, showing that the independence of the choice of words is more often than not compromised by lexico-grammatical as well as semantic constraints: as he puts it, words "begin to retain traces of repeated events in their usage, and expectations of events such as collocations arise". This line of reasoning is continued in Sinclair (1998b).

Sinclair (ibid.) maintains that language is realised in a dialectic relationship between the "terminological tendency"[5] and the "phraseological tendency"[6] and the question arises as to where is the boundary between a relatively independent item, such as the word as a technical term, and one where the environment becomes part of a phrase, which, Sinclair argues, is effectively a multi-word lexical item. One of the examples discussed by Sinclair (ibid.) is the phrase built around the collocation *naked eye*, which we will briefly report on here to illustrate the gist of the argument.

Extended units of meaning: the example of *the naked eye*

Sinclair (ibid.) identifies a number of constraints around this collocation, both at the lexico-grammatical and the semantic levels. Choices such as the definite article *the* at position N-1 or a preposition at N-2 are colligational features and their regularity seems to extend the phrase into a larger unit: *to/with the naked eye*. Still in the left co-text of the phrase, Sinclair locates other co-selected features: he posits, at N-3 or N-4, a semantic preference of "visibility", realised by strong collocations with words such as *see, visible*, etc. Even further to the left, he posits a semantic prosody of "difficulty" realised by a consistent collocation with words such as *difficult, faint, invisible* or *barely, just*, etc. that qualify the visibility as difficult to attain or problematic. Semantic prosodies will be discussed and exemplified in some detail below.

Having started with a core expression *naked eye*, by the end of the analysis, Sinclair demonstrates that the initial choice of a word or a phrase is therefore only the fixed element of a selection that involves several words. The other choices which are almost invariably co-selected with the initial node expression are realised at the lexical, the grammatical and the semantic levels.

One point is worth noting in Sinclair's analysis of *naked eye*, again concerning the interconnection that is obvious between different choices within the unit. This is clearly shown by the fact that there is a correlation between the word class of the word chosen by semantic preference - the "visibility" choice - and the word chosen by colligation[7], the preposition choice; adjectives, such as *visible*, take *to*, apparent as a convention of co-selection, and verbs, such as *see*, take *with*. Yet again form and meaning seem to merge, realised by the coming together of lexical features (the collocates embodying "visibility") and grammatical features (the preposition involved). Lexis and grammar appear to be ultimately co-selected.

The meaning arises from the largest and outermost units being chosen first, and its analysis as described by Sinclair (1996c:88) is as follows: first the speaker/writer decides to give expression to difficulty experienced (semantic prosody) in the area of visibility and seeing (semantic preference). Within the chosen semantic area there is now a sub-choice of word-class relating the semantic preference to its realisation in the stream of language - usually either a verb, typically *see*, or an adjective, typically *visible*. If a verb is chosen there is now a strong likelihood that the next sequential choice will be a modal verb, with the collocations *can, could* prominent among the modals, and the preposition *with* to link with the noun phrase at the end of the phrase. Where an adjective is chosen, the pattern of collocation is mainly with degree adverbs such as *just*; we note in passing that the prefix *in-* (cf. *invisible*) is particularly common, though co-occurrences below the word are not usually considered to be collocations. The final component is "the core", the almost invariable phrase *the naked eye*.

This kind of lexical structuring is built around a collocation; Sinclair claims that it is a common kind of pattern above the word level, one of the principal patterns and perhaps the dominant one. He hints at the fact that there may be another common pattern, sufficiently different to be developed as a second type. This he discussed in a previous paper (Sinclair & Renouf 1991) under the name of collocational frameworks, where the unit is based on a grammatical core, usually discontinuous, such as *the .. of*. If further research bears this out we would have then two types of unit, one - such as *naked eye* - based on a lexical core and extended to incorporate grammatical as well as other lexical choices, the other - such as *the .. of* - based on a grammatical core extended to incorporate lexical choices.

From the point of view of the present discussion, Sinclair's analysis of this type of extended units of meaning is important as it posits a core unit - whether initially lexical or grammatical - which is built up of inextricably linked lexicogrammatical and semantic choices. This is the type of connection that is regularly brought up by corpus evidence, and the language reference works that are that are compiled according to a corpus-driven approach focus more and more on phraseology. Gill Francis, who worked for many years as senior grammarian at Cobuild, outlines the goal of a corpus-driven lexical grammar along the lines set out by Sinclair:

> the end result will be that we will be able to specify all major lexical items in terms of their syntactic preferences, and all grammatical structures in terms of their key lexis and phraseology. (1993:155)

Although Sinclair is not the first scholar to advocate a lexical approach to grammar, he certainly takes it further than his predecessors. Stubbs points out the consequences of Sinclair's standpoint in the context of a systemic position: "if lexis and syntax are co-selected, then lexis cannot merely be `the most delicate syntax'" (1993:17). What then becomes obvious is the doubtful value of looking at lexis and syntax separately, of taking the stance of a grammar-observer and getting grammar-like answers, and conversely of a lexis-observer and getting lexis-like answers. The corpus seems to bring together the disciplines of lexicology and grammar and, on the other hand, make a true lexical grammar possible.

Extended units of meaning: the example of *proper*

We will consider here the example of the adjective *proper* which, by virtue of being consistently linked to certain contextual features, exemplifies the process that erases the dividing line between the individual item and its environment. When the item merges with its environment, and becomes part of it, then we can say that there is actually no difference between them and they both form part of a single choice. As in the example of *the naked eye* discussed above, we have therefore to query the boundaries of the unit of meaning. When patterns of co-selection are strong enough, some words tend to lose their initial (decontextualised) meaning and acquire a new function that predicts and, at the same time, carries the echo of the meanings realised in the environment. This, of course, becomes evident when the focus of the analysis is on a "functionally complete unit of meaning" (Tognini Bonelli 1996b, 2000b), in other words when patterns of co-selection are sufficiently present to become part of the unit and make their contribution to its overall function.

It is argued that this is the case of the adjective *proper* which, to an initial cursory consideration, may seem to have a fairly neutral meaning, something like "appropriate".

If we consider the concordance to the adjective *proper* from the BBC corpus we can very quickly divide it into three groups according to a grammatical distinction. Here we will only consider the adjective in attributive position, which is the most common usage, but for the sake of completeness will report below samples from the other two groups. First the predicative use which is the least common; we note here the pattern |*it is/was proper for* N *to*| which is always associated with this function. We should also note the very low frequency of this use:

> by Mr Tambo. He said **it was proper for** the head of an organisation ..
> their name. And **it's entirely proper for** literature to continue with ..

Then there is another use which is specific to *proper*, that is when the adjective follows the noun:

> currencies. In their **Council meeting proper**, the twelve are expected to ..
> yellow jersey for **the first stage proper** today -- but there's a long way to..
> the Arc de Triomphe, for **the summit proper**. Our correspondent describes it as..
> that one mustn't engage in **politics proper**, but in a time of transition, for ..
> could not get out into **the North Sea proper** because of the peat because the ..
> of emergency workers from **Serbia proper** and even ethnic Albanian government
> union leader not of **a politician proper**. NARR. Halina Bortnowska ..

Here the meaning is to emphasise that something is definitely a part of a particular place, object, etc. in order to distinguish it from other things which are sometimes regarded as parts of it and sometimes not (Cobuild English Language Dictionary). This usage is still quite infrequent compared with the third group, where the adjective *proper* is in attributive position; this is the one we will consider in more detail to illustrate the phenomenon of co-selection. The concordance is reported in Appendix 4.

Considering the noun that follows *proper*, some elements of co-selection can be noted at the collocational level: words such as *consideration, procedures, place* are repeated. What is more evident, though, is that there is a common semantic thread across most of the instances: the fact that these are all things that, as normal citizens, we expect to have. There is general consensus that things like *consultation, consideration, discretion, medicine, peace*, etc. are approved of; we are entitled to them. On the other hand, if we consider the left co-text of the adjective, we find that this list of "approvables" is invariably linked to the notion of "absence" realised by the negative polarity (*no, not, never*) at the grammatical level, as in:

> Baghdad, **has not** been given full and **proper** access ..
> feel that Japan **has still not** made a **proper** apology for occupying ..
> accused of **not** holding **proper** legal documents ..
> had **not** followed the **proper** procedures for staging it ..

This negative polarity can also be realised at the lexical level:

> **prevent or delay** the **proper** market response ..
> **failing to provide proper** medical aid ..
> **the absence** of a **proper** passenger list in Oslo ..
> **the lack** of **proper** rescuing equipment is hampering ..
> **without giving** any **proper** economic justification ..
> **without** a **proper** license ..

Other examples incorporate elements of modality, whether modal verbs as such, verbs with modal meaning or words which express modality:

> he really **wants** a **proper** border worked out ..
> BBC has said it **would** exercise **proper** discretion in reporting ..
> is really **needed to** provide **proper** homes ..
> which are **necessary** for the **proper** functioning of the organs ..
> measures to **try and ensure** **proper** monitoring ..
> he too is **anxious to get** **proper** guarantees ..

Yet other examples show the use of reporting structures as distancing devices; what is being reported is usually what someone says one should do or have. Yet again we read, between the lines, the element of 'absence':

> rather than providing **what it calls** **proper** child care facilities ..
> children to be in **what he calls** the **proper** place - the playground ..
> standards of **what the West sees as** **proper** respect for human rights ..
> games - **what Davies described as a** "**proper** thrashing" ..

In terms of semantic prosody, the common denominator between these different formal realisations is that whatever it is that *proper* qualifies as something that should be there, it is not there. This pattern is so consistent that it makes one wonder whether, in the language of BBC, *proper* really means something that should be had, something that we all think worth having, or rather something that, whatever we may think about it, we do not have.

Before we continue the discussion above by looking at the collocational profile of *proper* in the overall BBC corpus, let us open a brief parenthesis and consider the role that corpus evidence has had so far in the linguistic description of this adjective. The meaning we have identified, that is the semantic preference for 'approvables' and the semantic prosody for 'absence', 'lack of', has been established by bringing together functional and formal elements. Although this procedure is not new, and the connection between form and meaning is regularly invoked as necessary in language teaching for instance (see Berry 1999 among others), corpus evidence has offered a privileged perspective for the analysis specific function of *proper*; it has done so by bringing together three different formal levels which are usually seen, taught and analysed as discrete and separate levels. At the colligational level, we have observed the negative polarity on the one hand and the modals on the other. At the lexical level, the same function found its realisation in words such as *without, the absence of, the lack of* and *necessary, anxious to get, try to ensure*. At the discourse level, the reporting structures brought about the same meaning by operating as a distancing device between the speaker/writer and what (s)he reported.

ITEM AND ENVIRONMENT 109

We can claim therefore that the analysis of corpus evidence has brought together the different levels of linguistic description and has truly offered us the means to identify meaning as function in context.

We will now resume our discussion by reporting below the collocational profile of *proper* in the BBC corpus (see Table 1 below; the collocates that show the negative semantic prosody have been underlined for easier reading):

without	51	6.901580
for	109	6.288467
a	180	5.943743
not	55	5.305161
to	205	4.779065
give	20	4.110701
failing	16	3.946447
documents	15	3.816900
and	149	3.763362
procedures	14	3.711576
no	25	3.493171
lack	13	3.490735
should	20	3.438837
provide	13	3.409026
system	15	3.321021
how	17	3.318090
given	15	3.305540
get	15	3.298574
consideration	11	3.284249
abiding	10	3.157710
legal	10	2.984915
its	28	2.956171
keep	10	2.911401
facilities	9	2.910064

Table 1: collocates of *proper* (BBC corpus) ordered by t-score

The presence of negatives, with *without* at the top, is very visible and confirms the semantic prosody noticed in our initial analysis of the concordance. There are also elements that show that the type of thing that is qualified by *proper* is something which is *provide(d), given*, is therefore the focus of a transitive action on the part of someone. Other collocates like *documents, procedures, system, consideration, facilities, realising the semantic preference*, are also very noticeable and the list would be longer (here we just report the beginning of the list and, inevitably, grammatical words take priority because of their frequency).

In the case of *proper*, in spite of a lot of variation, the mere fact that we are able to scan the instances and analyse the different choices one next to the other on the one hand, and to find confirmation in the collocational profile on the other, allows us to identify an extended unit of meaning which does not coincide at all with the initial node. This type of unit can be called functionally complete and has been discussed and exemplified in the context of translation (Tognini Bonelli 1996b) where the equivalence between two languages has to be established functionally. It is important to understand that only when such a unit is functionally complete (that is, it has reached its semantic prosody) can it become available as a choice to the writer, the speaker or the translator alike. The choice represented by *proper*, as shown above, goes well beyond the qualification of something as 'appropriate' and entails the speaker/writer making a selection at a functional level. The function of *proper*, therefore, finds its place in an extended unit of meaning which is a "complaint for the absence of something that we all think should be present or available".

The data analysed here comes from the BBC corpus and the typical register of the news and such TV and radio programmes will be partially responsible for the patterning. The analysis should be integrated by adding a comparative dimension and considering *proper* in other corpora. Here, however, the intention is not so much to describe the adjective, but to exemplify the type of patterning that leads us to query the extent of the unit of meaning.

The remaining three sections of this chapter will examine three issues connected to the shape and the extent of the unit of meaning, and its discreteness. They will be illustrated with some examples from English and Italian corpora. We will first consider in more detail the notion of semantic prosody, as identified by Sinclair (1987f, 1991, 1996c and ff.) and elaborated by Louw (1993). Then we will illustrate the frequent phenomenon of de-lexicalisation which is entailed by the fact that words are often co-selected and build up multi-word units. Lastly, we will point to the ideological load carried by certain words when these are considered as starting points for extended units of meaning.

There is, perhaps, a certain amount of overlap between the three: semantic prosodies often reflect an ideological slant, and vice versa. A strong collocation always involves some kind of reciprocal delexicalisation and, as a consequence, the precise parameters of the pattern built around the collocation are difficult to define. All three of these features of the unit of meaning share the fact that before the advent of large computer-held corpora, they could be postulated but not easily observed and analysed; now, thanks again to the concordance, these phenomena are amenable to observation. But we are only just starting. It is hoped that more studies will systematically show the interrelations and the overlaps between different meaning dimensions and these will be reflected and reported accordingly in the reference works available to scholars.

Semantic prosodies

Perhaps one of the most obvious consequences of the extension of the unit of meaning is that, as noted above, words which are co-selected do not maintain their independence. If a word is regularly used in contexts of good news or bad news or judgement, for example, it carries this kind of meaning around with it; and, as noted by Sinclair above, the choice that a speaker/writer will make when selecting a multi-word unit will involve the more local grammatical and lexical constraints around the word, but will also include a perhaps more remote semantic preference and its correspondent on the pragmatic side, semantic prosody. While semantic preference, discussed above in the context of the phrase *naked eye*, identifies the semantic field within which an item operates, Sinclair (1996c:87) maintains that semantic prosodies are "attitudinal and on the pragmatic side of the semantics-pragmatics continuum". He defines them as "the functional choice which links meaning to purpose" (ibid.:88): they represent, in other words, the outer limit of the unit of meaning where, to put it in Firthian terms, the co-text merges with the context and a certain item achieves a purpose in a certain environment. And Sinclair (ibid.) insists that the initial meaning choice will actually be at the functional level of the semantic prosody.

Sinclair drew attention to the phenomenon that later became identified as semantic prosody in his discussion of the patterning associated with the verb *happen* and the phrasal verb *set in* (1987f, 1991). He pointed out for *set in* (1987f:155-56) that the typical subject of this verb is something unpleasant, and listed *rot, decay, malaise, despair, ill-will, decadence, impoverishment, infection, prejudice, vicious (circle), rigor mortis, numbness, bitterness, mannerism, anticlimax, anarchy, disillusion, disillusionment, slump* as examples; note how many of them are abstractions, often nominalisations of other parts of speech.

In his seminal article (1993) Louw discusses this phenomenon and names it semantic prosody, explaining the term in the Firthian sense of a "prosody" (in Palmer 1968:40), that is, the phonological colouring which is capable of transcending segmental boundaries. Louw explains:

> The nasal prosody in the word *Amen* would be an example: we find that the vowels are imbued with a nasal quality because of their proximity to the nasals *m* and *n*. In the same way, the habitual collocates of the form *set in* are capable of colouring it, so it can no longer be seen in isolation from its semantic prosody, which is established through the semantic consistency of its subjects. (Louw ibid.:158-159)

By analogy with the Firthian definition, Louw defines semantic prosody as "a consistent aura of meaning with which a form is imbued by its collocates" (ibid.:157). Whether or not the phenomenon is intuitively perceivable[8], Louw maintains that semantic prosodies can be properly assessed and systematically explored only with the input of computational tools (ibid.:159); the emphasis here is on the consistency of the phenomenon and, in this respect, Stubbs notes:

> This is a statement about probabilities: these are the most common uses of the word as attested in large corpora (..) Meaning is not regarded as a purely mental phenomenon, but is analysed distributionally on the basis of observable, objective textual evidence. (Stubbs 1996:173, 174)

Louw (ibid.) illustrates the concept of semantic prosody with examples such as the adverb *utterly* which carries a very negative semantic prosody and which was briefly referred to in Chapter Two. Other examples are the phrasal verb *bent on*, consistently followed by words such as *revenge, villainy, mischief, destroying, ruining*, etc., or the expression *symptomatic of,* again followed by "a multitude of sins", expressions such as *something deeply wrong, numerous disorders, clinical depression, parental paralysis, the quest which leads nowhere*, etc.

It is against the backdrop of these overwhelmingly bad semantic prosodies[9] that Louw explains what he calls the diagnostic potential of such patterning: when a consistent norm of meaning association with a set of undesirables is established, any apparently "good" collocate will be perceived as a deviation from the norm of meaning-choice that has been established, and the instance will be interpreted as ironic[10]. Louw explains:

> Irony relies for its effect on a collocative clash which is perceived, albeit subliminally, by the reader. In order for a potential collocative clash to attract the ironist's interest, there must be a sufficiently consistent background of expected collocation against which the instantiation of irony becomes possible. (Louw 1993:157)

This variety of irony, then, makes its impact because it runs counter to the choices that are established by the prevailing semantic prosody; this is a good example of how a wide variety of paradigmatic choices can be accommodated within a syntagmatic framework, including some which are not at all predicted by the prosody. Irony we interpret as deliberate, but it has a corresponding involuntary text effect which is a kind of insincerity - where a language user is hiding his or her real feelings but is caught out by the prosodies (s)he chooses; as Louw says (ibid.:157), it reveals "the speaker's real attitude even where (s)he is at pains to conceal it"[11]. This lack of control suggests that semantic prosodies operate mainly subliminally and are not readily available to the speaker as discourse devices at the conscious level.

As we can imagine, the phenomenon of semantic prosodies has far reaching implications in many fields. To name but two, which will remain unexplored in this study, Louw mentions radical stylistics, where the identification of ironical effects is of paramount importance, but he also mentions the industry of persuasion where a clear understanding of semantic prosodies will be of great assistance. At present in the market place, companies work hard and spend a lot of money making sure that bad prosodies do not impede their sales, and that brand names and slogans carry only positive and relevant overtones; the purchase of a suitable "new" word as a brand name can cost hundreds of thousands of dollars.

What is perhaps interesting to note again is that our initial assumption concerning the interdependence between form and meaning is further borne out with prosodies, since the specification of an attitudinal meaning is often very precise. So, concerning semantic prosodies, Louw (ibid.:173) observes that "the prosodies based on very frequent forms can bifurcate into "good" and "bad", using a grammatical principle like transitivity in order to do so" (ibid.:171). Therefore, we find that, in the case of the phrasal verb *build up*:

> Where *build up* is used transitively, with a human subject, the form of the prosody is uniformly good. People *build up* organisations, better understanding, and so on. Where things or forces, such as cholesterol, toxins, and armaments *build up* intransitively, of their own accord, they are uniformly bad. (Louw 1993:171)

Semantic prosodies: the example of *andare incontro*

We come now to illustrate the phenomenon of semantic prosodies with some data from the Italian corpus, drawing here on a combined concordance of the inflected forms of the verb [*andare incontro*]. The concordance is reported fully in Appendix 5. Here we will just quote a few examples to illustrate the points as we go along. The meanings of this verb cluster around two specific uses associated with two distinctive patterns. On the one hand we have the 'physical' use of *andare incontro* with the meaning of 'going towards someone to meet them'. This meaning is always associated with personal pronouns, either preceding the verb or built into the infinitive form. This meaning is relatively rare in the concordance:

> so tutta la notte. Non per **andargli incontro**, ma affinché la vedesse scappare ancora fuori. Lo so. Voglio **andargli incontro** per un pezzo di strada. Non ti di aprir bocca. Si alzò e **le andò incontro** con le braccia tese. "Cara Matilde

The other meaning, though, which we may call 'metaphorical', is much more common and accounts for 71.4% of the instances. A quick analysis of the concordance will reveal a consistent colligational patterning: we find either the preposition *a* (whether in its simple form or "articolata") at N+1, or, when that is not present, then the pronoun *cui* at N-1, which is to be expected as a normal replacement for a noun phrase in this case:

> giovani per parte loro possono **andare incontro ad altri inconvenienti,** di natura
> raddoppiare la probabilità di **andare incontro a un aborto spontaneo.** La notizia
> ed il paziente rischia di **andare incontro ad effetti collaterali indesiderati**
> Ma anche ora i ricercatori **andarono incontro a una delusione:** le installazioni
> ci assicura che non **sarebbe andato incontro a sofferenze peggiori?**". S'in
> degli **insuccessi a cui** Freud è **andato incontro** ogni volta che ha cercato "di

The most revealing insight into the behaviour of this metaphorical meaning, however, is again at the level of the semantic prosody. Out of thirty-five instances of noun phrases following or preceding the node expression, twenty-two could be grouped into a lexical set of definitely unpleasant things such as *perdizione, fallimento, obsolescenza, rifiuti, difficolta', disidratazione e ricovero in ospedale, tosse cronica* and *bocciatura*. The unifying feature here is the negative semantic prosody: these are all things that we would not wish upon ourselves or our best friends.

The remaining instances in the concordance all relate to a technical use involving a process of scientific modification: we have, therefore, technical terms and noun phrases such as *modificazioni molecolari, ricombinazione meiotica*, etc. The change in itself is in most instances presented as undesirable, therefore supporting the negative semantic prosody:

> attività specifiche senza **andare incontro a fenomeni di radiolisi.** Altri ti
> ucarioti l'm - RNA ottenuto **va ora incontro ad alcune modificazioni molecolari**
> regione del cromosoma Y che non **va incontro a ricombinazione meiotica.**
> i ridurre **le modificazioni cui va incontro** il mezzo di coltura, e i tossici
> veri e propri ammortizzatori, **vada incontro ad un processo degenerativo** . Il

As mentioned above, semantic prosodies are mainly engaged at the subconscious level; this is obvious when one looks at the entry for |andare incontro| in a dictionary, where examples are often chosen, or made up, to illustrate grammatical rather than semantic or lexical constraints. Thus, in the Collins Italian Dictionary, new-first edition (1995) we find an example such as *stiamo ormai andando incontro alla primavera* (we are moving towards spring now) which, although fitting in with the colligational constraints (the preposition *a* following the verb) is clearly unnatural and unlikely to occur in real language. Whereas before accessing the evidence of the corpus we would have probably felt that something odd was going on, now corpus evidence shows us exactly that it contravenes the semantic and lexical constraints systematically associated with the word.

The observations about the lemma |andare incontro| again lead us to question both the size and the semantic weight of the unit of meaning. The expression chosen consisted of two words - a verb form *andare* and a preposition *incontro*. Our first observation of a colligational nature made a first distinction between the physical meaning disambiguated by the presence of the pronoun and the metaphorical meaning by the presence of the preposition *a* in most cases. This is easy to accept as we are all used to verbs specifically entailing certain syntagmatic constraints, and yet it is not reported in most current dictionaries. Our second observation showed the consistent aura that seems to be carried by the verb in question in the metaphorical meaning: patterns such as these force us to query the choice we make when we decide to use a verb like *andare incontro*. It seems obvious to conclude that the choice must be primarily semantic, hence a loaded expression to introduce a dark result. And the two items - verb and complement - end up merging into a single unit of meaning: a verb that, in a specific pattern, is consistently associated with an unpleasant results ends up by being chosen with, and therefore prospecting, the unpleasant result.

To conclude this section we will report the extended context of citation n. 26 (cf. Appendix 5), where the verb |andare incontro| comes at the end of a question put by an interviewer to his/her interviewee and therefore is not immediately recognised as carrying a specific prosody:

> Qual'è il contatto diretto che Lei ha col suo pubblico? "È quello dell'intesa. Di un'intesa che nasce piano piano. E soprattutto quando parlo col pubblico, mi lascio andare totalmente". A cosa pensa che andremo incontro in campo musicale? (*What do you think we are facing in the musical field?*) "Secondo me, ci sarà sempre della musica mediocre, ma ci saranno sempre più anche delle cose eccezionali, perché ci sarà chi non vorrà più essere "usato e gettato"..

The expanded context gives us a chance to understand what is going on because the interviewee goes along immediately with the negative semantic prosody set out by the interviewer and answers that in her opinion "what we are facing" in the musical field is "rather mediocre music". However, she is quick to add that there will also be more and more exceptional things .. The interesting thing here is that the choice of the semantic prosody is made at the level of one participant in the discourse (the interviewer) while the realisation of it is done by another (the interviewee). An explanation of this tacit agreement might be that interviewer and interviewee had already rehearsed the questions and answers and therefore both knew what was coming next. Hence the question in a way predicted the answer and the answer went along with the implicit assumptions of the question.

The analysis of this last expanded instance exemplifies well the switch which can be made from the analysis of a corpus to the analysis of a text and the integration of the two types of evidence. The corpus had allowed us to identify the patterns of co-occurrence associated with |*andare incontro*| on the vertical axis and, by doing so, to evaluate the individual instance against the background of the established norm. The corpus, however, as pointed out in the Introduction, is made up of texts and therefore allows also the observation of an extended fragment of text if one calls for an expanded citation. In this case, we were able to query the interaction between the two participants and consider specifically the language event in which they were engaged.

Delexicalisation

The second item for discussion in this chapter again stems from positing an extended unit of meaning, and is what we have mentioned above as *delexicalisation*. As the term implies, this is the process through which a lexical item loses at least some of its original lexical value and often acquires other meanings and other functions within a larger unit[12]. This kind of semantic impoverishment is again triggered when the dividing line between an item and its environment becomes blurred; then, strong collocational and/or colligational patterns combine to create multi-word units where the function of the whole is of course different from the function of the individual parts. There may be different kinds, or stages, of delexicalisation; for this study we can define one kind only. Delexicalisation here can be defined as a collocational relationship where one word loses most or all of its specific semantic content, while its collocational partner appears to keep most of its characteristic meaning[13].

In *take a photograph, take a decision*, it is *photograph* and *decision* which retain their normal meanings while *take* loses its meaning. The delexicalised word disambiguates, where necessary, the sense of the other word: it selects a meaning, and of course it undergoes some kind of compensation by adopting a more grammatical role. So in the example of *take a photograph, take* carries the verbal function, allowing *photograph* to remain as a noun, and so making English a tiny bit more analytic than if *photograph* had been used as a verb, which is grammatically acceptable but not felt as colloquial.

This is an area of usage which seems to escape traditional grammar teaching as well as the type of vocabulary teaching that concentrates on single lexical items. The important fact, both from the point of view of description and applications, is that, as Sinclair observes, the phenomenon of delexicalisation is very common with words with high frequency which tend to lose their independent meaning (1997b:323).

Sinclair's point is also discussed and illustrated by May Fan (1999) in a study where she considers "delexical chunks", their pervasiveness in authentic language and the problems they present to L2 learners.

May Fan investigates a special type of VERB + NOUN collocation, in particular the patterning associated with the verb *make* (a very frequent verb). Of the several meanings of the verb *make*, she notes that the core meaning of *make* as "to construct" e.g. *make a table, make a dress,* etc. is not the most frequently used (only 18.1% of the utterances). The most prominent use of *make* is with the general meaning of "doing" (58.1%). In this respect, *make* has gone through a delexicalisation process where the logical core meaning has ceased to be the most important or the most commonly used.

May Fan also points out that 82% of the instances in her corpus are not free combination but on an idiomatic continuum ranging from delexical chunks (70%) to other idiomatic combinations (12%). Of the delexical chunks 90% are with corresponding verbs (*make a bid* [to bid], *make another arrangement* [arrange]) and this seems to affect the meaning because the VERB + NOUN collocations yields a meaning different from the verb and the noun combined, e.g. *make a speech*: 'speak formally to an audience on a specific subject'. The pervasiveness of this phenomenon should make it worth observing; however, it has not received much attention, either in descriptive studies or in the field of specific applications. In both, the emphasis is still on discrete items that are chosen individually and hardly any attention is paid to the overlap between units and its consequences in semantic and functional terms.

The examples discussed in the preceding sections have exemplified, at a less local level, the progressive erosion of the dividing line between item and environment through a systematic correlation between an individual word and its context. We have seen that when this "extension" takes place the item itself will acquire a new function very much linked to a specific environment. With the adjective *proper* this meant taking on shades of the meaning of its neighbours, almost to the extent of undermining what seemed the most basic meaning of the adjective. Similar cases were the adverbs *largely* and *broadly*, discussed in Chapter Two, which differentiated themselves one from the other because of the very precise pattern of co-selection they each favoured. At other times, as in the examples of *all but* and *except that*, discussed also in Chapter Two, the new function seemed to take on a structural role and change the grammatical function traditionally assigned to the phrase.

The phenomenon of delexicalisation discussed in this section poses a problem for the descriptive linguist and the teacher alike. Although it is mainly associated with words that are frequent, it operates at a subliminal level and therefore it goes unnoticed even to mother tongue speakers. This is another instance where the ability to observe it and analyse it is made possible by the large amounts of evidence available in a corpus. The sections that follow will present and discuss some examples.

Delexicalisation: the example of *real*

We will briefly consider now the example of the adjective *real* which is usually taken to mean "existing in reality". In Tognini Bonelli 1993a, the different functions of this adjective were analysed. Here we will just recall some of the findings to illustrate this phenomenon and the different functions a word can acquire because of the different patterns of co-selection it entertains. The concordance data used to exemplify its functions comes from the BBC corpus within the Bank of English.

Consider Table 2 below showing a concordance where the adjective is associated with the indefinite article or zero-article, or is preceded by a word like *any*.

```
       basis where both sides go into with a   real will to make progress." Mr
       to persuade Flamingos that 30 is a      real crowd. Apparently this encourages
       for speeding. It must have been a       real boneshaking ride, because in those
       Environment Committee says there's a    real risk of contracting minor infections
       be any wish to force the issue to a     real confrontation. The Algerian Foreign
       politician, Mr Major seems to take a    real interest in what is said by the
       and fatally marks the beginning of a    real and desperate crackdown. The
       and we have, as you can imagine, a      real problem with carpet-beetle and moths
       definitely form a real obstacle and a   real problem. REP: Today (02/08/91) the
       The Croatian leadership now faces a     real threat to some of the main Dalmatian
       First of all, they failed to show any   real interest in the directive. After
       His concern about the absence of any    real peace process is likely to be
       EC and Eastern Europe can make any      real claims to trade complementarity # to
       States has struggled to exert any       real influence on the deepening Yugoslav
       I don't think there will be any         real programs or witch hunts in the
       to be down by 40 # There are            real shortages of raw materials and the
       that it doesn't even want to debate     real questions. During the Gulf crisis we
       in the industry now, without having     real talent. REP: But in the meantime,
       announced that they had made            real progress on this matter at their
       Presidents have already secured         real achievements: first, agreement in
```

Table 2 - focusing *real*: emphasising typicality

In these cases the adjective is inward-looking with respect to the noun group; this is what Sinclair (1992a) refers to as the "focusing" function and gives examples such as *physical assault* and *scientific experiment,* pointing out that the adjectives *physical* and *scientific* repeat the meaning already inbuilt in the noun and appear delexicalised as a consequence. The adjective *real*, in this specific contextual pattern, is also delexicalised because, having lost its original meaning of 'existing in reality', it acquires a new function, that of emphasising certain characteristics already present in the noun. So, "a real problem" can be paraphrased as a serious problem, "a real crowd" is a very numerous crowd, "real progress" is a considerable progress. What is being emphasised is the typicality of the notion embodied in the noun. The type of nouns associated with the focusing function of *real* at the collocational level is a set of abstract nouns such as *problem, danger, difficulty, threat, concern, fear, hope, optimism, opportunity, possibility, democracy*, etc., almost to implying that reality here does not qualify the real world. We also note that in terms of semantic prosody there is a majority of negatives associated with this function.

As we have by now come to expect, a different contextual pattern will correspond to a different function. In Table 3 below, we can observe other instances from the same concordance of *real*.

```
                      gesture." The statement said its  real value would be given proper
                 to open the way for Romania's  real King, Michael I, to return to his
                 by police using teargas. The  real test will come when the university
              but said it was imperative that the  real cause be investigated and call for a
           negotiating positions disguise the  real wishes of both sides. While there is
            even by President Gorbachov. But the  real question to be decided is whether
             We are only at the beginning of the  real negotiations, he said. Adding that
                or the German president today. The  real power was in Parliament; and, in
               talk of postponing the deadline. The  real deadline, it's argued, is March 1st
                    at the outcome. He said the  real issues had not been focussed on in
                  in Warsaw, Jan Repa, says the  real contest is between the leader of the
           Accusing the Government of hiding the  real costs of unification appears to have
            unity problems will dwindle. The  real problems will be for East Germans.
                  omen for President Hrawi. But the  real stumbling block for Lebanon will be
                       of BCCI creditors said the  real question was not how BCCI itself
                 to tell the difference between the  real Elvis and his many imitators. The
                   in cars, to remind us who held the  real power. One afternoon I went for a
                  in practice, long ago become their  real currency. The *Times* says that for
```

Table 3 - Selective *real*: discourse and argumentation

Here the contextual patterning shows, very prominently, the presence of the definite article and, to a lesser extent, of possessives. Again we notice the loss of the original meaning of *real* as 'existing in reality' and this coincides with the acquisition of a new discourse role. So, *the real cause* is selected against a possible "other" cause, which is implicitly assumed to be not as genuine or perhaps of lesser importance. Similarly, a sentence like "the real problems will be for East Germans" presupposes other problems for other people, but, for the point being made here, not really as serious or as important.

What we have witnessed, in both cases, is the fact that the loss of the original meaning has coincided with the acquisition of a new function. In the first case, a focusing function where the adjective operated exclusively within the boundaries of the noun group emphasising the typicality of the noun; in the second case, a selective function where the adjective selected the noun group against the implicit background of other choices which were, as a result, dismissed as less important or less relevant. The adjective *real*, as a consequence, acquired a specific role outside the boundaries of the noun group, at the level of discourse argumentation.

Delexicalisation: the example of *bel*

We will now illustrate the phenomenon of delexicalisation with the Italian adjective |*bello*|[14]. The adjective is described here not in its traditional lexical meaning of beautiful, good-looking, etc. whether applied to physical or abstract beauty (we will come back to this point in next section on ideology); the lemma |*bello*| can have certain delexicalised uses and it is on these that we shall concentrate on in this section. As one might expect, not all the inflected forms of the adjective are susceptible to delexicalisation in the same way; while 46% of the uses of *bell'* and 27% of *bel* are delexicalised, we do not find *belli* and *begli* functioning in this way at all.

We will consider here three examples of delexicalisation of the adjective in question associated with different contextual features where the function varies accordingly. Let us then consider the first set of concordances (see Table 4 below).

1.	Continuammo a camminareper **un bel pezzo** nelle vie rumorose
2.	lupo? Il lupo se l'era svignata da **un bel pezzo**." Allora mi stavi seguendo
3.	reddy Malins salì dopo di lei e ci mise **un bel pezzo** a sistemarla sul sedile
4.	disse Cunningham." Non per niente è **un bel pezzo** che sono al mondo e ne ho
5.	guardo fisso ai piedi del dirupo. Dopo **un bel pezzo** il monologo s' interruppe
6.	. "Adoro i gatti. Oltre a visitarne **un bel po'**, faccio parte della Federazione
7.	della formula spicca senza dubbio **un bel po'**: almeno per altezza . GOL
8.	Non prese parte alla conversazione per **un bel po'**, limitandosi ad ascoltare
9.	due guardie del Parco ci accompagnarono **un bel po'** lungo la strada che scende
10.	si svegliò , era già buio , e ci mise **un bel po'** per ricordarsi dove si trova

Table 4 - *un bel pezzo, un bel po'*: 'a good bit'

In the citations above, *un bel pezzo* and *un bel po'* can both be translated into English as 'a good bit', and the adjective has lost completely the initial meaning to do with physical beauty and taken up the function of emphasising what follows.

A similar process has taken place with the instances where *bel* collocates with *niente, nulla* (meaning 'nothing') in Table 5 below.

1.	di paglia, perché io non ho insinuato **un bel niente**. Ho solo fatto una domand
2.	non riuscire a venire a capo proprio di **un bel niente**. A me e ad una signora di
3.	"Col bracciale sì, ma volontario **un bel niente**] Ci hanno arruolati in Fe
4.	questo: le proteste non hanno risolto **un bel niente**. La donna non viene ancor
5.	bbe riuscito a venire a capo proprio di **un bel niente,** e dopo avere inveito sul
6.	ismo è puramente epidermico e non educa **un bel nulla**. Il matrimonio di Bruna e
7.	lui se ne ricordasse non cambierebbe **un bel nulla**: già i redattori di " Lace

Table 5 - *un bel niente, un bel nulla*: 'nothing at all'

Here the meaning can be glossed as an emphatic 'nothing at all' or 'not at all'. Table 6 reports the concordance to *nel bel mezzo*, where *bel* again merges with the word that follows it (*mezzo*, 'middle') and emphasises its meaning:

1.	mattina, nei sobborghi, li si trovava **nel bel mezzo** degli scoli, con un piccolo
2.	intenso movimento turistico, si ferma **nel bel mezzo** dei crocicchi come un vigile
3.	in cucina a ringraziarlo e riverirlo. **Nel bel mezzo** del corteo avanzava la Prin
4.	grattacieli, Napoli ne ha eretto uno **nel bel mezzo** del panorama cittadino,
5.	e il primo atto. Noi siamo arrivati **nel bel mezzo** dell'atto successivo e,
6.	piscina e tennis. Che il professore **nel bel mezzo** di una lezione piombi sugli
7.	tilità specifica. Certo, è difficile **nel bel mezzo** di un accesso di tosse,
8.	studiarne gli effetti fisiologici. **Nel bel mezzo** di questo lavoro mi si pres
9.	gli scenari economici stessi, sono **nel bel mezzo** di un cambiamento radicale
10.	sposto per lui, ma all'improvviso, **nel bel mezzo** di una vicenda già iniziata
11.	li incauti. C'è sempre un momento, **nel bel mezzo** di una chiacchiera, in cui

Table 6 - *nel bel mezzo*: 'right in the middle'

In the three sets of citations reported above the adjective *bel*, having lost any reference to beauty, whether physical or abstract, is used to emphasise the great extent or degree of something; in the three cases, *bel* functions as an intensifier of whatever follows, having lost its independent meaning. As can be seen clearly from this concordance, the collocational and colligational patterns in which *bel* is embedded are very strong and show little variation: even a change of article would immediately project a totally different meaning[15].

Let us now consider another set of citations, still involving the form *bel*, but in a different colligational and collocational environment; again the reference to any type of beauty is lost and the adjective acquires a different meaning:

1. mi recai personalmente alla posta, ma **ebbi un bel dire** che avrei pagato (..) mi rifiutarono le lettere ..

2. Il giovane **ebbe un bel protestare**, chiese che lo lasciassero parlare col re: le guardie non gli diedero neanche ascolto ..

3. **Ebbe un bel affermare** che il suo articolo era mosso da nobilissimi intenti
(..) ma il deputato seppe dimostrare che ..
4. Guardie e servitori, dietro; ma **ebbero un bell'affannarsi**, lo persero di vista..

Here the adjective *bel* is found emphasising a nominalised infinitive, the nominalisation of a verb introduced in this case by the indefinite article *un*. The unit is further extended by the verb *avere* in N-1 position, always in the preterite (*ebbi, ebbe, ebbero*). So we now have a four-word unit: vb. *avere* (preterite) + indef. article + *bel/bell'* + nominalised infinitive. The colligational pattern is very strong and consistent. But let us also look at the collocational angle: three of the verbs qualified by *bel/bell'* in N+1 position have to do with verbal actions (*dire, protestare, affermare*), the fourth can be glossed as fretting and hurrying. But it is perhaps this last one that best conveys the semantic common denominator. These are all actions that, in spite of the effort involved, came to no avail, as it is invariably stated in the following clause. The expression, therefore, can be seen to have a discourse role; by emphasising the effort, it prospects that the action is doomed. While the original meaning of the adjective is lost in the multi-word unit, the whole expression has acquired a new dimension that goes beyond the qualification of a noun phrase.

We now come to the third example involving the delexicalisation of the adjective |*bello*|. Let us consider the following concordance:

1.	dei ministri gliel'avevano già data **bell'e pronta** i capipartito. C'erano
2.	to storico, che non è un oggetto dato **bell'e pronto** poiché risulta dalla cost
3.	esto capitolo e i due successivi erano **bell'e finiti**; contenevano in dettagli
4.	ne del Colombo dove trova la soluzione **bell'e fatta** senza perder tempo per cal
5.	farà sbigottire"). Il tema c'è, **bell'e pronto**. Non è ancor stato tratt
6.	ro. Guarda lui, indicò Mimì: Sembra **bell'e andato**. Dovremmo portarlo a dor
7.	noi stessi ed ecco la nostra storia è **bell'e fatta**. Tuttavia, irresistibilm
8.	ione del momento, che il regime fosse **bell'e liquidato**. Era appena al second
9.	mio Giuseppe] A quest'ora lui sarà **bell'e morto** e a me tocca la stessa bar

Table 7 - *bell'e* (..)

In this concordance we immediately identify the fixed core *bell'e* and the fairly consistent colligational pattern of the auxiliary *essere* in N-1 position and the past participles at N+1. The only two exceptions to this pattern are instances of the adjective |*pronto*|. These, however, are very much in line with the semantic common denominator of the past participles: whatever action is conveyed by the verb is over, done, finished. *Pronto*, meaning 'ready', although an adjective, shares this semantic preference with the rest of the collocates. In this context the meaning of *bel/bell'* could be glossed as "already", and its role is of emphasising the completeness of the action, which is already built in the chosen past tense.

To conclude this section, let us underline the point that "delexicalisation is the necessary correlate of co-selection" (Sinclair 1992:16). Delexicalisation has coincided invariably with an extension in the size of the unit of meaning whereby our initial node has become an inseparable part of a larger, multi-word unit. The principle at stake here is the phraseological tendency of language, the "idiom principle" (Sinclair 1991:110-12), which accounts for the patterns of mutual choice between words. As we have seen in the concordances discussed, delexicalisation very rarely is an end in itself. In most cases it signals a new role for the original unit; in the case of the adjective |*bello*|, that of emphasiser. More studies are needed to understand this phenomenon thoroughly; from the evidence available, however, it would seem that there is a tendency for delexicalisation to coincide with grammaticalisation, i.e. the process by which, with the passage of time, certain items lose their lexical meaning and acquire a grammatical function. It would also seem that it is very common words, which are used in a large number of contexts, that are more exposed to the phenomenon of delexicalisation and are more likely to lose their independence to "mean" with other words.

This is observable in the historical process; as Rissanen (1999) describes in a recent study, for example, the Old English adverb from which *rather* derives is the comparative form of *hræ_*, meaning "swift", "alert". This loses its link with speed of body or mind and becomes an indication of preference - "I'd rather walk". Now that it has become grammaticised it is available for duty as a degree adverbial modifying adjectives, e.g. "That's rather pretty". It thus join the class of "very" and "fairly", which themselves show evidence of similar lexical origins if you look closely at them.

Ideology

Words often carry an ideological weight that we sometimes guess, but very rarely prove. Firth (1935:27) said that "every man carries his culture (..) about with him wherever he goes", and Stubbs more specifically says that "by searching for frequent collocations, we can glimpse the recurrent wordings[16] which circulate in the social world, and glimpse how linguistic categories become social categories" (1996:194).

As an example of how the corpus can uncover these hidden meanings by exposing evidence of cumulative usage, we will discuss now certain ideological insights into language which become apparent by examining the concordance. This is a preliminary study mainly to establish openings for further research. If, as Firth maintained, language reflects culture and is realised in the interaction of the different contextual parameters (participants, relevant objects, relevant events, verbal actions, etc.), then the formal analysis of language should indeed yield insights into the cultural parameters that govern the interaction.

Firth advocates research into "the detailed contextual distribution of sociologically important words, what one might call *focal* or *pivotal* words" (1935, 1957:11) and, discussing the potential for an analysis of such words in a historico-sociological dimension, he offers a list of typical words - *work, labour, trade, employ, occupy, play, leisure, time, hours, means, self-respect* - and advocates the study of their derivatives, compounds and contexts. Other kinds of words whose study Firth says should be "enlightening" include those "associated with the dress, occupations, and ambitions of women", the language of advertising, "especially of quackery", that of the leisure industries, and that of political movements and propaganda (ibid.:13).

Firth had located this type of study in the realm of historical semantics, and this is understandable as in his days corpora existed only as collections of texts brought together on a historical basis. The advent of computerised corpora assembled along the same synchronic dimension makes it feasible for the scholar to examine how a certain *focal* word behaves in the society that uses it. Furthermore, the fact that we are focussing here on what Firth had called "the continuity of repetitions in the social process" (1957:183) makes this type of study ideal for gaining some help from the use of computers, which can identify frequency of occurrence in a large corpus almost instantaneously.

Empirical language work over the last half-century has demonstrated the importance of these research guidelines (Teubert 2000), and there are signs of renewed interest with the availability of corpora. Aston (forthcoming) in a demonstration of The BNC Sampler in 1998 showed that the adjective *pretty* meaning "nice-looking" is very much a woman's word, and that men seem to prefer to use it as a degree adverbial with a meaning similar to "rather" - in other words, men favour the delexicalised form while women the fully lexical one.

Stubbs (1996) in an important essay on "Keywords, Collocations and Culture", brings together Firth's notion of focal words and Williams' notion of keywords (1976). He talks of the insights that this type of analysis can offer into discourse, in the sense of "recurrent phrases and conventional ways of talking which circulate in the social world, and which form a constellation of repeated meanings"(ibid.:158). This is a broader, more sociological view of discourse than the term tends to have in linguistics, and Stubbs refers to Foucault 1972, Fairclough 1992 and Lemke 1989. For Stubbs these regularities of phrasing provide "familiar and conventional representations of people and events" and easy ways for the transmission of ideas, and can be documented and studied by looking at the evidence from large corpora (1996:158).

In order to exemplify and evaluate the above position, let us now turn to some data from the Italian corpus. In this study the type of key words that, for instance, Williams (1976) considered (e.g. *class, culture, democracy, capitalism*, etc.) would be so rich as to overbalance the general argument, although they would make for a very interesting corpus-driven study along the lines of Stubbs' proposal for "a Dictionary of Keywords in British Culture" (1996:181ff) transferred to the Italian context. Here we will pursue a more modest discussion of the collocational profile of some words that are gender-sensitive. Italian is a strongly inflected language and even the difference in grammatical gender yields some interesting insights into the cultural context in which the language is spoken.

To begin with, let us examine the collocational profile of the word *donna* in the Italian corpus and see what that reveals from the collocational angle. From there we will move to the adjective *bello*, and see if it shows different collocational behaviour in the masculine and the feminine forms, *bello* and *bella*. Finally we will consider the word *carriera*, specifically when the career person is a woman, to see whether the contextual features offer some insights into the way Italian society perceives career women. These steps are not unrelated, *bella* being one of the most frequent collocate of *donna*, while *carriera* ("career-woman") is not very common at all.

The collocational profile of *donna* locates immediately the most frequent collocates: it might come as no surprise that these are *giovane* and *bella*. Further analysis of the situational contexts (as realised in the co-text) in which this woman is likely to operate brings up words and expressions in the field of physical beauty and sex (*attraente, affascinante, femminile, gatta, sessualmente libera, rapporti sessuali*) and reproduction (*incinta, gravida, aspettava un bambino, partoriva, madre, mamma, fecondazione, gravidanza*) with occasional hints towards marriage (*sposare, moglie*). This type of *donna* can only exist in some role vis-a-vis a man or the family (see also Nakamura and Sinclair 1995). By way of comparison, a parallel search for *uomo* uncovered as the two most frequent lexical collocates *libero* and *politico*, neither of which refers, directly or indirectly to a woman.

We will move on to examine the collocational profiles of the two inflected forms of the adjective |*bello*|, masculine and feminine respectively, these are *bello* and *bella*. The lemma |*bello*| appears to have several meanings (cf. section on delexicalisation: the example of *bel*, discussed above), among which physical beauty is not necessarily the most prominent. In this section, though, physical beauty is what we will be concentrating on.

A first insight into what is in store is the relative frequency of this specific function of the two forms across the corpus. A total of thirty-seven instances of feminine beauty were found compared to only twenty-four of male beauty. This is unusual with respect to the language as a whole, and already indicative because the masculine form of adjectives in Italian is usually more common than the feminine one.

The collocational profile of the two words reveals insights which may confirm certain received ideas about the Italian culture, but which it would be difficult to pin down without the necessary support of quantifiable co-occurrence patterns in the corpus. On the one hand, we have *bella* collocating with words such as *corpo, bionda, rossa di capelli, attraente, giovane, giovanissima, capricciosa, vestiti, Rolls Royce*. On the other, we have *bello* collocating with words such as *forte, dolce, intelligente, generoso e niente affatto ricco, bravo, buono, giusto.* So, in the world of women, beauty is elaborated further with details about the body in question, coupled with characteristics of youth, capriciousness and sex-appeal and obvious references to expensive clothes and cars; on the other hand, in the social field where masculine beauty is valued and referred to, so are generosity, strength, justice, intelligence and compassion. This is where the co-text merges into the context, and language reflects culture and perpetuates ideology.

Given this initial picture, let us now consider a word like *carriera,* which is specifically associated with *donna* in a compound expression, *donna-in-carriera.* Interesting to note, there is no equivalent expression for man (**uomo-in/di-carriera*)[17]. Some other instances of *carriera,* although not specifically associated with the word *donna,* reveal feminine subjects, but the ratio is 10:90 to male subjects. The type of career involved, when this is specified, involves almost exclusively acting and modelling, in any case relying on a woman's major attribute, beauty:

1. Commenta la madre: "Se le piace tanto fare **l'attrice**, faccia pure. Ma gradirei facesse **carriera** con i vestiti addosso...

2. "Sono disposto a offrirti una **carriera nel cinema**, una carriera per la quale mille donne di talento darebbero l'anima...

3. Senza dubbio si aspettava che la **bellezza** le garantisse la **carriera**...

4 . Ripensava alla sua **carriera d'attrice** e capiva...

5. nella **carriera di modella**...

When a more general notion of career woman is referred to, this is usually qualified in some negative way, as on the way down, not really successful or, for some reason, not really exploiting its full potential:

6. La donna single, la **donna-in-carriera** che ha puntato più sulla professione che sui sentimenti, intanto **non suscita più particolari emozioni** ..

7. Attualmente queste donnne-quadro **non fanno carriera** perchè non riescono a fare il salto qualitativo, professionalmente parlando ..

8. il 90% delle donne **hanno figli,** e li hanno proprio negli anni in cui, se vogliono perseguire una carriera, **dovrebbero essere più libere** dai doveri domestici...

9. Da una ricerca condotta a livello europeo è emerso che il sessanta per cento delle **donne in carriera** ha la matemantica certezza di **non aver sfruttato in pieno le sue capacità** ..

10. Nonostante l'Oscar, non pensa che, essendo sorda, la sua **carriera sia limitata**?

The choice of a career is often associated with a dilemma and often a failure on the home front:

11. E diventato un dilemma: **maternità o** *carriera*? casa o ufficio?

12. Dopo **due matrimoni falliti** e **la fine della** *carriera*, ha saputo ..

13. **Il matrimonio finí** dopo un paio d'anni e lei continuò la sua *carriera da sola*

This type of career woman causes embarrassment to certain members of society; she can be terrifying for a poor priest with a chip on his shoulder, for instance:

14. era bieco, sfuggente, disperato, simulatore, **atterrito e stridulo (o falsamente mondano) con la donna in** *carriera* ..

but is also portrayed as the subject of violent passion/obsession that leads to a downwards spiral of violence, as in this report of the film "Fatal Attraction" by Adrian Lyne:

15. Lei, rampante **donna in carriera** dai prepotenti riccioli biondi .. Eppure per la società e per il suo equilibrio, Alex, la giovane signora bionda, è molto **più pericolosa dell'Aids.**

The observations above speak for themselves and clearly point to the fact that collocation, by showing the association that words entertain with other words, also shows their ideological load and the assumptions which go with it.

The patterns of *langue* relevant to the words examined above, as established by the paradigms of collocates on the vertical axis of the concordance, show many specific associations of form and meaning. Again the extra semantic dimension, the ideological slant, extends the semantic weight beyond the realm of the word: words very rarely exist as discrete, separate units and what Sinclair referred to as semantic preference and semantic prosody come to be included in the meaning. Our ideological statement - however subconscious that may be - seems to be entailed by our choice to refer to *donna* and *uomo*, *bella* and *bello* and even when we talk of a woman in the context of *carriera* we do not seem to be able to avoid the semantic load that our culture conveys with it. In other words, we may conclude, language is not neutral and we have little choice but to convey what our culture and our language convey. Of course, after this realisation, we can choose a more interventionist stand and explicitly avoid certain loaded words on ideological grounds[18].

Conclusion

The types of finding which are exemplified in this chapter is consistently shown up by corpus evidence, and lead the corpus-driven linguist to reassess radically the units of linguistic description. If this *change in currency* brought about by corpus studies proves to be all-pervasive, and studies so far have tended to demonstrate that this is so, then it will obviously have important consequences not only on the way we teach and in what we ask the students to learn, but in every possible application which has to do with language studies. The chapter that follows will take on this point of view from the stance of translation and contrastive linguistics. The examples discussed in this chapter are intended simply to open up the field of corpus-driven linguistics; a number of meaning-distinctions in quite unsuspected areas are suggested by the evidence provided by the corpus, and these tend to support, among many other things, the following conclusions:

- that many textual meanings arise from the co-selection of more than one word
- that habitual co-selection tends to specialise the function of one or more of the words concerned
- that co-selection is largely covert and subliminal, which increases its importance in communication.

Notes

1. The working definition of *co-selection* that follows was arrived at in a Corpus Linguistics Seminar on terminology held at the University of Birmingham on 23.11.1994.
2. See for example Hornby (1954). Hunston and Francis (2000:9) outline in a very succinct way some of the work done within the perspective of the phraseological nature of language, where language is seen to "occur in sequences of morphemes that are more or less fixed in form". They remark: "These sequences are called, variously, "lexical phrases" (Nattinger and DeCarrico 1989, 1992), "composites" (Cowie, following Mitchell in Cowie 1988), "gambits" (Keller in Cowie 1988), "routine formulae" (Coulmas in Cowie 1988), "phrasemes" (Melcuk 1988, 1995), "prefabricated routines and patterns" (Krashen 1981), "sentence stems" (Pawley and Syder 1983), "formulae" (Peters 1983), and "formulaic language" (Weinert 1995; Wray 1999)".
3. Well, almost. The Bank of English records 161 instances of *in the nick*, of which twenty (12.4%) are not followed by *of time*.

4. This is the IATEFL 1996.
5. See also the *open choice* principle in language (Sinclair 1991:109-10) which accounts for word as separate choices, independent items of meaning.
6. See the *idiom principle* (Sinclair 1991:110-15) which accounts for the tendency that the choice of one word affects the choice of others in its vicinity.
7. Sinclair (ibid.) points out that "the pattern observed here is not full colligation, because it is the co-occurrence of a grammatical class (preposition) with a collocating pair, but it is an extremely useful concept at this stage of our investigation". This is indeed the extended notion of *colligation* which we have referred to above.
8. Many neo-Chomskian linguists would maintain that what Louw describes "only confirms a chalk-and-blackboard demonstration of the same point" (Freeman 1995). Freeman explains: "I find excessive Louw's claim that `semantic prosodies have, in large measure and for thousands of years, remained hidden from our perception and inaccessible to our intuition' (p. 173). Rather, Louw's (quite sound) intuition found candidate semantic prosodies only confirmed by the corpus data". This position is what Louw refers to as `twenty-twenty hindsight', "the tendency to claim that one `felt' the presence of a form which was inaccessible to one's intuition until it was revealed through research" (1993:173) and suggests that "the only cure for twenty-twenty hindsight lies in constant exposure, of the most humbling kind, to real examples" (ibid.).
9. Although from published work on semantic prosodies it would appear that examples of the bad ones are given more frequently than of the good ones, (this perhaps reflects actual distribution), Stubbs (1995a,b and 1996) discusses a word such as *provide* as entailing a positive semantic prosody: its typical collocates are from semantic fields of care, food, help, money and shelter. In Chapter 5 we discussed the example of *saper* which also had a good semantic prosody.
10. Louw gives as an example, among others, the utterance: "oh how kind he was, oh how *utterly* good and what trouble he took .." taken from a telephone conversation where the participants are criticising someone else.
11. Here, against the collocational background around the expression *symptomatic of*, Louw (1993:169-70) quotes the example of a Director of the British Council who is being interviewed and asked specifically how wide is the network of links between the UK and the Zimbabwean University. His answer clearly reveals his attitude: "Well, it's very wide. I mean it's symptomatic of the University of Zimbabwe which has such a high reputation that there are fifteen links .. that is a huge number of links and reflects not only the closeness .. but, as I say, the level of the University of Zimbabwe.."
12. For an interesting study on historical delexicalisation and relexicalisation see Partington (1993). Delexicalisation is defined by Partington (ibid.:183) as "the reduction of the independent lexical content of a word, or group of words, so that it comes to fulfil a particular function but it has no meaning apart from this to contribute to the phrase in which it occurs".
13. This is the use of the term delexicalisation in the Cobuild project; not perhaps the best choice of word for the phenomenon described which is more 'semantic' than 'lexical'.
14. See Tognini Bonelli 1995. This data was prepared for a course in Italian Corpus Linguistics at the University of Birmingham offered by the present author and further elaborated in Ball (M.Phil:1995).
15. Consider for example *il bel pezzo di antiquariato resta ancora da vedere* which could be glossed as "the beautiful antique piece is still to be seen".
16. "Wordings" is the term that Halliday (1985:xvii) uses for the way something is expressed. He says "meanings are realised through wordings" (ibid.).

17. The closest synonym with *uomo* is not **uomo di/in carriera* but *uomo d'affari*. In spite of the differences (while the first could be glossed as "career woman", the second would be a "business man") they also share some prima facie semantic similarity in that they associate the words *donna* and *uomo* with some fairly general work context. A collocational profile of *uomo d'affari*, however, will show him as "ben noto al Ministero", or presidingover a board, or starting an archaological initiative of some importance; when he behaves "da uomo d'affari" he is successful, laughs and drinks some whisky.
18. See Stubbs' position (1996) concerning the use of the word *master*.

7 Working with corpora across languages

> *If meaning is function in context, as Firth used to put it, then equivalence of meaning is equivalence of function in context.* What the translator is doing when translating or interpreting is taking decisions all the time about what is the relevant context within which this functional equivalence is being established.
>
> (Halliday *1992b:16*)

Introduction

The preceding chapters have discussed, starting from an application and going on to the theoretical issues behind it, an approach where meaning is seen as encoded by and intertwined with formal lexical and grammatical realisations in the verbal context. Starting from such a perspective, we have argued that it would not make sense to identify a certain function in a language solely from a grammatical or lexical point of view and expect an equivalent grammatical or lexical match in another language. Whether the starting point is lexical or grammatical, an analyst sensitive to the cumulative effect of usage will be led by the evidence to identify multiword lexicogrammatical items that operate within well defined semantic platforms and perform specific functions at the pragmatic level. These have been discussed as *functionally complete units of meaning* (Tognini Bonelli 1996b and 2000b) and it has been shown that they extend beyond the boundaries of a word and incorporate elements of their environment.

In this chapter[1] we will continue the enquiry considering the comparative angle. We will argue that the notion of translation equivalence has to be revisited in the light of these units, and that the matching between two equivalents has to be verified when all the components that are necessary for the unit to function have been identified, that is, at the level of the ultimate pragmatic function, the semantic prosody. In the sections that follow we will first address the application to translation and some issues it raises. We will then consider an approach that aims to combine the use of different corpora and illustrate it starting from a given function in English with the aim of identifying a comparable one in Italian. We will then go on to exemplify the initial steps towards the definition of a network of equivalences between two languages.

Progressive steps between form and function

From the point of view of the comparison of two languages, this study argues that the assumptions of a correlation between form and meaning on the one hand, and the postulation of a functionally complete unit of meaning on the other, are the crucial stepping stones to identify a network of equivalences. As in the case of language teaching, this approach applied to translation entails of course a communicative view of language where the linguistic choices made are seen as primarily functional. This is where it becomes crucial to identify systematically the formal patterns associated with the semantic preference and the semantic prosody; only when functionally complete, will a unit of meaning be available as a possible choice to the translator or for comparison to the contrastive linguist.

Before we go on to propose a methodology that makes use of a set of corpora for translation and contrastive linguistics, we should say a few words on the *process of translation*[2] itself. The main - and perhaps the most obvious - point to be made is that both the text, encoding meaning, and the context in which the text itself is embedded, vary. Translation presupposes "displaced situationality"[3] both at the linguistic and the extra-linguistic levels. At the purely linguistic level the translator will negotiate equivalence of meaning in a displaced context, that is from SL to TL. This will involve the assessment of the two different linguistic systems and the analysis of the formal contextual features that realise the same function; the translator will identify two units of meaning which are comparable in spite of the displaced context.

At the extra-linguistic level the situational features will also be displaced, in that the context will invariably refer to, and reflect, a different culture, a different situation and different participants. Two different levels of interaction will also have to be assessed and accommodated: the original interactive process between SL writer and his/her SL audience and the one between translator and his/her TL audience. The translator here has the task of reproducing, or re-creating, the original interaction to a different audience in a different situation, taking into account the fact that the original text and the translation may even have a different purpose altogether [4].

The steps that the translator will take to negotiate equivalence at the extra-linguistic level will account for the strategies (s)he will adopt in order to transfer and report the original interaction to a new target audience. This stage can be seen as a reporting strategy, whereby the original interactive process has the status of a report within another, new, interactive process. The translator has to act as a bridge between SL and TL, source audience (i.e. the audience of the original writer, in the SL) and target audience (i.e. the audience of the translator in the TL). The specific genre and function of the text (narrative, technical, advertising, etc.) is going to affect the choice whether to translate certain elements or add some which are not included in the original text.

Given these two levels in the translation process, it is important to understand that we are positing a difference between a *unit of meaning*, whether in the source or in the target language, and a *unit of translation*; while units of meaning are defined *contextually* at the linguistic level - that is by examining the verbal co-text of the chosen word or phrase and identifying the patterns of co-selection - units of translation are defined mainly *strategically* as the result of explicit balancing decisions taken by the translator in order to achieve an equivalent effect or purpose to the original (Nida 1964). The identification of units of translation will be possible (a) once comparable units of meaning have been isolated in the source and the target language, in the light of (b) the perceived role of the translator as "go-between" linking two cultures and two specific situations, as well as (c) the function of the translated text vis-à-vis the new target audience.

Although both the linguistic and the extra-linguistic levels must be taken into account for the translation to be successful, this article will only present a methodology for identifying and evaluating sets of comparable units of meaning. The strategic steps that may influence the translator to opt for a specific unit of translation rather than another, and the linguistic realisations of these steps, are excluded from the present enquiry.

The approach proposed here, therefore, will aim to locate the words and phrases that encode a function in L1 and that of other words and phrases, inevitably different from the first set, that will yield a comparable unit of meaning in L2. In other words, the aim here is to trace, through a series of steps from formal patterning to function and from function to formal patterning, the correlations that establish the boundaries of sets of functionally complete units of meaning in the two languages.

It is argued that, ideally, the translator should have at his/her disposal both a set of *translation corpora* and a set of *comparable corpora*. These have been briefly described in the Introduction to this book. While comparable corpora, as the word suggests, can be "compared" according to external criteria (see Chapter Three) and give insights into two independent linguistic systems, translation corpora are corpora of texts which are in a translational relationship to each other and give insights into the way translators have tackled different problems. Sinclair (1996e), talking about the use of 'parallel' or 'translated' corpora, points out:

> An alternative possibility [to harnessing the expertise of several bilinguals] is to replace the direct evidence of bilinguals with indirect evidence from their translations. This leads us to consider *parallel* corpora, or translated corpora, which are quite popular at the present time. (..) For our purposes, they can be seen as large repositories of the decisions of professional translators, supplied together with the evidence they had for those decisions. (Sinclair 1996e:174)

Going back to the procedure for the identification of a network of translation equivalents, the initial hypothesis positing one or more tentative matches between two or more *prima facie* units of meaning in the two languages would traditionally have to rely on the translator's intuition and/or past experience in translating. The use of a *translation corpus*, if available, gives the benefit of such input in a more reliable manner; it offers a range of possible translation pairs that have already been identified and used by translators, in other words verified by actual translation usage. In the examples that are going to be presented below, however, access to a translation corpus has not been possible. This study, therefore, will be limited in this respect, but it is hoped that it can still offer a methodological pointer in the right direction.

We must note that, in the framework of a corpus-driven approach, the definition of a functionally complete unit of meaning cannot be confined solely to the evidence from a translation corpus because, although a lot of work is being done, not enough is known about the constraints and restrictions of mediated language. We discussed in Chapter Three how the authenticity of the language included in the corpus is one of the most basic tenets of the corpus-driven approach; here, although the study of the translated text can be valuable in itself for what it can show us on the process of translation, the starting point for the identification of the boundaries and the realisations of two comparable units of meaning has to be the naturally-occurring, un-mediated language. At this stage, therefore, the linguist will need to base his/her observations on two *comparable corpora* and the identification and matching between form and function in the equivalence pair will take place in each of the two sets of data.

The formalisation of the regularities exhibited by the evidence will allow a series of progressive steps which will deconstruct an initial chosen function into its formal components in L1 and reconstruct it in L2. The aim is to ascertain *functional equivalence*, that is, the equivalence obtaining between functionally complete units of meaning. In this respect, we will distinguish three methodological stages (cf. Table 1 below). Given an initial word or expression that one wants to translate or to compare across a language pair, the first step works within L1 and consists in identifying and classifying the formal patterning in the context of such word or expression against the evidence of a L1 corpus; to this will follow the matching of a specific meaning/function for each specific pattern[5]. Step 2 in the process will consider L1 and L2 and will posit a *prima facie* translation equivalent for each meaning/function. As already mentioned, if a translation corpus is available the process will be enriched by access to past translations. If this is not available, as in the case of this study, this step has to rely on information taken from traditional reference books such as dictionaries and grammars or past experience on the part of the analyst. Step 3 will start from a function in the L2, realised by the *prima facie* equivalent, and will deconstruct it into its formal realisations (collocational and colligational patterning); in a way it will replicate the process of step 1, but the other way around.

COMPARABLE CORPUS (L1)	TRANSLATION CORPUS /TRANSLATOR'S EXPERIENCE (SL/TL)	COMPARABLE CORPUS (L2)
Step 1 from Formal Patterning/L1 to Function(s)/L1	Step 2 identify a prima facie translation equivalent for each function --> Function/L2	Step 3 from Function/L2 (as realised by a translation equivalent) to Formal Patterning/L2

Table 1: procedural steps in the identification of translation equivalence

It is important to understand that although the above table presents a step-by-step separation between form and function, these are ultimately the same thing. The analysis and the separation are therefore purely methodological. They are necessary, however, in order to appreciate the formal realisations of the function before reproducing them in a different linguistic system. This is what Sinclair sees as a step in "degeneralisation" and points out:

> In looking for the distinctive patterns, the human researcher needs to abandon his or her preconceptions about the languages concerned, and review the evidence in a detached way. This amounts to a process of 'degeneralisation', or fragmenting the generalisations about meaning that have been consciously learned. By allowing the evidence of a large corpus to influence one's view of language and meaning, completely new observations can be made, leading to new generalisations, some of which, while intuitively satisfying in one's reconstructed state, might have seemed counter-intuitive before the evidence of the corpus was encompassed. (Sinclair 1996e:177-178)

It is therefore very important to be strict and systematic about the specific formal patterning associated with a certain item. By looking at the patterns on the vertical axis, of the concordance and identifying larger syntagmatic units on the horizontal axis and by considering the frequency distributions, the translator will not only be able to assess what is possible, but also what is likely with a given linguistic system. Specific appropriateness to context will be evaluated against the evidence, and the full value of the translator's own chosen or inadvertent deviations from the norm will be assessed against the range of variations present in the L2 corpus. Issues that could not really be addressed before the advent of corpora because of the need for a lot of evidence - the cumulative connotational tendencies or specific register characteristics, for example - can now be observed and become tangible, often simply identified by alphabetising the context of a word.

These points become very relevant when considering the implications of translating from and into one's own mother tongue. The process leading from formal patterning to function and vice versa can be related to the process of decoding and encoding in language. Usually in translation the norm is for the translator to translate - that is to encode - into his/her own mother tongue where it is assumed (s)he can be more sensitive to the demands of appropriateness. With corpus evidence at hand, and with a methodology to identify systematically the relevant lexical and grammatical profile of a word or an expression and relate them to connotational weight and pragmatic function, this approach will reduce the gap existing between translating from and into one's own mother tongue.

The example of *in (the) case (of)* and its Italian equivalents

The sections that follow below propose an analysis of two prepositions that incorporate the words *case* and *caso* in order to introduce a circumstantial element. The last section will present a third example where the conjunction *in case* will be compared with the Italian *se per caso*. Two sets of corpora, one of English and one of Italian[6], will be accessed. Although not explicitly put together according to the same criteria, they are both 'general-purpose' and were both assembled as samples of contemporary language; we take them here as comparable. The second procedural step, positing a *prima facie* translation equivalent for each function, will rely here on standard reference works and the translator's experience. The findings reported below are to be taken as indicative of the methodological steps proposed, but they would still need to be explored further and validated in the light of more exhaustive evidence.

From *in the case of* to *nel caso di*

The expression "*in the case of*" is, from a grammatical point of view, a complex preposition introducing what Halliday called a "circumstance of matter" (1985:142). Our first step will be to consider its co-text and analyse it into its formal lexico-grammatical constituents (for the concordance[7] see Appendix 6). Below we report only ten of the total 550 instances in order to show the patterning. Looking at the right co-text we find a noticeable presence of the definite article *the*. This, coupled with the other strong pattern - the presence of proper names - points to the strong function related to specificity. The function here is to present individual examples, considered for their particular characteristics.

1. of subsidies can be illustrated **in the case of** Australia, where the
2. on shifts in values. As we shall see **in the case of** London's motorways,
3. period is likely to be lengthier than **in the case of** Spain, because of the
4. end in itself. This is especially so **in the case of** experiments which can
5. even a reasonable thing to assume; and **in the case of** relatively minor ills,
6. the awakening of enlightened optimism **in the case of** the Liberals, and the
7. have allowed myself to break this rule **in the case of** the USSR - the data
8. an expert witness on the truth drug **in the case of** the Boston strangler.
9. children and primitive artists , but **in the case of** the caricaturist the
10. not be able to perform efficiently. **In the case of** the distance runner

Table 2: *in the case of*

The semantic preference associated with this is very varied and cannot be identified with a specific collocational pattern; people alternate with countries, tangible objects with less tangible ones. In terms of semantic prosody we are not associating a particular evaluation to the instance presented. We could see perhaps the introduction of specificity as the ultimate function of this complex preposition.

To understand better the neutrality attached to the specific instances introduced by *"in the case of"* it might be interesting here to open a brief parenthesis and consider the collocational profile of a grammatically parallel expression in English, namely *"in the event of"* extracted from the same corpus. For lack of space, we will not report here the concordance, but just report some of the collocates that are introduced by this preposition: *unavoidable nationalisation, a major disaster, a breach of the rules, great national emergency, a war, company failure, hostilities, trouble,* etc. The negative semantic prosody realised by these collocates is very strong and regular, so much so that even the only neutral word - *an election -* is revealed as negative by what follows: *..of a politically hostile party*. It seems that when the linguistic system offers a set of apparently parallel or equivalent expressions, these, if they ever were truly equivalent, do not stay so for long and they tend to find their own very specialised role in a specific domain. This is another pointer to the illusion of synonymity discussed in Chapter Two and exemplified with the adjectives *fickle* and *flexible*.

The Italian *prima facie* translation equivalent for *"in the case of"* posited in stage two is *"nel caso di"*, and stage three will go through the same process of deconstruction in the Italian concordance (see Appendix 7), identifying the formal patterning present in the co-text. Table 3 below reports ten instances from the concordance out of the 319 instances in total present in the Italian Corpus.

1. peggiorativa, come, per esempio, **nel caso degli** "homines novi", uomini
2. ambienti simulanti l'acqua di mare **nel caso degli** acciai superferritici e le
3. formaggio. Diverso è il discorso **nel caso dei** bambini. Poiché il loro organi
4. gnificato in passato, sulla Terra, **nel caso dei** giannizzeri: bambini che i
5. si riproduce, altre volte come **nel caso del** terzo sonetto vediamo emergere
6. la collaborazione del paziente: **nel caso del** fumo, deve voler smettere. Se
7. l'approccio più diretto, almeno **nel caso del** carcinoma midollare della
8. olidaristiche e corporative: come **nel caso del** "Lord Spleen" di Giovanni
9. rambe le eventualità si presentano **nel caso dell'** "Orlando furioso"
10. informazioni di tipo diagnostico **nel caso della** patologia neoplastica

Table 3: *nel caso di*

Here we note the merging of the preposition *di* with the definite article which gives rise to *del, dell', dei, degli, delle* as substitutable for *di*. The function of specificity is very obvious because this merging between the preposition and the article is present in all the instances. In the right co-text we find nouns which, as in the English counterpart, show quite a lot of variation with no strong collocational pattern. In terms of semantic preference it is interesting to note two rather prominent areas. Firstly, the area of technical and scientific terminology (words like *acciai superferritici, algoritmi, carcinoma midollare, amminoacido, patologia neoplastica*, etc.) which accounts for 31% of the instances; secondly, the area of literary analysis (*"homines novi", terzo sonetto, "Lord Spleen", l'Orlando Furioso*, etc.) which accounts for 21.5% of the instances. At the level of the semantic prosody, again we could say that a fairly objective function of specificity is the only identifiable one, as in the English equivalent.

We have now established a first set of translation equivalents. The correspondence is not only between two complex prepositions which incorporate the same lexical word *case/caso*, or indeed between grammatical functions. The equivalence has been evaluated at the level of functionally complete units of meaning. The evidence of a divergence in semantic preference and/or prosody will be of great help to the translator and will allow him/her to avoid those instances of rather infelicitous "translationese" (Gellerstam 1986) which may stem from an involuntary contravening of the unstated semantic preference. The case discussed above is, in spite of the differences in semantic preference, a fairly felicitous case of equivalence.

One word of warning is in line. The difference in semantic preference apparent between the English and the Italian in the concordance discussed above needs to be confirmedto check that it is not the result of an unbalance in the selection of the texts included in the corpus, and therefore skewed towards a language variety or reflecting a specific topic. Semantic prosodies are often linked to language varieties and seem to become more systematic and restricted the more specific and restricted the variety. This point raises again the issue of the representativeness of a corpus and, in our case here, the comparability of the L1 and L2 corpora. Unfortunately, it is still often the case that an analyst will gain access to a set of L1/L2 "comparable" corpora as a *fait accompli*, without any real access to information on the criteria according to which these corpora have been assembled, and certainly without any say in corpus design and assembly. This is partially inevitable, given the fact that corpora tend to be very large nowadays and beyond the undertaking of a single individual. However, it also means that the user all too often will not be in a position to evaluate the evidence properly for lack of information, and will not to be able to affect the representativeness of the texts included in the corpus.

Our position with respect to representativeness here can be seen as rather pessimistic; we would go along with Leech (1991:27), who says that the assumption of representativeness must be regarded largely as an act of faith, as at present we have still no way of ensuring it or evaluating it objectively, although a lot of work is being done in this direction. As a first step towards achieving a balanced statement in language description, we should remember that corpus work - whether monolingual or multilingual - is above all comparative work where the analyst must never tire of comparing across different varieties, different situations, different languages, different corpora.

From *in case of* to *in caso di*

From the grammatical point of view *"in case of"* is also a complex preposition which introduces, in Hallidayan terms, a circumstance of cause or condition (1985:140). It interesting to note that the difference between *in the case of* and in *case of* - the first one introducing a circumstance of matter, while the second one of cause or condition - is, from a solely grammatical point of view, only brought about by the presence or absence of definite article as an explicit signal of specificity.

From the corpus we get some information on frequency: compared with *"in the case of"*, this complex preposition is not very frequent and we have fifty-six instances in total, compared with 550 of the other, in twenty million words (the concordance is reported in Appendix 8).

Our first step focusing on formal patterning identifies some of the most frequent collocates as repeated co-occurrences in the right co-text: *accident(s), attack, emergency, fire, trouble, need* and *difficulty* are among the more frequent. This collocational profile already shows a strongly negative semantic preference for what could be termed as "disaster areas". We report in Table 4 below some instances that exemplify this tendency.

1.	being, and I wanted to be sure **in case of a sudden emergency** that we
2.	This will minimize your loss **in case of accident or theft**. One pound
3.	of milk, a jar of pureed prunes **in case of constipation**. Other tips.
4.	and sail were constructed **in case of engine failure**. There were
5.	We were only on the first floor **in case of a fire** happening. Lally said she
6.	the place up kept an eye on it **in case of further vandalism** or moves from
7.	it in polythene kitchen wrap **in case of involuntary incontinence**, and
8.	be there to pick up the pieces **in case of massive calamity**. Such
9.	not. One of us should be here, **in case of more Lady Alices** don't you think
10.	Under-ripe berries were preferred **in case of transport hold-ups**, and were

Table 4: *in case of*

This collocational profile is reinforced by other words which belong to the same semantic field:

a burn	an urgent telegram	distress	further questioning	death
danger	renewed difficulty	showers	massive calamity	war
resistance	immediate need	problems	shortages	loss

What we have called semantic prosody, the overall function of the expression, here could be termed as "provision for disaster". This prosody is so strong that the only instance where the noun following *"in case of"* is rather neutral as in:

> One of us should be here, **in case of more Lady Alices**, don't you think?

is understood along the same lines and the possibility of a "Lady Alice", or someone like her, appearing at the door is interpreted as unappealing to say the least. The statement here carries an obvious ironical intention, and the clash in semantic prosodies can be seen as the formal realisation of this ironical intention (Louw 1993) which we have discussed in Chapter Six.

Having thus identified an extended unit of meaning in English, we will posit, as a *prima facie* equivalent, the Italian *"in caso di"*. As a start we can say that *"in caso di"* has the same grammatical function of the English counterpart, and again, in terms of frequency, it is rather rare (the Italian corpus contains eighty-three instances in total, compared with 319 *"nel caso di"*). The concordance is reported in Appendix 9. In Table 5 below we will give just a few examples reduced from the overall concordance. At the collocational level we find repeated instances of the words *necessità, guerra* and *urgenza*. The semantic preference for "disaster areas" overlaps with the negative prosody which shows the evaluative stance of the speaker: this is a set of undesirable events. The other words present in the right co-text emphasise this preference for the negative.

1. posporre l'intervento dell'esercito. **In caso di calamità naturali** dirige
2. questa castagna e non aprirla se non **in caso di gran necessità**. Cammina
3. riguarda l'arruolamento volontario **in caso di guerra**. A sedici anni
4. avrebbe preso e come le avrebbe usate **in caso di incendio**. Accennava i
5. fossero più pericolose di quelle grandi **in caso di incidenti** a catena a
6. adeguati alle loro esigenze di vita **in caso di infortunio**,malattia,
7. epilessia che garantisce una copertura **in caso di morte** o invalidità
8. e cioè l'autorizzazione, **in caso di necessità**, a convocare
9. con Mitterrand alla presidenza poiché **in caso di successo** non sarebbe" né
10. meglio avere i capelli super - puliti. **In caso di un invito ultimo-momento**[7]

Table 5: *in caso di*

At the collocational level we find other words such as:

bisogno	brusca frenata	caduta
contrasto	risposta negativa	conflitto
disubbidienza	giudizio negativo	emergenze
dissenzo	debolezza organica	eruzione
controversie	riduzione del personale	malattie
dubbio	impedimento permanente	cellulite
siccità	rilascio accidentale	urgenza

The semantic prosody can again be termed as "provision for disaster", as the extended unit of meaning has the overall function of hypothesising the possibility of something unpleasant and offering a guarded damage-limitation statement about it.
Interesting to note that - as in the instance with "*more Lady Alices*" - we find here a citation apparently neutral:

con Mitterand alla presidenza poiché, **in caso di successo,** non sarebbe né servito a ..

This instance, though, is seen to fit the pattern once we look at a wider context: the spokesman who is talking is conservative, and for him the success of Mitterand is certainly perceived as a political disaster.

The equivalence established between *in case of* and *in caso di* takes account of the general semantic field and semantic prosody and is satisfactory at the wider functional level. In the light of evidence from larger corpora it will be possible to validate a stronger collocational profile which would offer a welcome guide to appropriateness for the translator, whether they are translating in or out of their own mother tongue.

From *in case* to *se per caso*

In this section we will briefly consider the conjunction *in case*. The conjunction works at the level of the clause and therefore it can be expected that the local patterning in terms of collocation will be less strong than with the prepositions. In the concordance analysed[8] there is no specific collocational restriction. At the colligational level one notices a strong presence of personal pronouns, *I, you, he, she, we*, which point to a certain interactiveness and colloquialness of the texts on the one hand, and an association with the narrative genre on the other[9]. The element of colloquialness seems to be confirmed by the frequent use of phrasal verbs, *lay ahead, put (..) off, turns out, catch up, mixed in, brushed against*, etc. In terms of semantic preference there is again a lot of variation, but a number of words and expressions certainly confirm the feeling of informality.

In most cases the analysis requires a wider context in order to identify the functionally complete unit. Below (Table 6) we report a few significative examples which can help identify the overall semantic prosody.

1.	He looked at her now with alarm,	**in case**	she might do the room an injury ..
2.	any questions. "I bought your way out,	**in case**	you are curious" his father said.
3.	it is better to be bribed than to bribe	**in case**	something goes wrong down the line
4.	Claude, Fernet and I will be there too	**in case**	the wolves start snapping ..
5.	Tear gas, small arms,	**in case**	they won't come back by themselves ..
6.	He poured himself another	**in case**	the abbess forgot to suggest it ..
7.	avoid passing them too close to the male's body	**in case**	they brush against him accidentally
8.	He didn't tell you how to get in touch with him	**in case**	I should arrange another party?
9.	The pistol's right there beside the bed, just	**in case**	the pimp has an attack of amnesia ..
10.	cannibals are perfectly nice people and just	**in case**	you are wondering what this team is doing in the bush ..

Table 6: *in case*

In these instances the tone, and what we have called the semantic prosody, are clear: there is an element of guarded damage limitation and provision for disaster (as with *in case of*) but also, whether we define it semi-ironical or "tongue-in-cheek", the speaker/writer/narrator seems to be smiling at some hypothetical situation and sharing with his/her reader a knowing wink.

A *prima facie* translation equivalent for Italian is *se per caso* and we will report below (Table 7) some examples selected from the overall concordance:

Una torre senza ragni è sospetta: **se per caso** ne trovaste una, fuggite via subito ..
E soprattutto non cadermi addosso **se per caso** c'è un urto violento ..

si guardavano intorno per vedere	**se per caso**	il lupo li seguiva, ma lui ovviamente ..
calzati con le scarpe da footing infangate e	**se per caso**	caso non si posino sul divano ...
Venne la ragazza per chiedergli	**se per caso**	il cibo non fosse stato cucinato ..
chiede notizie di Mozart,	**se per caso**	lei conosce la sua "Marcia Turca" ..
decise di scoprire	**se per caso**	si erano trovate a New York...
una pentola, dico una, con il coperchio?	**se per caso**	gli riesce a convincere una a...
Attraversava il sentiero; e	**se per caso**	un qualche grosso scarabeo zuccone ..

Table 7: *se per caso*

Again we find that the collocational patterning is not strong, but the verbs *vedere* (to see whether) and *chiedere* (to ask whether) are often present in the left context of the conjunction. Other verbs which occur only once, but reinforce a general semantic preference for "discovering whether", are: *scoprire* and *spiare*, often in the context of a fairy tale (see also the use of words such as *lupo/lupa* - wolf and she-wolf).

Perhaps the most noticeable difference between the English and the Italian, though, is the fact that *in case* is used when someone is mentioning a possible future situation or hypothetical event which is someone's reason for doing something. In Italian this reference to a future/hypothetical event is not there, so we have instances like "si guardavano intorno per vedere *se per caso* il lupo li seguiva", where the best translation would be perhaps a more neutral "they were looking around to see *if by any chance* the wolf was following/had followed them" which would allow a reference to a past situation.

At the level of the semantic prosody we find some instances - like the first one above, "A tower without spiders is suspect: *se per caso* you were to find one you should run away immediately .." - which share the tone of "tongue-in-cheek" with the English instances. Others, though, do not seem to take this light, semi-ironical attitude to the hypothetical event presented. In the example "she decided to discover *se per caso* they had been in New York at the same time ..", where we no longer have a conditional clause but an indirect interrogative clause, the writer is really talking of a fairly neutral possibility, and simply adding to it the element of discovery. A translator would probably decide for a translation that does not include *in case*, which is consistently associated with irony. We have to conclude that the prosody which was remarkably regular in English is not as systematic in Italian. The element of tongue-in-cheekness remains as a possible choice at the paradigmatic level, allowing a translator to use *se per caso* as an equivalent for *in case* when the time reference allows it. However, the type of special effects identified by Louw (1993) - irony, hidden attitudinal stance for instance - which depend on a clash with "a sufficiently expected background of expected collocations" (Louw: ibid.), cannot be reliably identified in the Italian data. If the translator was working with English as their TL, they would have to be aware that their neutral possibility introduced by *se per caso* could become tainted with ironic connotations when introduced by *in case*.

In terms of functionally complete units of meaning we have analysed here what seemed a possible translation equivalent, but the function of the two expressions has been shown to differ quite a lot after all. At the grammatical level, the difference in time reference is quite noticeable and could give rise to mistakes in the translation. At the level of the semantic prosody, it could generate a trap for the unaware translator because the correspondence is similar but not as systematic.

The example of *real* and its Italian equivalents

The adjective *real* was discussed in Chapter Six in connection with the phenomenon of delexicalisation brought about by the different patterns of co-selection it entertained with its environment. The patterns discussed on that occasion as 'delexicalised', though, only related to the focusing and the selective functions. Here we will complete the analysis by looking at all the major functions of *real* and address the issues that these raise in translation and comparative linguistics. Therefore, going through a series of steps in generalisation and de-generalisation between source and target language, we will trace the semantic and functional web of equivalence obtaining between this adjective and its Italian counterparts. The *prima facie* translation equivalent will be initially posited as the cognate Italian adjective *reale*.

The most recognisable function of *real*, although not the most frequent one, is of something "that actually exists and is not imagined, invented or theoretical" (Cobuild English Language Dictionary). This we have termed as the *lexical function* of the adjective to contrast it with the delexical one, and is realised by three different types of contextual features in the data we are considering (see Tognini Bonelli 1993a). First a colligational (grammatical) feature, when the adjective is modified by a grading adverb such as *very*:

> treatment, but also there was a **very real** risk of transmission..
> kept back from people who had a **very real** need of it ..
> the crisis continued there was a **very real** possibility of a further..
> at a time where there is **very real** danger of another major conflict..

In this connection the nouns qualified by *real* are invariably abstract nouns such as *risk, need, possibility, optimism, suffering*. The second type of contextual feature associated with the lexical use is again a colligational feature. It is when *real* is in predicative position with verbs such as *be, become, appear*:

> "And when one face **becomes real** all faces become real..
> The treat against him **is real**". Officials say a warrant..

The third type of formal patterning associated with this function is when we find *real* coupled, or contrasted, with another adjective as in *real and potential*:

> fatally marks the beginning of a **real and desperate** crackdown.
> Their responses often reflect **real and justifiable** apprehension..

In Italian we find a similar lexical function associated with the adjective *reale* but the formal realisations are different. The first pattern discussed (*a very real need*) has an Italian functional equivalent, but not modified; we note that the adjective here follows the noun[10].

> Riteneva che corrispondessero a **un bisogno reale**, al bisogno di governare ..
> Interessa solo perché ha **una funzione reale** nell'educazione (o diseducazione)..
> Il Sabba era **un evento reale**: un crimine punibile col rogo.

In terms of semantic preference this use is connected with a set of abstract nouns - *sviluppo, vantaggio, contesto, influsso, riferimento, aria* - like in English. If we consider the second use of *real*, however - the predicative use - we find that it does not have a match in Italian. This does not mean that the construction would be perceived as ungrammatical, quite simply that if we accept the corpus as representative, it is not used often enough to appear in the concordance. For the third type of patterning we do find a parallel in Italian, though to some extent with a different pattern; this is |*più* + adjective + *che* + *reale*| where the adjective belongs to a set of potential antonyms of *reale*:

> penso che la divergenza sia **piu' apparente che reale** ..
> il suo terreno, **piu' potenziale che reale** ..

A second function of the adjective *real* is related to the *financial* area. Consider:

> other indices showed **the real cost of living** rose by about 14%
> the MP's said **the real value** of benefits has fallen ..
> help to halt a slide **in real incomes**. At a news conference ..
> will shoot up overnight **in real terms**, productivity in East Germany ..
> it fell by about 5% **in real terms** ..

The financial function is not very common but very clearly realised, at the collocational level, by the presence of a set of financial nouns following *real*. Other nouns belonging to the same set are *growth levels, cost of production, economy, value*, and of course there is the phrase *in real terms*, belonging to the same financial domain where prices, incomes, etc. are considered in terms of purchasing power rather than nominal currency value.

The pattern in Italian is very similar; we have a set of financial terms such as *salario, tassi di interesse, valore, costo, potere d'acquisto, ricchezza*. The adjective *reale* is always in post-nominal position: |financial Ns + *reale*| as in:

> gli interessi versati danno luogo a **un costo reale** per le imprese ..
> almeno dieci volte superiore **al valore reale** ..

The symmetry between the two sets of nouns is quite reassuring for the translator; it may be worth noting, however, that while the English pattern is always associated with the definite article, the Italian pattern is sometimes found in the presence of the indefinite article. This is an important point to note, because when *real* is preceded by an indefinite article in English it completely changes its function to what has been referred to as the *focusing function*.

The other two functions associated with the adjective *real*, namely the *focusing* and the *selective* functions, were the ones discussed in Chapter Six and are the most frequent functions of the adjective, the selective function representing the marked and less frequent choice compared with the focusing one which is very frequent (80% of the instances).

The selective function is associated with the formal environment |*the* (or possessive) + *real* + N|; for the sake of convenience we report below some of the citations from the concordance already discussed in Chapter Six:

> of postponing the deadline. **The real deadline**, it's argued, is March 1st
> in Warsaw, Jan Repa, says **the real contest** is between the leader of the
> unity problems will dwindle. **The real problems** will be for East Germans.
> omen for President Hrawi. But **the real stumbling block** for Lebanon will be
> level to get a solution. **My real fear** is that the whole thing will

As we mentioned in our previous discussion, the noun group qualified by *real* is selected in contrast to another one; the latter is implicitly referred to as of lesser importance, or relevance. The adjective is delexicalised and has acquired a structural role at the level of discourse and argumentation. So, for instance, the *real problems* presuppose a value judgement about other problems, which are implied to be less serious or important. In these instances the existence of another element to make up the contrastive set and the value judgement associated with it are both inferential, since they are not explicitly stated in the text. The correlation between contextual and functional features associated with this pattern accounts for a wider type of meaning; the reference to the lesser term, as we have seen, could encapsulate unexplicit propositions, perhaps in the form of lengthy statements realised over whole paragraphs in the preceding text.

Considering now the possibility of an Italian translation equivalent, an adjective with a similar inferential and pragmatic function in discourse, it soon becomes evident that our *prima facie* translation equivalent *reale* does not perform a similar function in Italian. The adjective we will investigate here in order to assess the specific formal correspondences with the selective use of *real* is *vero*.

Indeed, one of the functions of *vero* in Italian, the pattern [definite article (or possessive) + *vero* + N], triggers a similar inferential correlation to *real* in its selective function, implying a value judgement and referring back to a lesser element. Consider for instance:

> Nessuno aveva mai saputo **il vero nome** del Gran Masten ..
> Poi risulto' che **il vero capo** non era Persico, ma Jo ..
> Non riuscivamo a cogliere **il vero bandolo della matassa** ..

Il vero nome is thus contrasted with another name which is not real - a pseudonym or an alias, perhaps. *Il vero capo*, Jo, is set against another "boss", Persico, perhaps officially in charge, but not quite.

The parallels between the English and the Italian structures are quite clear. We should note that in Italian the adjective here is always in pre-nominal position. What is perhaps not immediately noticeable at the beginning is that, at the colligational level, the English *real* seems to be found more often in thematic position and, at the collocational level, to collocate more consistently with words such as *motive, cause, reason, purpose, issue, key, problem, question, extent*, etc., showing a semantic preference for the world of discourse. The evidence from English therefore shows the specific use of *real* for argumentation purposes, when different points of view are evaluated and adopted, or dismissed, in the process of discourse. The Italian equivalent *vero* does not seem to favour quite as consistently the thematic position and, in terms of collocates, it is associated with words that do not specifically show the same semantic preference for discourse; we find, for example, *nome, sapiente, artista, centro, creatore, padrone, padre, problema, scandalo, viaggio, segreto*.

This is an interesting problem for the translator because, although the function of the two adjectives is very similar at the pragmatic level, the segmentation of experience in the two cultures, as reflected by the semantic preference, shows a clear mismatch. Any notation for a data-base of translation equivalents will have to take into account these differences which only become apparent in the light of frequency distributions made available by large corpora. A decision to ignore them should only stem from an explicit strategic stand on the part of the translator and not on an easy ignorance of the facts.

As we pointed out in Chapter Six, the adjective with a focusing function is co-selected with the noun and, as such, closely linked to the nominal choice rather than a choice in its own right. It is, therefore, another instance of the phenomenon of delexicalisation and in this case the delexicalised adjective emphasises the `typicality' of the noun, i.e. the consensus-based view that the meaning of it is what we all expect it to be: *a real surprise* is genuine surprise, *a real risk* is something we would all agree to call "risky", etc. For the sake of convenience, before we consider a possible translation equivalent, let us reconsider some examples of *real* with a focusing function:

> the British weather does offer **a real surprise** - instead of the habitually
> Environment Committee says there's **a real risk** of contracting minor infections
> in the Middle East has created **a real possibility** of direct talks between
> The Croatian leadership now faces **a real threat** to some of the main Dalmatian
> First of all, they failed to show **any real interest** in the directive. After

As we can see, the formal features associated with the focusing function of *real* are usually |(indefinite article) + *real* + N|. The type of noun qualified is again a set of abstract nouns like *problem, danger, difficulty*. A similar focusing function exists in Italian, but again it is not realised by *reale*. We have to resort to *vero* for a possible match to the English adjective. Let us consider some examples:

> Tisane, infusi, decotti, sono **un vero toccasana** contro i dolori ..
> Non credo che questo sia fare **un vero favore** a Fernandez ..
> di poteri paranormali. **Una vera donna** capisce al volo ..

The function of the adjective *vero* in these instances indeed seems to be the appropriate translation equivalent for the focusing *real*. The meaning can be glossed as proper, genuine, the function is one of intensification and of implicit reference to a consensus view: *una vera donna* is a woman, as society expects her to be. Considering the colligational angle, the adjective is found in pre-nominal position, preceded by the indefinite article - |un/una, etc. + *vero/vera* + N|. We note that the set of abstract nouns collocating with *real* in English has no equivalent in Italian where we find examples like *diavolo, filologo, mirmecologo, pubblico, temperamento, trionfo* which cannot really be grouped under the same lexical or semantic label.

From the point of view of frequency, it should be mentioned that while the focusing function of *real* accounts for about 80% of the instances in English, the same cannot be said for Italian, where the focusing function of *vero* is relatively rare (11%). In Italian the most frequent pattern associated with *vero* is the predicative use (*e'/non e' vero che* ..), often acting as a preface at the beginning of a sentence and with an overall frequency of 40%; the English equivalent in this case is not *real* but *true*, but this will be another element in the web of equivalences based on contextual patterning, and will not be investigated here. Further research is needed in order to identify such networks across languages; in the context of this chapter this possibility will be briefly outlined in the section on "items and their collocates" below.

In Italian there is another pattern that we should briefly mention because it has a very similar formal realisation to the focusing *vero* above, although it also shows a slightly different function. This involves the phrase *vero e proprio* in the pattern: |(indefinite article) + *vero e proprio* + N|. Let us consider some examples:

>non un semplice aggiornamento ma **un vero e proprio** progetto di ristrutturazione
>l'eremo, circondato da un muro e' **una vera e propria** cittadella ..
>turba moltissimo lo scontroso bestione, **vero e proprio** "orso" ..

These instances have a similar function to the focusing *vero* above, the appeal to consensus and typicality: *un vero e proprio progetto di ristrutturazione* (a real project of restructuring), thorough and complete, we all know what it is. It is important to note, though, that *vero e proprio* establishes also a cohesive link with a preceding element and its function is to re-qualify and in a way emphasise, in the light of typicality, the meaning of the other element. So, *un vero e proprio progetto di ristrutturazione* re-qualifies *un semplice aggiornamento* (a simple up-dating) and brings it one step further. Similarly, in the second example, *l'eremo* (a hermitage) becomes *una vera e propria cittadella*, a small enclosed town in its own rights; and in the third example the beast, already defined as *scontroso* (sullen), is further qualified as *vero e proprio orso*, where *orso* is the Italian word for bear, but also the stereotype for anybody totally introverted and antisocial.

In the light of this evidence we can say, therefore, that the pattern involving *vero e proprio* in Italian, although very similar in meaning to the use of focusing *real*, entails a different semantic prosody: it presupposes a cohesive link with another element and serves the purpose of re-qualifying it and emphasising its typicality. The translator will obviously have to be aware of this specific feature when encoding in the target language; equally, a data-base of translation equivalents will have to develop a system of annotation capable of accounting for these formal and functional differences between source and target language.

Items and their collocates: a web of relations across languages

In the sections above we have exemplified a method for the comparison of *primafacie* translation equivalents across languages. The starting point has been the observation of the linguistic context of a given word or phrase and the assumption has been that it is possible to correlate systematically the formal features in the environment of an item with its function in text and discourse. Once this is done in L1 and L2, equivalence can be investigated not so much at the level of individual words, phrases and structures but, as Halliday put it in the quote reported at the beginning of this chapter, as equivalence of function in context. This type of equivalence leads us to query very fundamentally the traditional belief that to a certain word in L1 will correspond another word L2, even if lip service is paid to a few mismatches where this is not possible. It is argued here that it would be altogether better if, at the level of the word or phrase, we simply started from an assumption of non-equivalence. Working with functions, we have seen, is different.

The corpus-driven approach entails the very strict correlation between formal and functional parameters and, in the presence of corpus evidence, it is now possible to define fairly precisely the formal boundaries of a function. We have seen that a function does not usually coincide with a word, although there may be a lot of overlaps: several functionally complete units of meaning may have the same word as their core but associated with a different environment. If what we are after is *functional equivalence*, in spite of the overlaps at the level of individual words in L1 and L2, we must remember that it is not the word but the contextual patterning associated with it that identifies a function. The correspondences between the two languages may at times leave out some blank areas of no match; at other times they offer more than one possible equivalent in L2 for an initial function in L1. The job of the translator is exactly that of bridging these gaps in the light of the linguistic and extra-linguistic constraints.

Here we would like to exemplify further the first steps towards a database of equivalences between functionally complete units of meaning in L1 and L2. This type of database, it is argued, could be seen a translation work-bench, and can offer the linguistic input upon which the translator can make informed decisions taking into account the extra-linguistic constraints discussed above. It is argued that such a platform, if the descriptive steps are systematised, can be semi-automatic and can provide a valuable input for translators.

The theoretical assumptions of this work go back to a project in multilingual lexicography sponsored by the Coucil of Europe in 1990-1991 under the direction of John Sinclair (see Sinclair et al. eds. 1996). This project proposed an approach to translation equivalence which went "beyond the word" and incorporated contextual features that consistently interrelated with the node word.

Sinclair summarises the project as follows:

> The foundations have been laid for a system of describing the shared meanings of languages in terms of the actual verbal context in which each instance is found. The attraction of the description is the way in which each instance is assumed to be carrying in its immediate environment sufficient differential information to indicate which of several possible meanings is the relevant one, and in the case of translation, what is the appropriate phraseology. If successfully pursued, the descriptive method could lead to applications such as translation aids which are likely to be simple enough to be computable and powerful enough to be worth the trouble. (Sinclair 1996e:174)

We will present below the initial steps for the establishment of a network of translation equivalents following Sinclair's guidelines. We will use an example already discussed in Chapter Two. This is the adverb *largely*[11]. The steps proposed here start from degeneralising the initial function of *largely* into its specific uses. We recall that these are connected with three major areas:

- the area of CAUSE and REASON (realised by words such as *because, thanks to, as a result, due to*)

- the area of BASIS and RELATION (realised by words such as *based on, depends/ed on, dependent on, rely/ied on*)

- the area of morphological and semantic NEGATIVES (realised by a set of adjectives with negative prefix: *ignored, incompatible, unaware, disappeared*, etc.).

The idea of extending the comparison to the context will mean that we will look for Italian equivalents to *largely* in the same type of contextual patterning associated with the three functions outlined above. So the match will be sought for *largely because, largely thanks to, largely as a result, largely due to* which are the functionally complete units of meaning encoding the first area of usage, the one of cause and reason. Here we note that a very frequent collocate such as *because* "keeps company" with other adverbs like *mainly, mostly, particularly*, while a phrase such as *as a result* seems to be only modified by *largely*. This is a point where frequency information can be of great value, adding a probabilistic dimension to paradigmatic choice. This information could also be very valuable for the comparison of L1 and L2, showing for instance that although *a causa di* can in principle be modified by *soprattutto*, in practice it is likely to go without modification. Looking at the Italian corpus we find an equivalent to this first function of *largely* operating in a comparable context (see Table 8 below). This is the adverb *soprattutto*:

— because (v. frequent) (*largely, mainly, mostly, particularly*)	• soprattutto (— *perché*)
thanks — to (*largely, mainly*)	• soprattutto (— *grazie a*)
— as a result (*largely*) due – to (*entirely, largely, mainly*)	• soprattutto (— *a causa di/de*l etc.) (*a causa —*) (usu. not modified)

Table 8 - *largely*: CAUSE and REASON

When we consider the second area associated with *largely*, the area of basis and relation (Table 9 below), the problem of modification mentioned above becomes very visible because the verbs modified by *largely* with this function are not usually modified in Italian. The exception is with forms like *dipende* or *è dipeso da*, but it is interesting to note that this does not apply to *dipendente da*, which is never modified. This is again a pointer to the fact that we should not expect different inflected forms to behave according to the same pattern of usage (see our discussion on lemmas and inflected forms in Chapter Five).

— based on (*largely, mainly, essentially*)	not modified (*basato su*)
— dependent on (*entirely, heavily, largely, totally, completely, more*)	not modified (*dipendente da*)
depends/ed — on/upon rely/ied — on	• — in larga misura (*dipende/è dipeso da*) • molto —, • — essenzialmente,

Table 9 - *largely*: BASIS and RELATION

The area where *largely* emphasises adjectives with negative prefixes is an important area of usage for *largely* and, as we have seen in Chapter Two, it is where this adverb is differentiated from a semantically connected word such as *broadly*. In Italian there is a match for this function in *largamente* which also has a role emphasising semantically negative adjectives. We note that, at the purely morphological level, the different possibilities allowed by the English system (*in**, *un**, *dis**) are only realised by the prefix **in* with the Italian equivalents. Consider Table 10 below:

largely	in*	• largamente
	ignored	illusoria,
	inaccessible	inattuale,
	incompatible	incompleta,
	incomprehensible	inconsapevoli,
	inconclusive	inesplorati,
	indefensible	inferiori,
	irrelevant, etc.	inutilizzati, etc.
—	un*	n.a.
	unanticipated	
	unattended	
	unaware	
	unchanged, etc.	
—	dis*	n.a.
	disappeared	
	discounting	
	dismantle	
	dismissed	
	disregarded, etc.	

Table 10 - *largely*: MORPHOLOGICAL and SEMANTIC NEGATIVES

Although *largely* and *largamente* can be considered as equivalents at the functional level in the specific area of semantic negatives, they are not so from other points of view. So, *largamente* is also found qualifying words such as *accettato, diffuso, condiviso, consolidato, popolare, presente, praticato* which are associated with the positive semantic prosody of general acceptance and popularity.

This is just the beginning of a definition of a network of equivalences. This can be seen as a series of steps in degeneralisation and generalisation whereby an initial item (*largely*) is defined in a number of specific functions associated with specific formal features. Each formal feature is then examined and a possible match is posited from the combination of item/environment in L1 to a comparable combination of item/environment in L2. We have found that what is not possible as a match between two items (for instance *largely* and *largamente*) is possible when *one* of the specific functions associated with *largely* is compared with one of the specific functions associated with *largamente*. The equivalence we posit therefore will be truly functional, that is, an equivalence between functions.

Conclusion

The approach to establishing functional equivalence, whether for contrastive or translation purposes, proposed in this article advocates the use of comparable corpora in stage one and three, and a translation corpus in stage two. The use of comparable - or even relatively comparable - corpora is seen as an absolute necessity to establish equivalence and it is argued that it would be impossible to identify reliably functionally complete units of meaning without the help of the evidence from the two corpora. We have argued that it is also necessary to use a translation corpus to posit a set of *prima facie* equivalents, but these corpora are still not very widely available, and unfortunately we have not been able to access one for this study. As a result, this study is only partially exemplifying the model it advocates, but it can be seen as a way forward to a methodology that will bring together the translator's experience (as from the translation corpus) and the input, the richness and the variability of two natural languages (as from the comparable corpora).

What we have illustrated in this study is a way of establishing and evaluating the comparability of units of meaning across languages which tries to take into account language events which, in Firth's words, are "typical, recurrent and repeatedly observable" (1957:35). The assumption that words do not live in isolation but in strict semantic and functional relationship with other words has led us to the notion of functionally complete units of meaning. To sum up, we can characterise them in this way:

1. They can be identified looking at patterns of co-selection in the context of a word or expression. They involve collocational (lexical) and colligational (grammatical) choices and therefore cannot be defined solely in lexical or grammatical terms. They also involve a semantic preference, realised by words which belong to the same semantic field, and they perform a specific semantic prosody at the pragmatic level.

2. They are syntagmatic units in that they interrelate linearly with other words and, through a process of co-selection, they form a multi-word unit which becomes available as a single choice on the paradigmatic axis.

3. Only when these multi-words units are functionally complete do they become available as translation equivalents or as comparable units of meaning between two languages.

4. A web of translation equivalents can be posited and defined using items and their frequent collocates as formal parameters to match with functional ones.

The information gathered from corpus evidence simply by observing the repeated patterns of co-selection cannot be found in standard works of reference. The examples chosen here may share the same grammatical function or the same lexical core, as in *in (the) case (of)* and its Italian equivalents. What accounts for their varying degrees of correspondence in terms of their semantic preference and semantic prosody cannot be severed from their very individual pattern of co-selection. It would not make sense to attempt a translation without first being fully aware of that specific semantic preference and that specific semantic prosody. It should never be assumed that the match is going to be adequate as the evidence from the corpus shows some large areas of mismatch which are often beyond the explicit perception of a native speaker.

Notes

1. This chapter was given as a paper at a conference on "Lexis in Contrast" at Louvain-la-Neuve, and will also appear on the proceedings of that conference (Altenberg and Granger, forthcoming). This version has greatly benefitted from the comments of colleagues in that occasion and in particular of the editors of the proceedings, Sylviane Granger and Bengt Altemberg.
2. For a more detailed discussion of this point see Tognini Bonelli 1996a.
3. The term "displaced situationality" is originally taken from Neubert (1985) and elaborated in Viaggio (1992).
4. This view is based on Sinclair's position on the function of *reporting structures* in discourse (1981).
5. This procedure is what Johns (1991:4) refers to as "Identify-Classify-Generalise" and applies to concordance-based learning research (*data-driven learning*).
6. The English corpus used here is the Birmingham Corpus. The Italian corpus is the Contemporary Italian Corpus; they are both briefly described in the Introduction.
7. Un "invito-ultimo-momento" is an invitation at the last moment. In Italy some people are rather sensitive to this because it implies not really having planned it at the party and having been invited only because someone has called out and the host has suddenly realised that thirteen people were going to sit at the table (this is usually taken to bring bad luck). This instance goes along with the trend *in case* + something unpleasant taking place.
8. A total of 532 instances of the conjunction *in case* were found in the Birmingham Corpus (twenty million words).

9. As discussed in Chapter Two, Biber (1994) identified text types - in contrast to register and genre - on the basis of shared linguistic co-occurrence patterns. Among the linguistic features analysed to identify text types, one is pronouns; Biber pointed out that they are "relatively interactive and colloquial in communicative function" (ibid.:389).
10. The Italian language allows adjectives both in pre-nominal and post-nominal position. For a discussion of the types of adjectives which favour pre-nominal position based on corpus data, see Ball 1995.
11. The data we will use comes again from the Birmingham Corpus of Contemporary Written English and the Corpus of Contemporary Italian.

8 The contextual theory of meaning

> *It is not sufficient that a word is found, unless it be so combined as that its meaning is apparently determined by the tract and tenor of the sentence.*
> (Dr. Johnson, *Preface:320*)

The theory of meaning that lies behind corpus-driven linguistics is that of J.R. Firth (1890-1960). Firth died just before the advent of computers and electronic corpora, and it is unlikely that he would have been well disposed towards them[1], but nevertheless he laid the theoretical foundation of a contextual theory of meaning which is central to our present-day view of corpus work. The central tenet of Firth's theory of language relies on the assumption that:

> We must take our facts from speech sequences, verbally complete in themselves and operating in contexts of situation which are typical, recurrent, and repeatedly observable. Such contexts of situation should themselves be placed in categories of some sort, sociological and linguistic, within the wider context of culture. (1957:35)

Very much in contrast, therefore, with other theoretical models (see Chapter Nine), the object of linguistic enquiry is above all the observable and the attested, embedded in the immediacy of social intercourse.

Concerning Firth's theory of meaning, we should start by noting two points. The first is that for Firth the main concern of descriptive linguistics is to make "statements about meaning". The second, very much implied by the first, is that meaning *can* be stated in linguistic terms. Both these assumptions are fundamental in the corpus-driven approach proposed here. What we have attempted to show in the preceding chapters has been driven above all by an interest in identifying, defining and, at times, disambiguating meaning. The fact that our chosen data has been corpus evidence shows that we start from the assumption that meaning, in its different forms (including connotational, inferential and ideological) is realised above all at the linguistic level.

In the history of linguistics, meaning has sometimes been seen as secondary or even dispensable from linguistic study on the grounds that it involved other non-linguistic, or extra-linguistic, enquiries (cf. Bloomfield, Z. Harris, Chomsky). Firth proposes to integrate the linguistic and the extra-linguistic by taking as the object of his enquiry the whole man, a man who is alive and active in the world around him. He asserts (1968:13) that human beings have a natural urge to communicate using speech, and the communication is broad and general, not just workaday interaction and getting things done; he sees us as being "endowed with an urge to diffuse (..) experience", constantly involved in "meaningful activity" with our fellow human beings. Man is, above all, a social animal who is immersed in his culture and gradually accumulates social roles from a very early stage in his life. Firth balances the social and individual sides of the individual by saying that although each new baby is an individual, its needs compel it to accept the process of socialisation, which Firth sees as the acquisition of "a bundle of roles and *personae*" (1957:27-28).

This kind of perspective brings language into the picture as simply one - perhaps the most important - of the meaningful activities through which man expresses himself in order to interact with his fellow human beings and his environment. Firth sees speech as vocal action in a social context, controlling other people and ourselves, getting, as he says, "on speaking terms with our environment". The basic principle behind this is what Firth calls "the unity, identity and continuity of the human personality"; basically, what we are, what we say and what we do are very strictly interrelated. Any human activity is, inescapably, meaningful. For Firth meaning is everywhere in situations, and all the parties involved are making meaning; the inanimate objects and the events are also meaningful. "Some of the events", he says, "are the noises made by the speakers" (in Palmer 1968:14).

We note here that "events" and "noises" are very much considered as two of a kind, showing the strict interconnection between linguistic and non-linguistic events in Firth's model. Statements about the first must take into account the second, and the linguist makes a presumption that people are inherently communicative, and predisposed to diffuse their experience (ibid.: 14). Communicativeness, of course, cannot exist in isolation, in complete abstraction from a specific environment; meaning cannot be analysed in itself and for itself if it is to handle speech events. These have to be apprehended "in their contexts, as shaped by the creative acts of speaking persons" (1957:193).

The central notion of this model is, as we can see, the *context of situation*; Firth's taxonomy of the context of situation portrays it as a schematic construct to be applied to language events. Its constituents are:

1. The participants: persons, personalities and relevant features of these.
    (a) The verbal action of the participants.
    (b) The non-verbal action of the participants.
2. The relevant objects and non-verbal and non-personal events.
3. The effect of the verbal action.

The context of situation is abstract; it is "a group of categories, both verbal and non-verbal, which are considered as interrelated" (1957:175). The text as such is "an integral part of the context, and is observed in relation to the other parts regarded as relevant in the statement of the context" (ibid.:176). Firth quotes Wittgenstein's famous dictum "the meaning of words lies in their use" and takes it as a key point in the development of his model: use cannot exist in isolation, use can only be recognised and analysed contextually and functionally.

Any linguistic statement about meaning will ultimately have to "renew the connection" with "the processes and patterns of life" (in Palmer 1968:19), abstractions will have to be validated in a "constant reapplication to the flux of experience" (ibid.:19). In other words, every utterance which occurs and functions in a culturally determined context of situation will have to be evaluated with respect to it. We can see that the approach we have advocated is very much in line with this view of language as function in context, hence the prominence of the stage of the semantic prosody in the creation and the attribution of meaning at the textual level, and as the crucial meeting point between text and context.

We are a long way away from the Saussurean concept of *langue* and *parole* where individual use had been dismissed as idiosyncratic, unobservable and too chaotic to be taken as the basis for a sound theory of language. Furthermore, *parole* was taken to be unrepresentative of the social norm governing language use. *Langue,* on the other hand, being an abstract notion, was taken to represent the norm, the social agreement underlying use, the only true object of linguistic enquiry. While the social element, for Saussure, could only exist at the abstract level of code crystallisation, with Firth we find that the individual instance of language use is physically embedded in the situation and pivotal in the social and cultural context; as such it can be accounted for only in so far as it has a function in the wider context. Meaning, in this framework, cannot be seen as what Firth, referring to Saussure, had named a set of "relations in a hidden mental process" (1957:19).

Firth was very quick to dismiss the well-known dichotomies such as "mind and body", "thought and word", etc. Meaning, according to Firth, could be regarded chiefly as "situational relations" and "modes of behaviour", and the language was "that kind of language which disturbs the air and other people's ears" (ibid.). Both the utterance under observation and the context in which it is embedded are observable rather than ontological or presupposed. The object of linguistic description, notwithstanding Firth's absolute refusal of the Saussurean dichotomies, would be (in Saussurean terms) very much *parole*, but the methodology would relate the physical events to an abstract model.

Another key concept in Firth's model, stemming from the fact that the utterances under consideration constitute real language in action, is the notion of "repeated events". Firth, having stressed the importance of studying individuals in their social roles or personae, proposes a view of language as the vector of "the continuity of repetitions in the social process" (1957:183). The assumption is that, linguistically speaking, human beings act systematically. So he proposes to identify and isolate the recurrent patterns from "the mush of general goings-on" (ibid.: 187), so that they can be handled systematically by a set of descriptive categories. We have seen the determining importance of frequency of occurrence in the shaping of linguistic categories based on corpus evidence. The corpus offers the linguist the ease to quantify this 'continuity of repetition' and derive typological statements from it.

Indeed, one of Firth's most important statements both links and separates the speaker as an individual from the speaker as a typical user of the language. The linguist must "abstract the impersonal from the personal by regarding it as typological" (ibid.:188); the feature by which we recognise facts as impersonal and typological is that they are recurrent. Only thus will the linguist achieve "the formalisation of observations of regularities exhibited" in the language (Tsui 1994:3). This, as we can see is a very empirical method where abstractions are not acceptable if they are not capable of extraction directly from, and corroborated by, linguistic facts[2].

In such a model, the social element in language is two-fold. On the one hand, Firth sees any utterance as functional - a way of acting on other people and influencing one's environment[3] (1957:36). Language thus viewed extends beyond words, phrases and sentences and achieves results in a context, which itself may not have linguistic realisations (the "context of culture"). On the other hand, the routine inbuilt in life and language[4] likens the cumulative effect of repeated events to typological statements and acts as a criterion of relevance: the object of linguistic study is the "typical", and yet again we note that the typical cannot be severed from actual usage.

Firth thus sets out to face squarely the full complexity of language in use, and only then suggests a division into levels of analysis (1957:183); each level or "component function" concentrates on an aspect of language such as grammar or phonetics, relating it to a context. The context may be another of the levels of analysis, or the context of situation as a whole - the important point is that all statements of meaning are statements of contextual relations (1957:19).

The statement of meaning can be achieved from the outer layer of social context inwards to grammar, vocabulary and phonology, or in the other direction, where sound and sense are ultimately linked. The analysis of meaning, therefore, is achieved by splitting it into different mutually congruent levels, and proceeding to "its dispersion into modes, rather like the dispersion of light of mixed wavelength into a spectrum" (1957:192).

According to F.R. Palmer, one of Firth's junior colleagues, Firth insisted that no priority should be given to any one of the levels within this cline of modes; Palmer reports that "the simile that Firth liked to use in his later years was of the lift that moved freely from one level to another, without giving priority to any one and without proceeding in any one direction" (Palmer, 1968:5). Firth himself, in his published writings, does not always make clear the interrelation between these various levels; meaning is taken to be "the whole complex of functions which a linguistic form may have" (1957:33). These functions are then subdivided into minor functions - the phonetic function, for example - and major functions: on the one hand, the lexical, morphological and syntactical function, which together would be the province of "a reformed system of grammar"; on the other, "the function of a complete locution in the context of situation, or typical context of situation, the province of semantics" (ibid.).

At times, however, Firth seems to postulate some kind of hierarchical structure and talks of the empirical analysis of meaning as "a serial contextualisation of our facts, *context within context* (my emphasis), each one being a function, an organ of the bigger context and all contexts finding a place in what may be called the context of culture"[5] (1957:32). A hierarchical structure of this kind poses the problem of what type of relationship really exists between lexis and grammar. Are we meant to understand that they are two clearly distinct levels and that lexis, as the lower of the two, will `slot into' the bigger context, i.e. a grammatical framework? Firth, however, comes back to point out that:

> Such an analytic dispersion of the statement of meaning at a series of levels (..) does not imply that any level includes or constitutes a formal prerequisite of any other. The levels of abstraction are only connected in that the resulting statements relate to the same language texts in the focus of attention in experience, and the theory requires them to be congruent and consequently complementary in synthesis on renewal of connection in experience. (in Palmer 1968:177)

One can't help feeling that the question of the interrelation of the different levels is left rather vague[6], and Firth's reliance on the "renewal of connection" is weakened by the fact that although he makes reference to this process at several crucial points in his various statements, he never expands on this notion. This is unfortunate, particularly since the study of language using corpora offers a methodology that permits just this renewal of connection - and also another Firthian notion, that language patterns may be interpreted directly in the context of situation no matter at what component level they originate.

One of the properties of a corpus is that it is always available; it does not go away, it is finite and clearly defined, so there should be no obscurities in its composition. Early critics of the use of corpora made these into drawbacks, claiming that since language was non-finite both in the set of well-formed structures and the range of variation, then no corpus could adequately represent it (see the Chomskian position). We should note that there is a positive side to placing at least cautious confidence in a corpus as a source of evidence about a language. Using a corpus, the "renewal of connection" advocated by Firth can be made at any time. The typical "word-in-context" concordance that corpus linguistics has been using for forty years allows generalisations to be made without obscuring for a moment the instances that for one reason or another do not follow the generalisation. While there is no record that Firth was aware of this model growing round about him in his later years, the analysis of "words in context", made possible by the concordance, satisfies the requirements of the model he describes in the above quotation, at least as far as all the verbal environments are concerned.

We must now consider one of the most original notions put forward by Firth, one that has had, and is still having, a revolutionary impact on modern linguistics. This is the notion of *collocation*. Meaning by collocation is a direct consequence of the fact that, for Firth, the meaning of words lies in their use, and established usage will recognise words "in familiar and habitual company". Firth states that:

> The habitual collocations in which words under study appear are quite simply the mere word accompaniment, the other word-material in which they are most commonly or most characteristically embedded. It can safely be stated that part of the `meaning' of cows can be indicated by such collocations as *They are milking the cows, Cows give milk*. The words *tigresses* or *lionesses* are not so collocated and are already clearly separated in meaning at the *collocational level*. (in Palmer 1968:180)

Meaning by collocation is placed at the lexical level, which is a constituent in the taxonomy of the context of situation, but Firth distinguishes collocational meaning from contextual meaning; meaning by collocation is "an abstraction at the syntagmatic level" (ibid.:196) and therefore purely co-textual. He goes no further, and we are left to wonder why collocation, which seems almost by definition to be the ultimate type of contextual - or at least co-textual - meaning (that is if we see meaning as usage), should not have a clear place in Firth's taxonomy - even a level for itself.

One reason could be that the pervasive nature of collocation in the general language was not observable in Firth's day; the amount of collocational data capable of accounting for the standard variety of language had not been made available at the time when he was writing and it is only now, with the development of large and representative computerised corpora, that we truly recognise the importance of the collocational criterion for statements of meaning.

Hence Firth saw the usefulness of collocation lying mainly in the description of restricted languages and in the stylistic analysis of selected texts; while he saw that collocation was the type of meaning that characterised a variety of communication, he did not fully recognise it as a mechanism for creating textual meaning.

But there are indications that, in spite of the fact that collocation is not explicitly seen as a component of the contextual meaning as such, according to Firth it can be regarded as a criterion "for setting up a system of distributed variants" (in Palmer 1968:20). Starting with the outermost level, there is life itself seen as processes and patterns; and language behaviour, called *text*, is part of these processes and patterns and central to linguistic description. Text has the abstract feature of *order*, and in text there are observable structures, of which the first patterning to be examined is collocation, which Firth sees distributionally. The text can then be seen as ordered series of items like words and morphemes, and *pieces* (a typically undefined Firthian term), and this ordering is interpreted as arising from the operation of *systems* and sets of systems, of which the "pieces" etc. are *terms* (Palmer 1968:24).

It is interesting to note here that for Firth the "system of distributed variants" at the collocational level must be matched by another at the colligational level. Firth says:

> The study of the collocations in which a word is normally used is to be completed by a statement of the interrelations of the syntactical categories within collocation. (in Palmer 1968:23)

This is what he calls *colligation*, i.e. the statement of meaning at the grammatical level, seen as the relationships between word classes and sentence classes. The word here is not considered as such but in terms of its belonging to a class such as adjective, verb or pronoun, for example. This point is extremely important, as we shall observe later; it is the first step towards recognising the strict interdependence of lexis and grammar, which is by no means to be taken for granted.

We should note, in this respect, that the link with colligation is made after the collocational patterns have been established, and this is very revealing of Firth's position and important in linguistic theory. Firth observes that while a word in usual collocation "stares at you in the face just as it is" (in Palmer 1968:182), colligations of grammatical categories constitute one step in abstraction; and abstraction, in the Firthian model, has to be derived from the actual, once the actual has been observed and attested. The most obvious consequence of this seems to be that, if we prioritise the immediately observable and the actual, statements of lexis should take precedence over grammar. Regardless of the sequence of events in an investigation, Firth's stance leads us to claim the inherent, theoretically recognised priority of syntagmatic patterns over paradigmatic abstractions.

In this position we recognise Sinclair's point concerning the theoretical and methodological steps leading to the identification of the unit of meaning (1996c,

1998b) based on corpus data. Collocation, as the first step in abstraction at the syntagmatic level, is given priority and colligation is defined with respect to the collocational patterns.

To conclude this section on the works of Firth, we may recall Saussure's dictum: *c'est le point de vue qui crée l'objet*. The aim - object[7] - of linguistic description is, in the Firthian model, the observable and the attested. Any linguistic abstraction is, for Firth, strictly related to use. If we wish to relate this to the Saussurean notion of *langue*, it is *langue* seen as the whole set of linguistic habits of the *masse parlante*, the repetition of similar linguistic events in *parole*, that is seen as relevant and determining for the linguistic statement. The notion of system is strictly related to the abstractions made from observation of patterns at the syntagmatic level.

Now that the study of corpora, particularly large corpora in today's terms (e.g. hundreds of millions of words), is commonplace, the magnificent vision offered by Firth's admittedly untidy model for language can be thoroughly explored. His words ring through the decades with ever greater accuracy and force, and phrases like one quoted early in this section have an uncannily prophetic depth to them:

> typical, recurrent, and repeatedly observable (1957:35)

Coming into prominence a generation after Firth, corpus linguistics could do worse than identify with phrases such as the above.

Notes

1. Firth often made cutting remarks against the use of "machines" in linguistic investigation and was certainly opposed to frequency studies.
2. This can be seen as the central tenet of corpus-driven linguistics.
3. In "The Use and Distribution of Certain English Sounds" (1935). In this article what Firth calls *Pragmatic Functionalism* is contrasted with the "purely systematological or structural analysis" of language attributed to Saussure.
4. One of the principles identified and discussed by Stubbs (1993:19-20) in the British tradition is the fact that "much language use is routine".
5. In "The Technique of Semantics" (1935). A similar point assuming a hierarchy between levels is made when Firth mentions that they should be dealt with "sometimes in a descending order, beginning with social context and proceeding through syntax and vocabulary to phonology and even phonetics, and other times in the opposite order". This seems to imply that, whatever order we may choose to adopt (see Palmer's simile of the lift), vocabulary - we take this to be the lexical level - would be considered a lower rank than syntax. This hierarchical view of levels is taken up by Lyons who explains that "[Firth] describes the `meaning' of units of each level in terms of their `function' as elements in the structure of units of the level above. The structures of the higher-level units are the contexts in which the lower-level units `function' and `have meaning' (1966:289).
6. This is pointed out by Langendoen (1968:37-38).
7. It is interesting to note that in French *objet* can mean equally "the object of description" and "the aim of description".

9 Historical Landmarks in meaning

This book has presented a new and fairly radical approach to the elucidation of the meaning of language, where the central evidence is provided by the repeated instance of items in context from a corpus. Contextual meaning has been specifically addressed in Chapter Eight as the underlying foundation of this type of approach to corpus linguistics at work. Other historical landmarks in the theory of meaning will be addressed here in a somewhat cavalier fashion. The selection of statements from different linguists that will be presented in this chapter, will not reflect sequentially and systematically the work of the linguists who made them, but will be used and discussed mainly as points of contact with the issues we have addressed in this book.

In the history of the study of language, meaning has not always been regarded as central; indeed, it has sometimes been seen as almost irrelevant to the study of language. Even when the study of meaning has been recognised as the true object of linguistics, it has been approached from such different perspectives that one may wonder whether the same notion has been investigated.

Considering at first the historical development in the perception and definition of meaning, we can distinguish three currents of theoretical development which, one after the other, have led the study of meaning into three very different directions, and as such have defined three very different objects of study for the discipline of semantics (see Tamba-Mecz 1988:10-11). First, one can identify comparative linguistics, historical and evolutionist in orientation. We will illustrate it here by looking at some statements made by Bréal.

The second period is structuralism, synchronic in orientation and where the emphasis is shifted to the notions of *system* and *function*. This movement has flourished and reached different form in different traditions; in France it is articulated by the Structuralist school proper, following Saussure. In the USA a rather narrowly-conceived brand was developed; in the UK the notion of system is contextualised and we have already discussed (Chapter Eight) the development of the contextual theory of meaning which is here taken as central to the corpus-driven approach proposed. In parallel with the later structuralism, there is also a strand of language formalism, emanating from USA, where the emphasis is on the well formed sentence and meaning ceases to be related to the description of language in use, the primary concern being to rewrite and reproduce.

The presentation here is first European and then American structuralism; then language formalism, mainly with reference to the figure of Chomsky. The subdivision of the history of semantics into these periods, although convenient from the point of view of our argument, is as all generalisations, rather too simplistic. As we will see below, the seeds of the synchronic and functional study of meaning, for example, were already present in the first period; the divisions therefore are not altogether clear-cut.

The historical and evolutionist period

From this period we will draw attention to some statements from Bréal who is usually considered as the father of semantics. His work shows some very modern intuitions, but for him meaning, although "data-oriented" in today's terminology, is realised in the historical dimension and determined by evolution. Although the origins can be seen of a theoretical differentiation between what is the synchronic and what is the diachronic study of a language, the period remains mainly within the realms of historical linguistics. The work of this period could be summarised along three general lines: (1) meaning is seen mainly as a psychological and a historical process - semantics studies the evolution of meanings in languages; (2) this evolution is regulated by certain general laws which apply to different languages across time; (3) these laws must be studied through the observation of actual "facts" of meaning.

   1. *L'homme n'est pour rien dans le développement du langage, et les mots
   - forme et sens - mènent une existence qui leur est propre.* (Bréal, 1897, 2-3)

An interesting quotation, showing how, at this very early stage, Bréal was positing a separate linguistic system which had to be accounted for in its own terms and according to its own rules, without reference to an external world which responded to a different set of rules. Bréal's main work, the *Essai de Sémantique* (1897), outlines new scientific criteria for the study of language based on observation. Semantics studies the universal, panchronic *laws* governing the development of meaning, and a law is defined as "le rapport constant qui se laisse découvrir dans une serie de phénomènes"[1] (1897:9).

It is important to realise that Bréal is talking of observable phenomena. Language is meant to be studied as it is actually used; as for meaning, the only good "distinctions" are the ones made by the people involved in the language activity themselves, as is clear from quote n. 2 below:

2. *Il n'y a de bonnes distinctions que celles qui se font sans préméditation, sous la pression des circonstances, par inspiration subite et en présence d'un réel besoin, par ceux qui ont affaire aux choses elles-mêmes. Les distinctions que fait le peuple sont les seules vraies et les seules bonnes.* (Bréal, 1897, 27)

This is a very modern position and indeed we could take it as underlying one of the major issues in corpus work, namely the one of authenticity. It could be understood also in functional terms as underlying the modern communicative approach to language (see for example Brumfit 1984): language meaning as actual usage in communicative situations.

European structuralism: Saussure

Saussure moved the point of view of linguistics - and therefore the object - from accounting for data to projecting an abstract system that is implied, and even entailed, by the data.

3. *Bien loin que l'objet précède le point de vue, on dirait que c'est le point de vue qui précède l'objet.*[2] (Saussure, CLG:23)

This is one of Saussure's best known aphorisms: it is the point of view that creates the object. Our attempt to define the field of corpus linguistics will inevitably be affected by the fact that we have chosen to investigate meaning in context. In turns, the fact that we have started by assuming as the focus of our enquiry the notion of meaning has necessarily influenced the way we have gone about the enquiry itself. But there is another way in which we can apply Saussure's famous dictum. Using Sinclair's words "the language looks rather different when you look at a lot of it at once" (1991:100), we could paraphrase them by saying that in this case it is the point of view which creates the discipline. This, we argue, is particularly true of corpus linguistics, where the input of the new technologies has changed the point of view on the subject.

Saussure postulated one of the major distinctions in linguistics, the one between synchronic and diachronic study of language. Synchronic study should be made without any reference to the historical dimension or the outside world:

4. *La langue est un système de pures valeurs que rien ne détermine en dehors de l'état momentané de ses termes.* (Saussure, CLG 116)

This statement can be connected to the one made by Bréal (quote n. 1 above). For Saussure, all science dealing with the notion of *"valeur"* has to draw a very firm dividing line between the system of values considered in itself and the same values considered in relation to time. From this stems his division between synchronic and diachronic linguistics. Within synchronic linguistics "le seul object réel de la linguistique, c'est la vie normale et regulière d'un idiome déjà constitué" (ibid.:105). Hence:

> 5. *La valeur de n'importe quel terme est déterminée par ce qui l'entoure.*
> (Saussure, CLG: 160)

Although this could seem as an early pointer to the notion of context, we should remember that Saussure is operating here within the sphere of *langue* (see quotes n. 6, 7, 8 below) and therefore the environment of a sign is seen as the relationships this sign entertains with other signs at the abstract level of the syntagmatic and the paradigmatic axes.

Saussure identified the sign as the basic linguistic unit and defined it as acquiring its value within an abstract system by differentiation with other signs. More relevant to our discussion on corpus linguistics here, he maintained that language in its totality in unknowable, for it lacks homogeneity: it is at the same time physical and psychological, individual and social, it simultaneously implies the presence of an established system and of an evolution. Taken as such, language has no discernible unity. Thus Saussure posits the dichotomy between *langue* and *parole*. The two parts of language are:

> 6. *L'une, essentielle, a pour objet la langue, qui est sociale dans son essence et indépendante de l'individu; cette étude est uniquement psychique; l'autre, secondaire, a pour objet la partie individuelle du langage, c'est-à-dire la parole y compris la phonation: elle est psycho-physique. (Saussure,CLG:37)*

> 7. *La langue, distincte de la parole, est un objet qu'on peut étudier séparément (..) Non seulement la science de la langue peut se passer des autres éléments du langage, mais elle n'est possible que si ces autres éléments n'y sont pas mélés. (Saussure,CGL:31)*

> 8. *(la langue) ... est un trésor déposé par la pratique de la parole dans les sujets appartenant à une même communauté un système grammatical existant virtuellement dans chaque cerveau, ou plus exactement, dans les cerveaux d'un ensemble d'individus; car la langue n'est complète dans aucun, elle n'existe parfaitement que dans la masse. (Saussure,*CLG:30)

Langue can be seen as a linguistic schema, i.e. "forme pure"; it is the theoretician's task to determine the structural principle of *langue* and, as Hjelmslev points out, "there is no question of whether the individual structural types are manifested, but only whether they are manifestable" (1943/1961:106). We can see that for Saussure the study of *langue* takes the shape of delimiting the object of study and in a way excluding from it the observable. A second angle on *langue* is one where it is seen as "norme de réalisation", comparable to a dictionary or a grammar (CLG:32) and, as De Mauro points out, here *langue* "n'éxiste que pour gouverner la parole" (CLG:420). But what is *parole*? Although *parole* might be realised by more than one individual, there is nothing social in it; its manifestations are individual and ephemeral. *Parole* is no more than an aggregate of particular cases (CLG:38). *Langue*, on the other hand, is never complete at the level of the individual, it can only exist perfectly in a "masse parlante".

But there is a third angle, where *langue* could be probably be called *usage*:

9. *La langue est nécessaire pour que la parole soit intelligible et produise tous ses effets; mais celle-ci est nécessaire pour que la langue s'établisse (..) Enfin c'est la parole qui fait évoluer la langue: ce sont les impressions reçues en entendant les autres qui modifient nos habitudes linguistiques. (Saussure,CLG:37)*

Langue here is seen as the whole set of linguistic habits which enables the speaker to understand and to make him/herself understood; it is the awareness of the repetition of similar linguistic events in *parole* and it has almost lost the total abstractness of the linguistic schema. This is the closest Saussure comes to relating *langue* to individual manifestations. This third angle on *langue* is the one that interests us most in the context of corpus linguistics because this version of *langue* has become now observable for us on the vertical axis of the concordance. It is the awareness of the social habit underlying the presence of repeated patterning. The concordance can thus reunite for us the instance of *parole* on the horizontal axis and the awareness of *langue* on the vertical one.

We could sum up the work of Saussure, as the major figure in this period of European structuralism, by noting three points. First, meaning is not seen any more as an inherent property of words, belonging to the sphere of man's intellectual activity; the emphasis is now on the notion of system, and meaning is identified with a set of relations within the system. In other words, the meaning of a word is no more just the relationship between a word and a concept or a thing, but the set of relationships that a specific word may entertain within a relational network. Second, the word, mainly for lack of a more easily definable "concrete" entity (cf. CLG:148 and 172), remains the basic unit of meaning of a semantic system and the study of meaning is mainly confined to vocabulary; semantics is mainly lexical semantics. Third, the relational perspective brought about by the notion of system goes along with the more and more marked differentiation of a synchronic and a diachronic approach to the study of meaning. Saussure was the first to use the term "lexicologie" meaning the study of "les rapports syntagmatiques et associatifs entre mots"(CLG:187-88). Although this remains a mixed period, the separation between the synchronic and the diachronic approach to language study is more and more taken for granted after Saussure.

The structuralist approach to meaning - Bloomfield and Zelig Harris

In this section we will first consider the work of Leonard Bloomfield, who dominated the American scene from the thirties to the sixties. Bloomfield restricts the object of linguistics to the description of language in a synchronic state, whether or not the description aims to account for an *état de langue* or to study the historical development of a language, the latter being a series of synchronic slices of evidence at different times. He also at times shows a reluctance to recognise meaning as a criterion, and tends to dismiss it as a matter mainly for psychology:

> 10. *In the division of scientific labour, the linguist deals only with the speech-signal (r ... s); he is not competent to deal with problems of physiology or psychology. (Bloomfield, 1933:32)*

> 11. *Our knowledge of the world in which we live is so imperfect that we can rarely make accurate statements about the meaning of a speech-form. (Bloomfield, 1933:74).*

Meaning (as stimulus + response) is, therefore, an unstable entity: the same forms are used for more than one typical situation, so we speak of the *head* of an army, of a procession, of a household, etc. (ibid.:149). Given one central meaning, the other "deviant" meanings are identified only through situational features. It is interesting to note here that Bloomfield accepts that "in some cases a transferred meaning is linguistically determined by an accompanying form"; he gives the example of the verb *give out* which, used intransitively (*his money gave out; our horses gave out*) has always a transferred meaning (become exhausted). In this case, he argues, "the structure of language recognises the transferred meaning" (ibid.:150). For him, though, this observable correlation between form and meaning is still not considered reliable enough to make it the object of linguistic study. In contrast to this position, consider the point made by Sinclair (1991:74-75) about the phrasal verb *set in* which, he notes, is consistently associated with subjects referring to "unpleasant states of affairs" such as *rot, disillusion, decay,* etc. Sinclair sees this "transferred meaning" (in Bloomfieldian terms) as determining and incorporates it into the Cobuild dictionary definition.[3]

Another pointer for the instability of meaning is *connotation*, i.e. "the presence of supplementary values", usually arising from the social standing of the speakers who use a form (ibid.:152). These are, according to Bloomfield, to be avoided at all costs, and he remarks that:

> 12. *We combat such personal deviations by giving explicit definitions of meaning; this is a chief use of our dictionaries. (Bloomfield, 1933*:152)

We can see in this quote that Bloomfield, in spite of its acceptance of the value of observation, is at the opposite end of the Firthian tradition which underlies our approach and where semantic prosodies are seen as crucial to the creation of meaning and the overall function of language. The instability of meaning outlined above joins forces with its unpredictability, that is the "uncertainty as to the forms that a given speaker will utter (if he speaks at all) in a given situation" (ibid.:142). The result is clear:

> 13. *The statement of meanings is therefore the weak point in language study, and will remain so until human knowledge advances very far beyond its present state. (Bloomfield, 1933:140)*

For Bloomfield, as for many of the linguists who adopted behaviourism, a mentalist approach to language analysis was firmly rejected in favour of the observable "stimulus + reaction" features in utterances. Although contextually sensitive, this position is, however, very different from Firth's contextual theory of meaning in that the element of purpose which forms the basis of the latter is totally absent from the former. With Bloomfield the object of study is, if we define it in Saussurean terms, *parole*. No abstraction from the data is necessary or indeed desirable; the method of study is inductive and confines itself to the observable.

The other American structuralist whose work bears upon the origins of the corpus-driven approach is Zellig S. Harris (1951, 1952, 1954, 1957, 1988). The methodology adopted by Harris prioritises at first the syntagmatic relationship between signs, whereby the units are defined by their linear environment. Subsequently, through chains of equivalences, i.e. the substitution of items for environments and vice versa, a specific unit is seen to acquire its value through different steps of "decontextualised" paradigmatic equivalence and the link with actual environments is lost. Harris dismissed the study of meaning more decisively than even Bloomfield, and insisted that:

14. *The method is formal, depending only on the occurrences of morphemes as distinguishable elements; it does not depend upon the analyst's knowledge of the particular meaning of each morpheme. By the same token, the method does not give us any new information about the individual morphemic meanings that are being communicated in the discourse under investigation.* (1952, rep. 1964:355)

We should note, at this point, that meaning had been invoked by Bloomfield as the criterion for defining distinctive units in language. Harris in this adopts a truly scientific methodology and, having excluded meaning from his object of study, also excludes it from being a criterion for the classification of his data:

15. *The observed co-occurrences thus have to be taken as raw data for classification and comparison; they cannot be adequately derived from some nonlinguistic source such as "the desired combinations of meanings". (1957, rep. 1964:157)*

There are three other important points in the theoretical position of this American scholar. First, there is the fact that with him there is a shift in the object of study: the object of linguistic inquiry is not any more the behaviour of a single unit in a specific situation, as in Bloomfield, but the distributional or combinatorial analysis of different units. This is achieved through the comparison of individual co-occurrences of morphemes. The second point which is worth noting is that distributional analysis for Harris goes across sentence boundaries and the object of study becomes "connected discourse" - a view of language that was ahead of its time.

The term "discourse", thanks to more recent studies on discourse analysis, has been seen as focusing on the way language is structurally communicative (Hymes 1964). Here, though, Harris takes it to mean simply a stretch of text above the level of the sentence "the sentences spoken or written in succession by one or more persons in a single situation" (1957, rep. 1964:357). The fact that quite often he uses the term "discourse" as a countable noun also implies a connection with situational features. See, for example,: "distributional analysis within one discourse at a time yields information about certain correlations of language with other behaviour" (Harris 1957, rep. 1964:357).

The third important point in Harris' approach is his postulation of classes which are defined by "a diagnostic environment" (1957: 157); this step led of course to the notion of transformations, which were transferred into another theoretical perspective by Chomsky (see below). For our purposes here Harris is notable in making use of the environment of an item as part of its discoursal function.

Formal grammars - Chomsky

> *Lawyers are fond of saying that an accused who undertakes his own defense has a fool for a lawyer. The same might be said of a grammarian who uses his own intuitions as the source of his grammar. But not so long ago this was the preferred method.* (N. Francis, 1992:28)

Nelson Francis, one of the pioneers of corpus linguistics, spent more than two decades as a prophet without hounour in his own country. He shaped his corpus in the early 1960s, just as language usage was going out of fashion with the rapid rise of generative transformational grammar. By the time the Brown corpus became available for use in the late 1960s, most descriptive linguists had concluded that it was no use to them. The above quote can be read in sharp contrast with the position that will be discussed in this section.

Chomsky dominated linguistics in the second half of the twentieth century, and we are only concerned here with two minor aspects of his position - minor from his point of view, that is; these are his stand on observed data and his position on the relevance of meaning for his grammatical theory.

On the first point he broke with the American tradition we saw in Bloomfield and Harris - a close preoccupation with data which characterised US linguistics in the first half of the century. In contrast to them, Chomsky, throughout his work, has been strongly opposed to the descriptive method; for him "linguistic theory is mentalistic since it is concerned with discovering a mental reality underlying actual behaviour"(1965:4), therefore:

> 16. *It is obvious that the set of grammatical sentences cannot be identified with any particular corpus of utterances obtained by the linguist in his field work.* (Chomsky, 1957:15)

The nearest Chomsky comes to recognising corpora as linguistic objects is the following:

> 17. *Any grammar of a language will project the finite and somewhat accidental corpus of observed utterances to a set (presumably infinite) of grammatical utterances.* (Chomsky, 1957:15)

The object of the linguist is to uncover the underlying set of rules determining the interpretation of an indefinitely large number of sentences in a given language.

Chomsky insulates his theory from actual usage by postulating *competence* and *performance* as a contrast somewhat similar to the Saussurean *langue* and *parole*. However, *langue* and *parole* were seen as interdependent by Saussure, while Chomsky is very careful to point out that *competence* and *performance* are not and, referring to Saussure's distinction, he claims that "it is necessary to reject his concept of *langue* as merely a systematic inventory of items" (1965:4) - presumably *langue* as "habitudes linguistiques", the sum of all our linguistic habits, *langue* as cumulative usage. *Competence* is for Chomsky closer to the Hjelmslevian notion of linguistic schema, in Saussurean terms "forme pure". *Competence*, therefore, has really nothing to do with usage. We have discussed the consequences of this stance with respect to corpus-based linguistics in Chapter Four (see section on 'insulation').

In this way Chomsky steered American linguistics away from observable data and questioned the importance - or indeed the relevance - of the context in which an utterance is embedded at the time of occurrence. This position is clearly stated by Katz and Fodor in their famous article on The Structure of a Semantic Theory:

> 18. *Grammars seek to describe the structure of a sentence in isolation from its possible settings in linguistic discourse (written or verbal) or in non-linguistic contexts (social or physical). The justification which permits the grammarian to study sentences in abstraction from the settings in which they have occurred or might occur is simply that the fluent speaker is able to construct and recognise syntactically well-formed sentences without recourse to information about settings, and this ability is what a grammar undertakes to reconstruct.* (Katz and Fodor 1963, rep. 1964:484)

It is important to note that Chomsky is only concerned with a very idealised man-in-the-street:

> 19. *An ideal speaker-listener, in a completely homogeneous speech-community, who knows his language perfectly and is unaffected by such grammatically irrelevant conditions as memory limitations, distractions, shifts of attention and interest, and errors (random or characteristic) in applying his knowledge of the language in actual performance.* (Chomsky, 1965:3)

Given the strict formalism within which grammars were to be constructed, it is not surprising that, especially in his earlier work, Chomsky should reject any interference on the part of a theory of meaning. In particular he is very opposed to the notion of "semantic significance as a general criterion for grammaticalness" (1957:100), and claims that "only imperfect correspondences hold between formal and semantic features in language". The conclusion is obvious:

20. *Grammar is best formulated as a self-contained study independent of semantics.* (Chomsky, 1957:106)

After some years, and under pressure from his own school, Chomsky identified with the work of Katz and Fodor, especially their article in 1963 which represents the first opening to a semantic theory within Transformational Generative Grammar. But it is important to note that for them, as Lyons observes (1977:410), "as far as well-formedness was concerned, semantics was residual" in that it took over where grammar left off; a theory of grammar, in other words, remained logically and methodologically prior as the seat of the generative capacity of the whole integrated model. Semantics is, therefore, "interpretive" and "non-generative":

21. *The semantic component determines the semantic interpretation of a sentence. That is, it relates a structure generated by the syntactic component to a certain semantic component and representation. Both the phonological and semantic components are therefore purely interpretive.* (Chomsky, 1965:16)

To summarise, we should note that the shift towards formalism and the new transformational generative orthodoxy in the second half of the century have brought about several important changes in the approach to meaning and semantics. In the structuralist period proper the object of semantic study was identified more or less explicitly with the lexicon, conceived as a network of relations with self-regulating meaning; the shift made by Chomsky is from a lexical semantics to a sentence-based semantics. This in turn entails the shift from conceptual meaning, intended as the relationship of *signifiant/signifié* within the semiotic system, to relational meaning prioritising the grammatical interconnections and "slotting in" a lexico-semantic component (see Katz and Fodor 1963).

The prioritisation of grammar over lexis and semantics, and the view of semantics as "residual", has had a serious effect on linguistics, an effect that is still quite difficult to dispel; this is the fact that "research has been biased heavily in favour of syntactic solutions to problems" (as pointed out by Jackendoff 1972:2). Indeed, still now, for many scholars "a grammar of the language L is essentially a theory of L" (Chomsky 1957:49); from this follows that, once we have stated the grammatical (generative) rules, we have described the language as a whole. This view, of course, leaves very little scope for an investigation into patterns of lexis for example and, as we have shown, relegates semantics to the role of a futile appendix, a ragbag for the leftovers after the grammatical banquet.

Notes

1. It is interesting to note that with Bréal *laws (lois)* take the place of the old *rules (règles)*, cherished by traditional prescriptive grammar.
2. Here and hereafter, unless otherwise specified, the page numbers relating to F. de Saussure refer to the *Cours de Linguistique Générale* edited by Tullio de Mauro, Payot, Paris 1972. Hereafter this will be called CLG. The English translation I am adopting has the title *Course in General Linguistics* (Harris 1983) which is here referred to as CGL.
3. See the definition in the Cobuild Dictionary: "if something unpleasant *sets in*, it begins and seems likely to continue or develop".

10. Conclusion

Corpus-driven linguistics (CDL): position statement

This book presents a case, through argument and example, for the establishment of a new discipline within linguistics, and within corpus linguistics. The provisional name of *Corpus-driven Linguistics* (CDL) is offered in order to point the contrast with corpus-based linguistics.

One question we should ask ourselves is: what are the basic requirements of a new discipline, to differentiate it from those nearby? This book has argued for the establishment of such a new discipline starting from the assumption that these are:

- a set of goals toward which the research hopes to move, in careful stages.

- a philosophical standpoint, an orientation to the data that is not as well developed elsewhere.

- a unique, or at least particular methodology.

- a set of theoretical and descriptive categories for articulating the content of the research.

- an accumulating body of knowledge that would be difficult if not impossible to acquire from other sources (though it may be confirmed or questioned by alternative approaches).

We will discuss each of these assumptions in turn.

Goals

The primary goal of CDL is to make exhaustive and explicit connections between the occurrence and distribution of language items in text, and the meanings created by the text. There are two principal issues here:

1. Texts are physical objects and meanings are unobservable, so claims could be made to justify a direct association between formal and functional elements. The safeguard here is the intuition of the language user, who must in some sense be satisfied that the connections offer an illuminating explanation of the way language text creates meaning.

2. This goal is not unique, in that every adequate theory of language might be seen to adopt an identical goal. That does not invalidate the distinctiveness of the discipline, indeed it confirms that it is in the mainstream of linguistics. But the precise phrasing of the goal is not already adopted by other linguistic theories, so there are aspects of emphasis and priority that may still serve to give CDL a distinctive flavour.

Standpoint

CDL considers axiomatic the statement that meaning arises as much because of the combination of choices in a text as because of the individual contribution made by the meaning of each choice. The combinations of choices are recognised as relevant to meaning in several areas of language patterning, but not in the comprehensive way that is implied in the above statement. Grammatical structure deals with combinations, and their relative sequencing, but not the specific choices of linguistic items - only linguistic abstractions like classes, elements of structure, etc. The study of idiom, and the recent flowering of phraseology, are concerned with specific combinations, but idioms are seen as occasional events, and phraseology is not tightly associated with meaning creation.

In CDL, the approach to language patterning is holistic. Any step away from the physical data is taken with care, and regarded as a weakening of the description unless compensated for by much greater generalisation.

Methodology

The essential methodology of CDL is to exercise the researcher's intuition in the presence of as much relevant data as can be assembled. It is accepted that there is no such thing as a theory-neutral stance, but in CDL the attempt is made to suppress all received theories, axioms and precepts and to rely on the standpoint above to guide the initial stages of any investigation. Obviously, as experience grows there will be new hypotheses that arise from the investigations, and if those are generally accepted they will form part of CDL methodology.

Specifically in the present intellectual climate, CDL does not accept *prima facie* those theories, axioms and precepts that were formulated before corpus data became available. These are not rejected or dismissed - the accumulated insights of centuries of research are not to be put aside lightly - but they are to be re-examined in the new frameworks where, instead of the scholar having to struggle to gather a sufficient amount of data, (s)he has now a plethora of data at his/her disposal.

CDL is not immediately concerned with positioning itself vis-à-vis the tradition of theoretical and descriptive linguistics. The results of research probes so far, e.g. those presented in this book, show convincingly that there are substantial differences between the patterns that are discovered in language corpora and those that are anticipated by the mainstream linguistic work of the last century, and especially of the last half-century. CDL does not, therefore, accept the agendas that are popular in other branches of linguistics, but will pursue its own goals probably for some time, until the theoretical position is more fully articulated and the descriptive system is elaborated.

For some time this may seem a laborious way of working, since so much of language structure seems to be non-contentious, but the methodology of CDL requires different standards of attestation from other approaches, and joins other strict sciences in expecting that all results are replicable.

Categories

As the main lines of description become clear, it is to be expected that a descriptive apparatus will take shape in response to the descriptive needs. Some basic categories are already postulated, clustering round the central concept of a *functionally complete unit of meaning*; this concept is explained and illustrated copiously in the book.

Body of knowledge

The awareness that there was special knowledge to be gained from a corpus, not available from any other source, and certainly not from unaided introspection, was the original impetus to establish CDL as a separate branch of linguistics. This knowledge has accumulated over years in several centres, and an *ad hoc* terminology has grown up around it because it could not be described with the normal apparatus of linguistics.

This Book: assumptions and issues

We will now turn to outlining how this position is brought out in the organisation of the book. We will consider first the theoretical background to corpus linguistics (explored in *Chapters Eight* and *Nine*), then the issues related to corpus work (*Chapters Three* and *Four*), thirdly the corpus-driven approach, and finally the applications to language teaching (*Chapter Two*) and translation (*Chapter Seven*).

From the point of view of the theoretical standpoint, the central assumption behind the present enquiry has been, as mentioned, the centrality of the notion of meaning and its relevance to linguistic theory and description. The relations between language structures (in the most general sense) and meaning which are highlighted by corpus evidence are not new in linguistics. Chapter Nine has explored different theoretical standpoints in relation to meaning. It identified the general tendency of linguistics of the last hundred years in the search for order against the apparent chaos and unsystematicity of `real' language. This need for order has usually led the linguist to define well-delimited and orderly niches, carved out of the whole of language which is felt as too disorderly, too changeable to define. The starting point of this study therefore could be Lecercle's notion of tidiness:

> Any theory of language constructs its `object' by separating `relevant' from `irrelevant' phenomena, and excluding the latter. As a result, all theories of language leave out a `remainder'. This remainder is the odd, untidy, awkward, creative part of how all of us use language all the time. (Lecercle 1990:i)

The first major step in this direction is perhaps the one taken by Bréal, positing a separation between the language and the real world and claiming that "les mots - forme et sens - mènent une existence qui leur est propre" (1897:2-3), in other words positing a language system, complete in itself, that could be explained with reference to its own data and not to a world outside. For Bréal, if the study of language is a study of meaning, then this meaning can only be safely identified with respect to the historical development of words. It could be argued that Bréal's is an early data-oriented approach, but delimiting the object of his enquiry to selected texts along the historical dimension.

Other attempts at order are surely Saussure's dichotomies, separating the diachronic dimension of language from the synchronic on the one hand, and *langue* from *parole* on the other. Saussure's stance differs from Bréal in that, by separating *langue* from *parole*, he proposes to explain the actual and the observable by postulating and examining an abstraction. Meaning is analysable, but only as an abstract possibility rather than an everyday reality. Thus, the domain delimited for the study of meaning avoids contact with the domain of individual, concrete - and chaotic - language manifestations.

Although for Bloomfield the study of language is still centred around concrete language manifestations, i.e. language use, what is excluded is the study of meaning itself, "the weak point in language study" (1933:140) that stems from our imperfect knowledge of the world. Again, the domain of language study is made `tractable' by eliminating potentially disruptive factors.

Chomsky contrasts with both Bloomfield and Saussure. His search is for order in the mind and the emphasis is on the mental language faculty as capable of generating all and only the grammatical sentences of a language. This "language" is not systematically related to anything attested in human communication, but exists only with reference to faculties of mental discrimination. Again the chaotic world of individual and idiosyncratic manifestation is kept out.

Contrasting with the theorists mentioned above is Firth, with his contextual theory of meaning discussed in *Chapter Eight*, and the group of scholars that followed him. Firth also attempts to find order in the infiniteness of language, but his stance differs from those of his predecessors and contemporaries because he accepts the wholeness of language and he does not try to erect boundaries separating what is orderly and what is chaotic, what is abstract and what is observable, what is grammatical and what is meaningful. The order that Firth finds in language is an abstraction in so far as the typological can be seen as an abstraction. This is related to the cumulative effect of language events and therefore does not discard the *parole* side of language; it is related to the social side of language, but only in so far that it reflects the individual; it accepts the formal side of language, but still sees this a meaningful activity.

All these theorists agree that human language behaviour is more complex than any description is ever likely to encompass. The difference lies in how to relate a possible description to the experience of language. Bréal, Saussure and Chomsky decide in advance what will be their object of study, and use their stance as theoreticians to evaluate the evidence of the senses, thus leaving behind the "remainder". On the other hand, Firth uses his stance as a theoretician to lay down principles for investigation, leaving no coherent or systematic remainder. Nothing that has meaning potential is excluded, and what is left after a Firthian study is merely those phenomena that have not, as yet, been found a place.

Concerning the issues related to corpus work, we should note a few points. None of the early theorists had a corpus in electronic form to refer to, and this book dealscentrally with the issues related to a corpus seen as a large electronic receptacle of language use. *Chapter Three* looked into the definition of a corpus and considered the underlying theoretical assumptions, such as the authenticity of the texts included, their cumulative representativeness and the sampling criteria necessary to build a corpus adequate for its function. The debate around these issues has brought in scholars from all traditions, and yet, when it comes to considering an approach capable of handling and making sense of corpus evidence, the discussion led to what could be seen as a sequence of *discrepancies*.

The mismatch has been outlined as the one between theory and practice whereby, while the corpus as `more data' is welcomed by the community of scholars, and the fact that this body of language is meant to be representative of language is also taken for granted, yet the full implications of this stance are avoided. Yet again the wish for order induces many, in the face of massive corpus evidence, to separate the clearly tractable from the apparently intractable (where the intractable is defined as that which does not reflect the categories of the system) and to superimpose *ad hoc* criteria that allow them to carve out a tidy world. It is important to note here that the `order' is superimposed on the evidence of language use, rather than derived from it.

Thus, *Chapter Four*, in the framework of what was defined as the *corpus-based* approach, discussed three instances of discrepancies between theory and practice. In the first instance, what we have referred to as *insulation*, this *ad hoc* separation operates at the theoretical level and the insights obtained from corpus evidence are accepted only as an ancillary extention to the theoretical statement as such (they may affect the interpretative process, but not the grammar). In the second instance, what we have referred to as *standardisation*, the input of `order' is at the level of the corpus evidence that, before being processed, is sieved through, or labelled with, pre-existing theoretical parameters. The result is that what may contravene the ready-made categories is not allowed to have a say in the matter: the standardised evidence fits the data. In the third instance, what we have referred to as *instantiation*, corpus evidence again provides a probabilistic extension to a pre-existing system, but is not allowed to affect the system as such.

The shadows of the search for order, outlined above, are therefore still transparent in the *corpus-based* approach outlined in Chapter Four. The questions that the corpus-based linguist can ask are limited in scope because they are restricted within the theoretical stance according to which they are formulated. What would not be accountable in terms of the existing criteria is not really allowed to surface. The qualitative revolution, heralded by many, is only accepted by a few.

The *corpus-driven* approach, discussed and exemplified in *Chapters Five* and *Six*, was initially identified as a methodology which is more innovative than the corpus-based one. The representativeness of a corpus, here, is fully accepted as an initial assumption; and once the corpus is accepted as a representative sample of the target population (be it a specific language variety or the language system as a whole), the corpus-driven linguist will take stock of what the cumulative effect of language use shows. The language events which Firth (1957:35) defined as "typical, recurrent and repeatedly observable" provide the basis for the establishment of theoretical categories. Language events which are not "repeated events" will not figure prominently in the theory, and the absence of a pattern will be taken as significant. The initial assumption about the representativeness of the corpus will be constantly evaluated in the light of external and internal criteria, but the point here is that in the corpus-driven approach the `order' - reflecting the categories of the linguistic system under observation - is derived from, and not superimposed on, the evidence of language use. The system, therefore, does not pre-exist the evidence.

The first consequence of this approach is that it exposes theoretical weaknesses in language descriptions that are not derived from a corpus. For instance, traditional categories that merge under the same functional heading 'lemmas and inflected forms' are seriously jeopardised by corpus evidence (see Chapter Five). The cluster of frequency of occurrence is such that new distinctions have to be posited, and often traditional ones become less relevant. The basic notion of what is a unit of meaning is also revisited in the light of a systematic patterning that defines new functional units. The idea of a multiword unit, defined as function in context, is not a new concept in linguistics and, as mentioned above, is usually accepted in traditional descriptions under the heading of idioms; however, thanks to the evidence of corpus it can now be identified precisely and shown to be an all-pervasive phenomenon rather than a sporadic one.

The idea that language is a "mode of action, not a countersign of thought" was articulated by Malinowski in 1923; the fact that the function of language has to be derived from looking at its use was also a well established idea in certain linguistic traditions. What the CDL approach allows, that was not possible before, is a systematic description of language use as purposeful activity. Also, if before the advent of the computer as a processing device, the notion of purpose had remained at an abstract and rather extra-linguistic level, now it is possible to locate meaningful units that achieve a specific function in a given linguistic context. *Functionally complete units* are easily identified by scanning the patterns on the vertical axis of the concordance line; they can be empirically validated and can be shown to be the building blocks of communication, the driving force behind language activity. It is claimed that this is the most important achievement of CDL, the qualitative change that is likely to revolutionise linguistics. It is argued that these new units constitute the new currency of linguistic description; they were discussed and exemplified in some detail in *Chapter Six*.

The results of the corpus-driven approach, even in these early stages, are quite distinctive, and are not easily accountable, if accountable at all, in terms of existing theories and descriptions; therefore the safest course is to recognise CDL as separate until further research is able to reconcile its results with the others, if indeed this can be attained. Recent work on *Pattern Grammars* (Hunston and Francis, 2000) suggest that reconciliation may be possible, since movements in *delicacy* of grammatical description seem to be simultaneously movements towards semantic coherence in the realisation classes.

Chapters Two and *Seven* can be seen as illustrations of the corpus-driven approach and explored the new type of findings that the linguist can gain in the field of two major applications: *language teaching* and *translation*. We recapitulate below the general issues raised by CDL at work as exemplified in these two chapters.

First, the type of observations made lead to the identification of formal *patterns of co-selection* involving both lexical and grammatical choices, collocation and colligation. The interrelation between lexis and grammar was so consistent in the case studies reported that it cast doubts on the possibility of making a choice that does not involve them both.

Second, the identification of such formal patterns could not be seen as a separate activity from the attribution of meaning. Meaning is the driving force behind formal choices, and the achievement of outcomes in a certain context is what determines the lexico-grammatical structures selected by a speaker/writer. We are here at the opposite end of the Chomskian view that "grammar is autonomous and independent of meaning" (1957:17).

Third, the units of meaning defined by such patterns of lexico-grammatical co-selection were seen to be above all syntagmatic units. It was argued that only when they are functionally complete do they become available as paradigmatic choices. The linear relationship between words, as the actualisation of function in context, has to be the first step in the analysis, as it is in the process of encoding; the relationship between categories realising abstract possibilities inevitably comes second and has to work within the established linear patterns. If the paradigm is not excluded from this view of language, it is seen as secondary with respect to the syntagm. CDL is thus above all a linguistics of *parole*.

Concluding remarks

A corpus is a record of language in use, and most of the linguistic information in it should be familiar to users of the language. It is important to note, however, that only a very small proportion of the available linguistic information can be reliably predicted by a user, even an expert researcher. The discrepancy between what can be retrieved by introspection, and the much greater detail that can be retrieved by corpus study, underlies some of the major differences between CDL and other linguistic theories.

In most modern societies people learn about languages, particularly their native language, and educational traditions arise that make assumptions about the nature

CONCLUSION 185

and structure of language; these then colour the perceptions and even the observations of the users, and at times conflict with corpus evidence. Such traditions are slow to change and are deeply integrated with the social structure; researchers adopting a corpus-driven approach can find it difficult to maintain the stance with respect to the data that characterises CDL.

CDL often faces the charge of abandoning the intuitions of a fluent user of a language in favour of the patterns of a corpus, which might not precisely reflect a state of a language. This, it is argued, is an empty charge, because without intuition the central relationship between form and meaning cannot be established. What distinguishes CDL is that the researcher's intuition is brought to bear on corpus evidence, which we have said is far richer than anything that a user can retrieve in isolation from the data. Intuition is "essentially, arriving at decisions or conclusions without explicit or conscious processes of reasoned thinking" (Gregory 1987:389).

No conclusion is worth its name if it does not announce that this is just the beginning. This one goes along with this trend. We maintain that the corpus-driven study of language has only just started, although its roots go back to the beginning of this century and before. Although some corpus-driven reference works have already been published, we are still mainly at the stage of feasibility studies, where the tools are tested and assessed and the first results are evaluated. In order to allow this powerful new methodology to flourish, this book argues for a separate status for it.

Nevertheless, the discrepancies between traditional descriptive categories and corpus evidence are likely to become less visible (unless supported by a theory that dismisses the evidence of language use altogether) when new corpus-driven descriptions become the standard. Then, the application of proven corpus-driven categories to different corpus data will lead to refinement of such categories and this can only be beneficial to language description.

Work on corpus representativeness is only beginning, especially when it comes to the internal criteria for the evaluation of corpus typology. We are still at the stage where representativeness is "an act of faith" and the problem is complicated further by the fact that large corpora of 200 million words and over are usually assembled as collective ventures involving national and commercial bodies. Therefore we often have a situation where the corpus builder is not directly answerable to the corpus user. The corpus, then, has to be taken as a fait accompli, and this often means that the scholar is not in a position to evaluate the parameters of his/her own enquiry. As corpora become more and more the normal tools of linguistic enquiry, this problem will also be improved and standard ways of stating and evaluating corpus representativeness will become normal practice.

The two pillars of CDL - the explicit connection of meaning with corpus data and the exhaustive exploration of the data - both fit well into the computer-oriented research and development programmes of the new millennium; computer applications of linguistic knowledge have given disappointing results so far, and there is plenty of room for this promising new approach.

References

Aarts, B. 1996. "The Rhetorical Adverb *simply* in Present-day British English". In Percy et al. (eds.), 59-68.
Aarts, J. 1991. "Intuition-based and Observation-based Grammars". In Aijmer et al. (eds.), 44-62.
Aarts, J. 1992. "Comments on S. Greenbaum Contribution". In Svartvik (ed.), 180-83.
Aarts J., de Haan P. and N. Oostdijk (eds.). 1993. *English Language Corpora: Design, Analysis and Exploitation*. Amsterdam: Rodopi.
Aarts, J., de Mönnink I. and H. Wekker (eds.). 1997. *Studies in English language and teaching: in honour of Flor Aarts*. Amsterdam and Atlanta: Rodopi.
Aarts, J. and T. van den Heuvel. 1985. "Computational Tools for the Syntactic Analysis of Corpora". *Linguistics* 23, 303-35.
Aarts, J. and N. Oostdijk. 1988. "Corpus-related research at Nijmegen University". In Kyto et al. (eds.), 1-14.
Aijmer K. 1985. "Just". In Bäckman S. and G. Kjellmer (eds.) *Papers on Language and Literature Presented to Alvar EllegDrd and Erik Frykman*, Gòteborg: Acta Universitatis Gothoburgensis, 1-10.
Aijmer, K. and B. Altenberg (eds.). 1991. *English Corpus Linguistics. Studies in Honour of Jan Svartvik*. London and New York: Longman.
Aijmer K., Altenberg, B. and M. Johansson (eds). 1996. *Languages in Contrast: Papers from a Symposium on Text-based Cross-linguistic Studies, Lund 4-5 March 1994*. Lund: Lund University Press.
Alderson, C. 1996. "Do Corpora Have a Role in Language Assessment?". In Thomas and Short (eds.), 248-259.
Alexander, L.G., Allen, W.S., Close, R.A. and R.J. O'Neil. 1975. *English Grammatical Structures*. London: Longman.
Alexandrova, O. and S. Ter-Minasova. 1987. *English Syntax: Collocation, Colligation and Discourse*. Moscow: University of Moscow Press.
Aston, G. 1995. "Corpora in Language Pedagogy: Matching Theory and Practice" in G. Cook and B. Seidlhofer (eds.) *Principle and Practice in Applied Linguistics: Studies in honour of H.G. Widdowson*, 257-270. Oxford: Oxford University Press.
Aston, G. 1997. "Enriching the Learning Environment: Corpora in ELT". In Wichmann et al. (eds.), 51-64.
Aston, G. (forthcoming)."Learning English with the British National Corpus". Paper presented at the *6° Jornata de Corpus*, UPF, Barcelona, May 1998. Forthcoming in the Proceedings.
Atkins, S., Clear, J. and N. Osler. 1992. "Corpus Design Criteria". *Literary and Linguistic Computing*, 7.1, 1-16.
Austin, J.L. 1962. *How to Do Things with Words*. Oxford: Oxford University Press.
Bahl, L.R., Jelinek, F. and R.L Mercer. 1983. "A Maximum Likelihood Approach to

REFERENCES

Continuous Speech Recognition". In IEEE*Transactions on Pattern Analysis and Machine Intelligence*, PAMI- 5.2, 179-90.

Baker, C.L. 1989. *English Syntax*. Cambridge, Massachusetts and London: MIT Press.

Baker, M. 1992. *In Other Words: a Coursebook on Translation*. London: Routledge.

Baker, M. 1996. "Corpus-based Translation Studies: the Challenges that Lie Ahead". In Somers H. (ed.) *Terminology, LSP and Translation: Studies in Language Engineering, in Honour of Juan Sager*. Amsterdam and Philadelphia: Benjamins, 175-186.

Baker, M. 1998. "Réexplorer la Langue de la Traduction: une Approche par Corpus".*META*, 43.4, 480-485.

Baker, M., Francis, G. and E. Tognini-Bonelli (eds.). 1993. *Text and Technology: in honour of John Sinclair*. Amsterdam and Philadelphia: Benjamins.

Ball, J.A. 1995. *An analysis of the Evaluative Adjective in Italian*. Unpublished M.Phil Thesis, University of Birmingham.

Barlow, M. 1996. "Corpora for Theory and Practice". *International Journal of Corpus Linguistics* 1.1, 1-37.

Barnbrook, G. 1996. *Language and Computers. A Practical Introduction to the Computer Analysis of Language*. Edinburgh: Edinburgh University Press.

Bassnett, S. 1980. *Translation Studies*. London: Routledge.

Bazell, C.E., Catford, J.C., Halliday, M.A.K. and R.H. Robins (eds.). 1966. *In Memory of J.R. Firth*. London: Longman.

Benson, J.D., Cummings, M.J. and W.S. Greaves. 1988. *Linguistics in a Systemic Perspective*. Amsterdam and Philadelphia: Benjamins.

Beaugrande, R. de. 1991. *Linguistic Theory. The Discourse of Fundamental Works*. Harlow: Longman.

Beaugrande, R. de and W. Dressler. 1981. *Introduction to Text Linguistics*. Harlow: Longman.

Bernardini, S. and F. Zanettin. (eds.) 2000. *I Corpora nella Didattica della Traduzione - Corpus Use and Learning to Translate*. Bologna: CLUEB.

Berry, R. 1994. " 'Blackpool would be a nice place unless there were so many tourists': Some Misconceptions about English Grammar". *Studia Anglica Posnaniensia* XXVIII, 101-12.

Berry, R. 1999. "The Seven Sins of Pedagogic Grammar". In Berry et al., 29-40.

Berry, R., Asker, B., Hyland, K. and M. Lam (eds.). 1999. *Language Analysis, Description and Pedagogy*. Language Centre: The Hong Kong University of Science and Technology.

Biber, D. 1988. *Variation across Speech and Writing*. Cambridge: Cambridge University Press.

Biber, D. 1989. "A typology of English Texts". *Linguistics* 27. 3-43.

Biber, D. 1990. "Methodological Issues Regarding Corpus-based Analyses of Linguistic Variation". *Literary and Linguistic Computing* 5, 257-269.

Biber, D. 1994. "Representativeness in Corpus Design". In *Current Issues in Computational Linguistics: in Honour of Don Walker*, Zampolli A., Calzolari N. and M. Palmer (eds.). Linguistica Computazionale IX.X. Giardini Editori e Stampatori in Pisa and Kluwer Academic Publishers.

Biber D., Conrad, S. and Randi Reppen. 1998. *Corpus Linguistics. Investigating Language Structure and Use*. Cambridge: Cambridge University Press.

Biber, D. and E. Finegan, 1991. "On the Exploitation of Computerized Corpora in Variation Studies". In Aijmer and Altenberg (eds.), 204-20.

REFERENCES

Bindi, R. Monachini, M. and P. Orsolini. 1991. *Italian Reference Corpus: General Information and Key for Consultation.* Istituto di Linguistica Computazionale, CNR, Pisa. Unpublished Report.
Bloomfield, L. 1933. *Language.* London: Allen and Unwin.
Bod, R. 1992. "A Computational Model of Language Performance: Data Oriented Parsing". In *Proceedings of the Fifteenth International Conference on Computational Linguistics: COLING-92,* III, 855-59.
Bod, R. 1995. *Enriching Linguistics with Statistics: Performance Models of Natural Language.* Amsterdam: ILLC Dissertation Series, 14.
Bod, R. 1998. *Beyond Grammar. An Experience-based Theory of Language.* Leland Stanford Junior University: CSLI Publications.
Bondi, M. (ed.) 1998. *Forms of Argumentative Discourse. Per un'Analisi Linguistica dell'Argomentare.* Bologna: Clueb.
Botley, S. and A.M. McEnery. 2000. *Corpus-based and Computational Approaches to Discourse Anaphora.* Amsterdam and Philadelphia: Benjamins.
Bowker, L. 1998. "Using Specialized Monolingual Native-Language Corpora as a Translation Resource: a Pilot Study". In Laviosa (ed.), 631-651.
Bréal, M. 1883. "Les Lois Intellectuelles du Langage: Fragment de Sémantique". In *Annuaire de l'Association pour l'encouragement des études grecques en France,* XVII, 132-142.
Bréal, M. 1897. *Essai de Sémantique.* Paris: Hachette.
Brumfit, C.J. 1984. *Communicative Methodology in Language Teaching.* Cambridge: Cambridge University Press.
Bussi, G.E., Bondi, M. and G. Gatta (eds.). 1997. *Understanding Argument. La Logica Informale del Discorso.* Bologna: Clueb.
Butler, C.S. 1985. *Systemic Linguistics: Theory and Applications.* London: Batsford Academic and Educational.
Butler, C.S. 1985. *Computers in Linguistics.* Oxford: Blackwell.
Butler, C.S. 1992. (ed.) *Computers and Written Texts.* Oxford: Blackwell.
Calzolari, N., Kruyt, T. and M. Baker. (eds.). 1994. *Report of the NERC (Network of European Reference Corpora) Project.* Giardini Editori e Stampatori in Pisa.
Carter, R. and M. McCarthy (eds.) 1988.*Vocabulary and Language Teaching.* London: Longman.
Cermák, F. 1994. "Idiomatics". In P. A. Luelsdorff (ed.) *Prague School of Structural and Functional Linguistics.* Amsterdam and Philadelphia: Benjamins, 185-195.
Cermák, F. 1998. "La Identificación de las expresiones idiomáticas". In J. de Dios Luque Durán and A. Pamies Bertrán (eds.) *Léxico y Fraseología.* Serie Collectae. Departamento de Lingüística General y Teoría de la Literatura de la Universidad de Granada. Granada Linguistica y Método Ediciones, 1-18.
Chafe, W. 1992. "The importance of Corpus Linguistics to Understanding the Nature of Language". In Svartvik, J. (ed.), 79-97.
Chi M.L., Wong P.Y., and C.P. Wong. 1994. "Collocation Problems Amongst ESL Learners: a Corpus-based Study". In Flowerdew & Tong (eds.), 157-165.
Chomsky, N. 1957. *Syntactic Structures.* The Hague: Mouton.
Chomsky, N. 1959. "A review of B.F. Skinner's *Verbal Behaviour". Language,* 35. 1, 26-58. Reprinted in Fodor and Katz (eds.) 1964. 547-578.
Chomsky, N. 1964. "Current Issues in Linguistic Theory". In Fodor and Katz (eds.), 50-118.

REFERENCES

Chomsky, N. 1965. *Aspects of the Theory of Syntax*. Cambridge. Mass: MIT Press.
Church K., and P. Hanks. 1990. "Word Association Norms, Mutual Information and Lexicography". *Computational Linguistics*, 16.1, 22-29.
Church, K., Gale, W., Hanks, P. and D. Hindle. 1991. "Using Statistics in Lexical Analysis". In U. Zernick (ed.), *Lexical Acquisition*. Englewood Cliffs, NJ: Lawrence Erlbaum, 115-165.
Church, K. and R. Moon. 1994. "Lexical Substitutability". In Atkins and Zampolli (eds.) *Computational Approaches to the Lexicon*. Oxford: Oxford University Press, 153-177.
Clear, J. 1987. "Trawling the Language: Monitor Corpora". In Snell-Hornby (ed.) *ZuriLEX 1986 Proceedings*. Francke, Tubingen.
Clear, J. 1992. "Corpus Sampling". In G. Leitner (ed.), 21-31.
Clear, J. 1993. "From Firth Principles: Computational Tools for the Study of Collocation". In Baker et al. (eds.), 271-292.
Collins, P.C. 1991. *Cleft and Pseudo-cleft Constructions in English*. London: Routledge.
COLLINS English Dictionary (3rd Edition).
COLLINS Italian Dictionary. 1995. (New 1st Edition).
COLLINS COBUILD English Language Dictionary. 1987. (2nd edition 1995).
COLLINS COBUILD English Grammar.1990.
COLLINS COBUILD English Usage.1992.
COLLINS COBUILD Grammar Patterns 1: Verbs. 1996.
Coniam, D. 1997. "A Practical Introduction to Corpora in Teacher Training Language Awareness Programme". *Language Awareness* 6.4, 199-207.
Cook, G. and B. Seidlfofer (eds.). 1995. *Principle and Practice in Applied Linguistics*. London: Oxford University Press.
Coppen, P.A., van Halteren, H.and L.Teunissen. 1998. *Computational Linguistics in the Netherlands*. Amsterdam and Atlanta: Rodopi.
Cowie, A.P. 1988. "Stable and Creative Aspects of Vocabulary Use". In Carter and McCarthy (eds.), 126-139.
Culler, J. 1984. *Saussure*. London: Fontana Press.
Darmesteter, A. 1887. *La Vie des Mots Etudiées dans Leurs Significations*. Paris: Librairie Delagrave. (Rep. Editions Champ Libre, Paris 1979).
D'Addio, W. 1988. "Nominali Anaforici Incapsulatori: un Aspetto della Coesione Lessicale". In *Dalla Parte del Ricevente. Percezione, Comprensione, Interpretazione*. Atti del XIX Congresso Internazionale di Studi della S.L.I. 1985. Roma: Bulzoni.
Davies, F. 1988. "Reading Between the Lines: Thematic Choice as a Device for Presenting Writer Viewpoint in Academic Discourse". *The ESPecialist*, 9.1/2.
Davies, M. and L. Ravelli (eds.).1992. *Recent Advances in Systemic Linguistics*. London and New York: Pinter.
Delin, J. 1996. Review of Chafe 1994. *Functions of Language*. 3.1, 29-33.
Dijk, T.A. van (ed.). 1985. *Handbook of Discourse Analysis*. London: Academic Press.
EAGLES Interim Report. 1994. 2.1 "Corpus Typology, a Framework for Classification". In *http://www/ilc/pi/cnr.it/EAGLES96/corpustyp/*.
Eco, U. 1975. *Trattato di Semiotica Generale*. Milano: Bompiani.
Erjavec, T., Lawson, A. and L. Romary. 1998. *East meets West - A Compendium of Multilingual Resources*. TELRI CD-ROM.
Fairclough, N. 1992. *Discourse and Social Change*. Cambridge: Polity.
Favretti Rossini, R. (ed.) 2000. Linguistica e Informatica: Corpora, Multimedialità e

Percorsi di Apprendimento. Roma: Bulzoni.
Ferrari, G. 2000. "Livelli di Analisi del Testo: Due Approcci a Confronto". In Favretti R. (ed.) (in press).
Fillmore, C. J. 1992. "`Corpus Linguistics' or `Computer-aided Armchair Linguistics' ". In Svartvik (ed.), 35-60.
Fjelkestam-Nilsson, B. 1983. "*Also* and *too*: a Corpus-based Study of their Frequency and Use in Modern English". *Stockholm Studies in English* 58. Stockholm: Almqvist & Wiksell.
Firth, J.R. 1935. "The Technique of Semantics". In *Transactions of the Philological Society*. Reprinted in Firth (1957).
Firth, J.R. 1935. "The Use and Distribution of Certain English Sounds". *English Studies*, XVII, 1. Reprinted in Firth (1957), 34-46.
Firth, J.R. 1950. "Personality and Language in Society". In The *Sociological Review* 42, 37-52. Reprinted in Firth (1957).
Firth, J.R. 1957. *Papers in Linguistics* 1934-51. London: Oxford University Press.
Firth, J.R. 1968. "Linguistic Analysis as a Study of Meaning". In Palmer (ed.), 12-25.
Firth, J.R. 1968. "A Synopsis of Linguistic Theory 1930-55". In Palmer (ed.), 168-205.
Flowerdew, L. and A.K. Tong (eds.). 1994. *Entering Text*. University of Science and Technology, and Department of English, Guangzhou Institute of Foreign Languages. Language Centre: Hong Kong.
Foucault, M. 1972. *The Archaeology of Knowledge*. London: Tavistock.
Francis, G. 1986. *Anaphoric Nouns*. Discourse Analysis Monograph 11. University of Birmingham: English Language Research.
Francis, G. 1991. "Nominal Group Heads and Clause Structure". *Word*, 14. 2.
Francis, G. 1993. "A Corpus-driven Approach to Grammar. Principles, Methods and Examples". In Baker et al. (eds.), 137-56.
Francis, W.N. 1982. "Problems of Assembling and Computerizing Large Corpora". In Johansson, S. (ed.), 7-24.
Francis, W.N. 1992. "Language Corpora B.C.". In Svartvik (ed.), 17-32.
Francis, W.N. and H. Kucera 1979. *Manual of Information to Accompany a Standard Sample of Present-day American English*. Providence: Brown University Press.
Freeman, D.C. 1995 "Review of *Text and Technology: in Honour of John Sinclair*" in LINGUIST List, 6.469 (Thu. 30th March 1995).
Fries, U., Tottie, G. and P. Schneider. 1994. *Creating and Using English Language Corpora* Amsterdam: Rodopi.
Gellerstam, M. 1986. "Translationese in Swedish novels translated from English". In Wollin, L. and H. Lindquist (eds.),*Translation Studies in Scandinavia*, 88-95. Lund: CWK Gleerup.
Gellerstam, M. 1996. "Translations as a Source for Cross-linguistic Studies". In *Languages in Contrast*, Aijmer, Altenberg and Johansson (eds.), 53-62. Lund: Lund University Press.
Geluykens, R. 1988. "Five Types of Clefting in English Discourse". *Linguistics* 26, 823-41.
Granger, S. 1993. "International Corpus of Learner English". In Aarts, de Haan and Oostdijk (eds.), 57-72.
Granger, S. 1994. 'The Learner Corpus: a revolution in applied linguistics'. *English Today* 39, 25-29.
Granger, S. 1996a. 'Learner English around the World'. In: Greenbaum (ed.), 13-24.
Granger, S. 1996b. 'From CA to CIA and back: An integrated approach to computerized bilingual and learner corpora'. In: Aijmer, Altenberg and Johansson (eds.), 37-51.

Granger, S. 1997a. 'Automated retrieval of passives from native and learner corpora: precision and recall'. *Journal of English Linguistics* 25.4, 365-374.
Granger, S. 1997b. 'On identifying the syntactic and discourse features of participle clauses in academic English: native and non-native writers compared'. In: Aarts, de Mönnink and Wekker (eds.), 185-198.
Granger, S. (ed.) 1998. *Learner English on Computer*. London and New York: Longman.
Granger, S., Meunier, F. and S. Tyson. 1994. 'New insights from the learner lexicon: a preliminary report from the International Corpus of Learner English'. In: Flowerdew and Tong (eds.), 102-113.
Granger, S. and S. Tyson. 1996. 'Connector usage in the English essay writing of native and non-native EFL speakers of English'. *World Englishes* 15, 17-27.
Greenbaum, S. 1992. "A New Corpus of English: ICE". In Svartvik (ed.), 171-79.
Greenbaum, S. (ed.). 1996. *Comparing English Worldwide: The International Corpus of English*. Oxford: Clarendon Press.
Greenbaum, S. 1996 'Introducing ICE'. In: Greenbaum (ed.), 3-12.
Habert, B., Nazarenko, A. and A. Salem. 1997. *Les Linguistiques de Corpus*. Paris: Armand Colin.
Halliday, M.A.K. 1961. "Categories of the Theory of Grammar". *Word*, 17.3, 241-92. (Extract in Kress, G.R. 1976, 84-7)
Halliday, M.A.K. 1964. "Language and the Consumer". *Monograph Series in Languages & Linguistics* 17. Washington D.C.: Georgetwon U.P., 14-23. Reprinted in Halliday and Martin (1981) 21-28.
Halliday, M.A.K. 1966. "Some Notes on Deep Grammar". *Journal of Linguistics* 2, 57-67. Reprinted in Kress (1976).
Halliday, M.A.K. 1966b. "Lexis as a Linguistic Level". In Bazell, C.E. et al., 148-62.
Halliday, M.A.K. 1975. *Learning how to Mean*. London: Edward Arnold.
Halliday, M.A.K. 1976. *System and Function in Language* (Selected papers edited by G. Kress). Oxford: Oxford University Press.
Halliday, M.A.K. 1978. *Language as a Social Semiotic: The Social Interpretation of Language and Meaning*. London: Arnold.
Halliday, M.A.K. 1981. "Structure". In *Readings in Systemic Linguistics*, Halliday and Martin (eds.), 122-131. London: Batsford.
Halliday, M.A.K. 1984. "On the Ineffability of Grammatical Categories". In Manning et al. (eds.), 3-18.
Halliday, M.A.K. 1985. *An Introduction to Functional Grammar*. London: Edward Arnold.
Halliday, M.A.K. 1987. "Spoken and Written Modes of Meaning". In Horowits et al. (eds.), 55-82.
Halliday, M.A.K. 1991a. "Corpus Studies and Probabilistic Grammar". In Aijmer et al. (eds.), 30-43.
Halliday, M.A.K. 1991b. "Towards Probabilistic Interpretations". In Ventola, E. (ed.), 39-61.
Halliday, M.A.K. 1992a. "Language as System and Language as Instance: the Corpus as a Theoretical Construct". In Svartvik (ed.), 61-77.
Halliday, M.A.K. 1992b. "Language Theory and Tranlslation Practice". *Rivista Internazionale di Tecnica della Traduzione*. Scuola Superiore di Lingue Moderne per Interpreti e Traduttori, Università di Trieste, 15-25.
Halliday, M.A.K. 1992c. "How Do You Mean?". In Davies and Ravelli (eds.), 20-35.

Halliday, M.A.K. 1993a. "Language as a Cultural Dynamic". *Cultural Dynamics* VI, 1-2: E.J. Brill.
Halliday, M.A.K. 1993b. "Towards a Language-Based Theory of Learning". *Linguistics and Education*, 5, 93-116.
Halliday, M.A.K. 1993c. "Quantitative Studies and Probabilities in Grammar". In Hoey (ed.), 1-25.
Halliday, M.A.K. and R. Hasan. 1976. *Cohesion in English*. London and New York: Longman.
Halliday, M.A.K. and Z. James. 1993. "A Quantitative Study of Polarity and Primary Tense in the English Finite Clause". In Sinclair et al. (eds.), 32-66.
Hanks, P. 1994. "Linguistic Norms and Pragmatic Exploitations or, why Lexicographers Need Prototype Theory, and Vice Versa". In Kiefer, Kiss and Pajzs (eds.) *Papers in Computational Linguistics: Complex '94*, 89-113. Budapest: Research Institute for Linguistics.
Hanks, P. 1996. "Contextual Dependency and Lexical Sets". *International Journal of Corpus Linguistics*, 1.1, 75-98.
Hanks, P. 1997. "Ferocious Empiricism: Review of J. Sinclair's *On Lexis and Lexicography*". *IJCL* 2.2, 289-295.
Harris, R. (ed.) 1983. *Course in General Linguistics* (F. de Saussure). London: Duckworth.
Harris, R. 1987. *Reading Saussure*. London: Duckworth.
Harris, R. and T.J. Taylor. 1989. *Landmarks in Linguistic Thought. The Western Traditon from Socrates to Saussure*. London: Routledge.
Harris, Z.S. 1951. *Methods in Structural Linguistics*. Chicago: University of Chicago Press.
Harris, Z.S. 1952. "Discourse Analysis". *Language*, 28, 1-30. Reprinted in Fodor and Katz (eds.) 1964. 355-383.
Harris, Z.S. 1954. "Distributional Structure". *Word*, 10, 2-3, 146-62. Reprinted in Fodor and Katz (eds.)(1964), 33-49.
Harris, Z.S. 1957. "Co-occurrence and Trasformation in Linguistic Structure". *Language*, 33, 3, 283-340. Reprinted in Fodor and Katz (eds.) 1964. 155-210.
Harris, Z.S. 1988. *Language and Information*. New York: Columbia University Press.
Hasselgård, H. and S. Oksefjell (eds.). 1999. *Out of Corpus Studies in Honour of Stig Johansson*. Language and Computers: Studies in Practical Linguistics 26. Amsterdam and Atlanta: Rodopi.
Higgins, J. and T. Johns. 1984. *Computers and Language Learning*. London: Collins.
Higgs, T.V. 1985. "Language Acquisition and Language Learning: A Plea for Syncretism". *Modern Language Journal* 69, 8-14.
Hjelmslev, J. 1953. *Prolegomena to a Theory of Language* (translated from the Danish 1943). Bloomington, Ind.: Indiana University.
Hoey, M. (ed.) 1993. *Data, Description, Discourse. Papers on the English Language in Honour of John McH. Sinclair*. London: HarperCollins.
Hornby, A.S. 1954. *A Guide to Patterns and Usage in English*. London: Oxford University Press.
Horowitz, R. and S.J. Samuels (eds.). 1987. *Comprehending Oral and Written Language*. New York: Academic Press.
Hunston, S. 1995. "A Corpus Study of Some English Verbs of Attribution". *Functions of Language*, 2.2, 133-58.

Hunston, S. and G. Francis. 2000. *Pattern Grammar. A Corpus-driven Approach to the Lexical Grammar of English*.. Amsterdam and Philadelphia: Benjamins.
Jackendoff, R. 1972. *Semantic Interpretation in Generative Grammar*. Cambridge, Mass.: MIT Press.
Jarvinen, T. "Annotating 200 Million Words: The Bank of English Project". In *Proceedings of Coling 94*, Kyoto: Japan, Vol. II, 565-568.
Jelinek, F. 1986. "Self-organized Language Modelling for Speech Recognition". Continuous Speech Recognition Group, IBM Thomas J. Watson Research Center. [Unpublished]
Johansson, M. 1996. "Contrastive Data as a Resource in the Study of English Clefts". In Aijmer et al., 127-52.
Johansson, S. 1980. "Corpus-based Studies of British and American English". In S. Jacobson (ed.) *Papers from the Scandinavian Symposium on Syntactic Variation, Stockholm, May 18-19, 1979*. Stockholm: Almqvist & Wiksell, 85-100.
Johansson, S. (ed.). 1982. *Computer Corpora in English Language Research*. Bergen: Norwegian Computing Centre for the Humanities.
Johansson, S. 1995. "Mens Sana in Corpore Sano: On the Role of Corpora in Linguistic Research". *The European Messenger* IV.2, 19-25.
Johansson, S. and K. Hofland. 1994. "Toward and English-Norwegian Parallel Corpus". In Fries et al., 25-37.
Johansson, S. and S. Oksefjell. 1996. "Towards a Unified Account of the Syntax and Semantics of *Get*". In Thomas et al. (eds.), 57-75.
Johns, T. 1986. "Micro-concord: a Language-learner's Research Tool". *System* 14.2.
Johns, T. 1988. "Whence and Whither Classroom Concordancing?". In Bongaerts et al. (eds.) *Computer Applications in Language Learning*. Foris.
Johns, T. 1991a. "Should you be Persuaded: Two Examples of Data-driven Learning". In Johns and King (eds.), 1-16.
Johns, T. 1991b. "From Printout to Handout: Grammar and Vocabulary Teaching in the Context of Data- driven Learning". In Johns T. and King P. (eds.), 27-45.
Johns, T. and P. King (eds). 1991. *Classroom Concordancing*, ELR Journal 4. CELS University of Birmingham.
Jordan, M.P. 1998. "The Power of Negation in English: Text, Context and Relevance". *Journal of Pragmatics* 29, 705-752.
Karlsson, F., Voutilainen, A., Heikkilae, J, and A. Anttila (eds.). 1995. *Constraint Grammar, A Language Independent System for Parsing Unrestricted Text*. Berlin: Walter de Gruyter.
Katz, J.J. and J.A. Fodor, 1963. "The Structure of a Semantic Theory", *Language*, 39, (170-210). Reprinted in Fodor and Katz (eds.), (1964),479-518.
Kennedy, G. 1990. "Collocations: Where Grammar and Vocabulary Teaching Meet". In Anivan, S. (ed.) *Language Teaching Methodology for the Nineties*. Singapore: RELC Anthology Series, 215-229.
Kennedy, G. 1991. "*Between and Through*: the Company they Keep and the Function they Serve". In Aijmer et al., 95-110.
Kennedy, G. 1992. "Preferred Ways of Putting Things with Implications for Language Teaching". In Svartvik (ed.), 335-373.
Kennedy, G. 1996. "Over *once* lightly". In Percy et al., 253- 62.
Kennedy, G. 1998. An *Introduction to Corpus Linguistics*. London & New York: Longman.
Kenny, D. 1998. "Creatures of Habit? What Translators Usually Do with Words". In Laviosa (ed.), 515-523.

Kettermann, B. 1995. "Concordancing in English Language Teaching".*TELL and CALL*, 4/95, 4-15.
Kettermann, B. 1997. "Using a Corpus to Evaluate Theories of Child Language Acquisition". In Wichmann et al. (eds.).
Kiefer, F., Kiss, G. and J. Pajzs (eds.). 1999. *Papers in Computational Lexicography*: COMPLEX '99. Budapest: Linguistic Institute, Hungarian Academy of Sciences.
Krashen, S.D. 1981. *Second Language Acquisition and Second Language Learning*. Oxford: Pergamon Press.
Kytö, M., Ihalainen, O. and M. Rissanen (eds.). 1988. *Corpus Linguistics Hard and Soft*. Amsterdam: Rodopi.
Langendoen, A. 1968. *The London School of Linguistcs: A Study of the Linguistic Theories of B. Malinowski and J.R. Firth*, Research Monograph No. 46, MIT Press, Cambridge, Mass.
Larsson, B. 1984. *Some English Emphasisers*. MS Lund University.
Laviosa, S. (ed.). 1998. *L'approche basée sur le Corpus. The Corpus-based Approach. META* 43.4.
Lecercle, J. 1990. *The Violence of Language*. London: Routledge.
Lecercle, J. 1994. *Philosophy of Nonsense*. London: Routledge.
Leech, G. 1991. "The State of the Art in Corpus Linguistics". In Aijmer et al. (eds.), 8-29.
Leech, G. 1992. "Corpora and Theories of Linguistic Performance". In Svartvik (ed.), 105-122.
Leech, G. 1997. "Teaching and Language Corpora: a Convergence". In Wichmann et al. (eds.).
Leech, G. and Fligelstone, S. 1992. "Computers and Corpus Analysis". In Butler (ed.), 115-140.
Leech, G., Myers, G. and Thomas, J, 1995. *Spoken English on Computer*, Harlow: Longman.
Leitner, G. (ed.). 1992. *New Directions in English Language Corpora. Methodology, Results, Software Developments*. Berlin: Mouton de Gruyter.
Lemke, J.L. 1989. "Semantics and Social Values". *Word*, 40, 1/2, 37-50.
Levinson, S.C. 1983. *Pragmatics*. Cambridge: Cambridge University Press.
Ljung, M. 1990. *A Study of TEFL Vocabulary*. Acta Universitatis Stockholmiensis 78. Stockholm: Almqvist & Wiksell.
Louw, W.E. 1989. "Computer-assisted Materials Evaluation: Content vs. National Policy". *Language and Ideology*, ELRJ 3, English Language Research, University of Birmingham.
Louw, W.E. 1991. "Classroom Concordancing of Delexical Forms and the Case for Integrating Language and Literature". In Johns and King (eds), 151-178.
Louw, W.E. 1993. "Irony in the Text or Insincerity in the Writer? the Diagnostic Potential of Semantic Prosodies". In Baker et al. (eds.), 157-174.
Louw, W.E. 1997. "The Role of Corpora in Critical Literary Appreciation". In Wichmann et al. (eds.), 240-251.
Lyons, J. 1966. "Firth's Theory of meaning". In Bazell et al. (eds.), 288-302.
Lyons, J. 1977. *Semantics*. Cambridge: Cambridge University Press.
Lyons, J. 1995. *Linguistic Semantics. An Introduction*. Cambridge: Cambridge University Press.
McEnery, T. and A. Wilson. 1996. *Corpus Linguistics*. Edinburgh: Edinburgh University Press.
McEnery et al. (eds.) 2000
Malinowsky, B. 1923. "The Problem of Meaning in Primitive Languages". In Ogden, C.K. and Richards, A.I. *The Meaning of Meaning*. London: International Library of Psychology, Philosophy and Scientific Method, 451-510.

Malmkjaer, K. (ed.) 1998. *Translation and Language Teaching.* Manchester: St. Jerome.
Manning, A., Martin, P. and K. McCalla (eds.). 1984. *The Tenth LACUS Forum 1983.* Columbia, South Caronia: Hornbeam Press.
Martin, J.R. "Logical Meaning, Interdependency, and the Linking particle {*na/-ng*} in Tagalog. *Functions of Language* 2. 2, 189-228.
Martin, J.R. 1991. "Intrinsic Functionality: Implications for Contextual Theory". *Social Semiotics,* 1.1, 99-162.
Mauranen, A. 1993. "Theme and Prospection in Written Discourse" in Baker et al. (eds.), 95-114.
Mauro, T. de. 1972. (ed.) *Cours de Linguistique Générale* (F.de Saussure). Paris: Payot.
Mauro, T. de, Mancini, F., Vedovelli, M. and M. Voghera (1993) *Lessico di Frequenza dell'Italiano Parlato.* Fondazione IBM Italia: Etaslibri.
May Fan, C. 1999. "An Investigation into the Pervasiveness of Delexical Chunks in Authentic Language Use and the Problems they Present to L2 Learners". In Berry et al. (eds.), 162-175.
May Fan, Greaves, C. and M. Warren. 1999. "Identifying Characteristic Patterns in Students' Writing Using a Corpus of Learner Data" in Berry et al. (eds.), 176-188.
Melčuk, I. 1988. "Semantic Description of Lexical Units in an Explanatory Combinatorial Disctionary: Basic Principles and Heuristic Criteria". *International Journal of Corpus Linguistics* 1.3, 165-188.
Melčuk, I. 1995. "Phrasemes in Language and Phraseology in Linguistics". In Everaert et al. (eds.) *Idioms: Structural and Psychological Perspectives.* Hillsdale; New Jersey: Lawrence Erbaum Associates, 167-232.
Mindt, D. 1991. "Syntactic Evidence for Semantic Distinctions in English". In Aijmer et al. (eds.), 183-196.
Mindt, D. 1995. *An Empirical Grammar of the English Verb. Modal Verbs.* Berlin: Cornelsen Verlag.
Mindt, D. 1996a. "A Corpus-based Empirical Grammar of English Modal Verbs". In *Synchronic Corpus Linguistics* . Percy, E., Meyer, C.F. and I. Lancashire, 133-41.
Mindt, D. 1996b. "English Corpus Linguistics and the Foreign Language Teaching Syllabus". In Thomas et al., 232-247.
Mindt, D. 1997. "Corpora and the Teaching of English in Germany". In Wichmann et al. (eds.), 40-50.
Moon, R. 1994. "The Analysis of Fixed Expressions in Text". In Coulthard M. (ed.) *Advances in Written Text Analysis,* 117-135. London and New York: Routledge.
Moon, R. 1998. *Fixed Expressions and Idioms in English. A Corpus-based Approach.* Oxford: Clarendon Press.
Mounin, G. 1972. *Clefs pour la Sémantique.* Paris: Senghers.
Murison-Bowie, S. 1996. "Linguistic Corpora and Language Teaching". *Annual Review of Applied Linguistics* 16, 182-199.
Nakamura, J. 1993. "Statistical Methods and Large Corpora. A New Tool for Describing Text Types". In Baker et al., 293-312.
Nakamura, J. and J.M. Sinclair, 1995. "The World of Woman in the Bank of English: Internal Criteria for the Classification of Corpora". *Literary and Linguistic Computing,* 10.2, 99-110.
Nattinger, J. and J. De Carrico. 1989. "Lexical Phrases, Speech Acts and Teaching Conversation". In AILA Review 6, Nation P. and Carter R. (eds.)*Vocabulary Acquisition.*

Amsterdam: AILA, 118-139.
Nattinger, J. and J. De Carrico. 1992. *Lexical Phrases and Language Teaching*. Oxford: Oxford University Press.
Neubert, A. 1985. *Text and Translation*. Leipzig: VEB Verlag Enzyklopadie.
Ooi, V. B. Y. 1998. *Computer Corpus Lexicography*. Edimburgh: Edimburgh University Press.
Osborne, G. 1992. *Computational Analysis of Idiomatic Phrases in Modern English*. Mphil Thesis, Birmingham: University of Birmingham.
Palmer, F.R. 1968. *Selected Papers* of J.R. Firth 1952-59. London and Harlow: Longman Linguistic Library.
Palmer, F.R. 1976. *Semantics*. Cambridge: Cambridge University Press.
Partington, A. 1993. "Corpus Evidence of Language Change - The Case of the Intensifier". In Baker et al. (eds.), 177-192.
Partington, A. 1998. *Patterns and Meanings. Using Corpora for English Language Research and Teaching*. SCL 2. Amsterdam and Philadelphia: Benjamins.
Pawley, A. and F.H. Syder. 1983. "Two Puzzles for Linguistic Theory: Native-like Selection and Native-like Fluency". In Richards J.C. and R.W. Schmidt (eds.) *Language and Communication*, London: Longman, 191-227.
Pavel, T.G. 1986. *Fictional Worlds*. Cambridge Massachusetts: Harvard University Press.
Pearson, J. 1996. "Electronic Texts and Concordances in the Translation Classroom". *Teanga* 16. Dublin: IRAAL. 86-96.
Pearson, J. 1998. *Terms in Context*. SCL 1. Amsterdam and Philadelphia: Benjamins.
Percy, C.E., Meyer, C.F. and I. Lancashire (eds.). 1996. *Synchronic Corpus Linguistics. Papers from the Sixteenth International Conference on English Language Research on Computerized Corpora* (ICAME 16). Amsterdam: Rodopi.
Peters, A.M. 1983. *The Units of Language Acquisition*. Cambridge: Cambridge University Press.
Phillips, M.K. 1988. "Text, Terms and Meanings". In Benson et al., 99-118.
Prince, E. 1978. "A Comparison of *wh*-clefts and *it*-clefts in Discourse". *Language* 54, 883-906.
Qereda Rodriguez-Navarro, L. and J. Santana Lario (eds.). 1992. *Homenaje a J.R. Firth en su Centenario* (1980-1990). Granada: Universidad de Granada.
Quirk, R.S., S. Greenbaum, G. Leech and J. Svartvik. 1972. *A Grammar of Contemporary English Language*. London: Longman.
Quirk, R.S., S. Greenbaum, G. Leech and J. Svartvik. 1985. *A Comprehensive Grammar of the English Language*. Harlow: Longman.
Renouf, A. 1998. *Explorations in Corpus Linguistics*. Amsterdam and Atlanta: Rodopi.
Renzi, L. and G. Salvi. 1991. *Grande Grammatica Italiana di Consultazione*. Bologna: Il Mulino.
Rettig, H. (ed.) 1995. TELRI*Trans-European Language Resources Infrastructure) Proceedings of the First European Seminar "Language Resources for Language Technology"*. Tihany, Hungary, September 15 and 16, 1995.
Rissanen, M. 1999. "On the Adverbialisation of *rather*: Surfing for Historical Data". In Hasselgård H. and S. Oksefjell (eds.), 49-59.
Rutherford, W.E. and M. Sharwood-Smith, 1985. "Consciousness-Raising and Universal Grammar". *Applied Linguistics* 6, 274-282.
Saussure, F. de. 1916. *Cours de Linguistique Générale*. T. de Mauro (ed.) 1972. Paris: Payot.

REFERENCES

Sampson, G. 1996. "From Central Embedding to Corpus Linguistics". In Thomas et al., 14-26.

Schegloff, E.A. and H. Sacks. 1973. "Opening up closings". *Semiotica* 8, 289-327.

Shchekina, I. 1995. "The Communicative Intent of Text as a Problem of Translation". *Rivista Internazionale di Tecnica della Traduzione* 1. Udine: Campanotto Editore.

Sinclair, J.M. 1966. "Beginning the Study of Lexis". In Bazell, Catford, Halliday and Robins (eds.) *In Memory of J.R. Firth*. London: Longman, 410-30.

Sinclair, J.M. 1972. *A Course in Spoken English: Grammar*. London: Oxford University Press.

Sinclair, J.M. 1980. "Some Implications of Discourse Analysis for ESP Methodology". *Applied Linguistics*, 1.3, 253-61.

Sinclair, J.M. 1981. "Planes of Discourse". In S.N.A. Rizvi (ed.), *The Two-fold Voice: Essays in Honour of Ramesh Mohan*. Saltzburg: University of Saltzburg, 70-89.

Sinclair, J.M. 1985. "On the Integration of Linguistic Description". In T.A. Van Dijk (ed.), 13-28.

Sinclair, J.M. 1986. "Fictional Worlds". In M. Coulthard (ed.), *Talking about Text*. University of Birmingham: English Language Research, 43-60.

Sinclair, J.M. 1987a. "Mirror for a Text". *Journal of English and Foreign Languages* 1. Hyderabad.

Sinclair, J.M. 1987b. "Collocation: a Progress Report". In Steele, R. and T. Threadgold *Language Topics: Essays in Honour of Michael Halliday*. Amsterdam and Philadelphia: Benjamins, 319-31.

Sinclair, J.M. 1987c. "The Nature of Evidence". In Sinclair (ed.), 150-159.

Sinclair, J.M. (ed.). 1987d. *Looking Up: an Account of the COBUILD Project in Lexical Computing*. London: Collins.

Sinclair, J.M. 1987e. "Grammar in the Dictionary". In Sinclair (ed.), 104-15.

Sinclair, J.M. 1989. "Uncommonly Common Words". In *Learners' Dictionaries: State of the Art* (Anthology Series 23). Singapore: SEAMEO Regional Language Centre.

Sinclair, J.M. 1991. *Corpus Concordance Collocation*. Oxford: Oxford University Press.

Sinclair, J.M. 1992a. "Trust the Text: the Implications are Daunting". In Davies and Ravelli (eds.), 5-19.

Sinclair, J.M. 1992b. "The Automatic Analysis of Corpora". In Svartvik (ed.) *Directions in Corpus Linguistics*, Berlin and New York: Mouton de Gruyter.

Sinclair, J.M. 1993. "Written Discourse Structure". In Sinclair et al. (eds.), 6-31.

Sinclair, J.M. 1996a. *Lexis and Lexicography*, J.A. Foley (ed.). Singapore: Unipress.

Sinclair, J.M. 1996b. "The Empty Lexicon". *International Jounal of Corpus Linguistics* 1.1, 99-119.

Sinclair, J.M. 1996c. "The Search for Units of Meaning". *TEXTUS IX*, 1, 75-106.

Sinclair, J.M. 1996d. "Prospects for Automatic Lexicography" (The Otto Jespersen Lecture). In Zettersten and Pedersen (eds.), *Symposium on Lexicography VII*; Proceedings of the seventh Symposium on Lexicography May 5-6, 1994 at the University of Copenhagen. Tübingen: Max Niemeyer Verlag, 1-10.

Sinclair, J.M. 1996e. "Multilingual Databases: An International Project in Multilingual Lexicography". In Sinclair et al. (eds.), 171-178.

Sinclair, J.M. 1997a. "Corpus Evidence in Language Description". In Wichman et al. (eds.), 27-39.

Sinclair, J.M. 1997b. "Corpus Linguistics at the Millennium". In Kohn et al. (eds.) *New Horizons in CALL*. Szombathely: Bersenyi Dániel College.

REFERENCES

Sinclair, J.M. 1998a. "Large Corpus Research and Foreign Language Teaching". In de Beaugrande, Grosman and Seidlhofer (eds.) *Language Policy and Language Education in Emerging Nations*. Volume LXIII, Advances in Discourse Processes. Stamford, Connecticut: Ablex Publishing Corporation, 79-86.

Sinclair, J.M. 1998b. "The Lexical Item". In Weigand, E. (ed.) *Contrastive Lexical Semantics*, Amsterdam and Philadelphia: John Benjamins, 1-24.

Sinclair, J.M. 1999a. "A way with common words". In Hasselgård and Oksefjell (eds.) *Out of Corpus Studies in Honour of Stig Johansson*. Language and Computers: Studies in Practical Linguistics 26. Amsterdam and Atlanta: Rodopi, 157-179.

Sinclair, J.M. 1999b. "The internalisation of dialogue". In Rossini Favretti, Sandri andScazzieri (eds.) *Incommensurability and Translation Essays in Honour of Thomas S. Khun*. Cheltenham: Edward Elgar, 391-406.

Sinclair, J.M. 1999c. "Data Derived Multilingual Lexicons". In E. Arcaini, (ed.) *La Traduzione, Saggi e Documenti (IV)*. Quaderni di Libri e Riviste d'Italia 43, Ministero per i Beni e le Attività Culturali Ufficio Centrale per i Beni Librari, Le Istituzioni Culturali e l'Editoria Divisione Editoria Istituto Poligrafico e Zecca dello Stato, 33-46.

Sinclair, J.M. 1999d. "New roles for Language Centres: the mayonnaise problem". In Bickerton and Gotti (eds.) *Language Centres: Integration through Innovation*. Cercles (Confédération Européenne des Centres de Langues de l'Enseignement Superieur) Secretariat, Department of Modern Languages, University of Plymouth, 31-50.

Sinclair, J.M. 2000. "The Computer, the Corpus and the Theory of Language". In Azzaro and Ulrych (eds.) *Transiti linguistici e culturali* II, Proceedings of the XVIII AIA Congress *Anglistica e .:metodi e percorsi comparatistici delle lingue, culture e letterature di origine europea"*. Trieste EUT, 1-15. Reprinted 1999 LMS Lingua 1.9, 24-32.

Sinclair, J.M. (forthcoming). "The Deification of Information". In Thompson and Scott (eds.) *Patterns of Text: in Honour of Michael Hoey*. Amsterdam and Philadelphia: Benjamins.

Sinclair, J.M. (forthcoming). "Passion Speechlesse Lies". In Tong, Pakir, Ban and Goh (eds.) *Ariels: Departures and Returns*. Essays for Edwin Thumboo. Singapore: Oxford University Press.

Sinclair, J.M. (in preparation) *English Words in Use: a Dictionary of Collocations*. HarperCollins

Sinclair, J.M., Jones S. and R. Daley. 1970. "English Lexical Studies", Report to OSTI.

Sinclair, J.M. and A. Renouf. 1988. "A Lexical Syllabus for Language Learning". In *Vocabulary and Language Teaching*, Carter and McCarthy (eds.). Harlow: Longman, 140-158.

Sinclair, J.M. and Renouf, A. 1991. "Collocational Framework in English". In Aijmer et al., 128-143.

Sinclair, J.M., Hoey, M. and G. Fox (eds.) 1993. *Techniques of Description: Spoken and Written Discourse*. London and New York: Routledge.

Sinclair. J.M., Payne, J. and C. Perez Hernandez (eds.). 1996. *Corpus to Corpus: a Study of Translation Equivalence. IJCL* 9.3.

Sinclair, J.M. and S. Hunston. 2000. "A local grammar of evaluation". In S. Hunston and G.Thompson (eds.) *Evaluation in Text: Authorial Stance and the Construction of Discourse*. Oxford: OUP, 74-101.

Sinclair, J.M. and G. Barnbrook (in press). "Specialised corpus, local and functional grammars". In Ghadessy et al. (eds.) *The Use of Small Corpora in the Teaching of Language*. Amsterdam and Philadelphia: Benjamins.

REFERENCES

Sperber, D. and D. Wilson. 1986. *Relevance: Communication and Cognition.* Oxford: Blackwell.
Stubbs, M. 1983. *Discourse Analysis. The Sociolinguistic Analysis of Natural Language.* Oxford: Blackwell.
Stubbs, M. 1992. "Institutional Linguistics: Language and Institutions, Linguistics and Sociology". In M. Pütz (ed.) *ThirtyYears of Linguistic Evolution.* Amsterdam: Benjamins, 189-211.
Stubbs, M. 1993. "British Traditions in Text Analysis". In Baker et al. (eds.), 1-33.
Stubbs, M. 1994. "Grammar, Text, and Ideology: Computer-assisted Methods in the Linguistics of Representation". *Applied Linguistics,* 15.2, 201-223.
Stubbs, M. 1995a. "Collocations and Semantic Profiles: on the Cause of the Trouble with Quantitative Studies". *Functions of Language* 2.1, 23-55.
Stubbs, M. 1995b. "Corpus Evidence for Norms of Lexical Collocation". In Cook and Seidlfofer (eds.), 245-256.
Stubbs, M. 1996 *Text and Corpus Analysis: Computer-assisted Studies of Language and Culture.* Oxford and Cambridge, Mass.: Blackwell.
Stubbs, M. and Gerbig, A. 1993. "Human and Inhuman Geography: on the Computer-assisted Analysis of Long Texts". In Hoey (ed.), 64-85.
Svartvik, J. (ed.) 1992. *Directions in Corpus Linguistics. Proceedings of Nobel Symposyium 82, Stockholm, 4-8 August 1991.* Berlin and New York: Mouton de Gruyter.
Svartvik, J. 1999. "English Corpus Studies: Past, Present, Future". *English Corpus Studies* 6. Japan Association for English Corpus Studies, 1-16.
Swales, J. 1990. *Genre Analysis.* Cambridge: Cambridge University Press.
Swan, M. and C. Walter. 1997. *How English Grammar Works.* Oxford: Oxford University Press.
Tamba-Mecz, I. 1988. *La Sémantique.* Paris: Presses Universitaires de France.
Tadros, A. 1985. *Prediction in Text.* Discourse Analysis Monograph 10. Birmingham: University of Birmingham.
Taglicht, J. 1984. *Message and Emphasis.* London: Longman.
Taylor, J. 1989. *Linguistic Categorisation: Prototypes in Linguistic Theory.* Oxford: Oxford University Press.
Teubert, W. 1996. "Comparable or Parallel Corpora?". In Sinclair et al. (eds.), 238-264.
Teubert, W. 2000. *"Corpus Linguistics and Lexicography".* In Lawson and Teubert (eds.) Text, Corpora and Multilingual Lexicography. Manchester: St. Jerome.
Teubert, W., Tognini Bonelli, E. and N. Volz (eds.). 1998. *Translation Equivalence. TELRI: Proceedings of the Third European Seminar, Montecatini Terme Oct. 16-18 1997.* TELRI Association, IDS-Mannheim and TWC.
Thomas, J. and M. Short. 1996. *Using Corpora for Language Research. Studies in Honour of Geoffrey Leech.* London and New York: Longman.
Thomson, A.J. and A.V. Martinet 1960. *A Practical English Grammar.* Third Edition 1980. Oxford: Oxford University Press.
Tognini Bonelli, E. 1992. "'All I'm saying is' .. the Correlation of Form and Function in Pseudo-cleft Sentences". *Literary and Linguistic Computing,* 7.1, 30-42.
Tognini Bonelli, E. 1993a. "From a Reliable Source: Uses and Functions of the Adjective *real*". In *Dialogueanalysis IV, Proceedings of the 4th Conference. Basel 1992,* Tubingen: Niemeyer, 385-392.
Tognini Bonelli, E. 1993b. "Interpretative Nodes in Discourse: *actual and actually*". In Baker et al. (eds.), 193-212.
Tognini Bonelli, E. 1995. "Italian Corpus Linguistics: Practice and Theory". TEXTUS VIII, Merlini Barbaresi and Sinclair (eds.), 391-412.

Tognini Bonelli, E. 1996a. "Appeals to Reality in the World of Discourse: Structuring Interpretation". In Siciliani, Intonti, and Sportelli (eds.), *Le Trasformazioni del Narrare. Atti del XVI Convegno Nazionale (Ostuni 14-16 Ottobre 1993)*. Bari: Schena Editore, 679-712.
Tognini Bonelli, E. 1996b. "Translation Equivalence in a Corpus Linguistics Framework" in *International Journal of Lexicography. Special Issue on Corpora in Multilingual Lexicography*, 9.3. Oxford: Oxford University Press, 197-217.
Tognini Bonelli, E. 1996c. *Corpus Theory and Practice*. Birmingham: TWC Monographs.
Tognini Bonelli, E. 2000a. "Things that can and do go wrong in language teaching: Revisiting 'the seven sins' in the light of corpus evidence". *Linguistica e Filologia* 11. 1-28.
Tognini Bonelli, E. 2000b. " 'Unità Funzionali Complete' in Inglese e in Italiano: verso un Approccio Corpus-driven". In Bernardini e Zanettin (eds.), 153-175.
Tognini Bonelli, E. 2000c. "Il Corpus in Classe: da una nuova Concezione della Lingua a una Nuova Concezione della Didattica". In Favretti (ed.).
Tribble, C. and G. Jones. 1990. *Concordances in the Classroom*. Harlow: Longman.
Tsui, B.M.A. 1994. *English Conversation*. Oxford: Oxford University Press.
Valla, M. 1990. *Nomi e Aggettivi nel Processo Anaforico*. Tesi di Laurea, Università di Pavia.
Van Eynde, F., Schuurman, I. and N. Schelkens. 2000. *Computational Linguistics in the Netherlands 1998*. Amsterdam and Atlanta: Rodopi.
Ventola, E. (ed.). 1991. *Functional and Systemic Linguistics: Approaches and Uses*. Berlin and New York: Mouton de Gruyter.
Viaggio, S. 1992. "Contesting Peter Newmark". *Rivista Internazionale di Tecnica della Traduzione*. Scuola Superiore di Lingue Moderne per Interpreti e Traduttori, Università degli Studi di Trieste, Udine: Campanotto Editore, 27-58.
Ullmann, S. 1951. *The Principles of Semantics*. Oxford: Blackwell.
Ure, J. 1969. "Lexical Density and Register Differentiation". *The International Congress of Applied Linguistics*. Cambridge: Cambridge University Press. 443-52.
Weinert, R. 1995. "The Role of Formulaic Language in Second Language Acquisition". *Applied Linguistics* 16, 180-205.
Wichmann, A., Fligelstone, S., McEnery, A. and G. Knowles (eds.) 1997. *Teaching and Language Corpora*. London and New York: Longman.
Widdowson, H.G. 1991. "The Description and Prescription of Language". In J.E. Alatis (ed.) *Georgetown University Round Table on Languages and Linguistics 1991. Linguistics and Language Pedagogy: the State of the Art* . Washington D.C.: Georgetown University Press, 11-24.
Williams, R. 1976. Keywords. London: Fontana, (2nd edition: 1983).
Willis, D. 1990. *The Lexical Syllabus. A New Approach to Language Teaching*. London: Collins ELT.
Winter, E. 1982. *Towards a Contextual Grammar of English*. London: George Allen and Unwin.
Wittgenstein, L. 1921. *Tractatus Logico-Philosophicus*. London: Routledge.
Wittgenstein, L. 1953. *Philosophical Investigations*. Oxford.
Wray, A. and M.R. Perkins. 2000. "The Functions of Formulaic Language: an Integrated Model". *Language and Communication* 20, 1-28.
Zanettin, F. 1998. "Bilingual Comparable Corpora and the Training of Translators". In Laviosa (ed.), 616-630.
Zipf, G.K. 1935. *The Psychobiology of Language*. Cambridge, Mass.: MIT Press.

Appendix 1

**Concordance of *all but* from the *Economist* and the *WSJ Corpus*
55 out of a total 411 instances.**

1.	sterling 113m Dollars 180m). Forte sold	**all but 24.8 %** of its Gardner Merchant
2.	and is extended by the United States to	**all but a handful**. China has had the
3.	achieving a decent standard of living than	**all but a handful** of tribes. If they
4.	posed the heart of darkness that beats in	**all but a few** men. Those with a
5.	, Yegor Gaidar, who lifted controls on	**all but a few** goods a year ago. Peace
6.	Ababa, since the Eritreans have already	**all but achieved** independence after
7.	Ministers. Earlier this year ministers	**all but agreed** on a directive on working
8.	job less attractive. A successor would be	**all but bound** by the tax increases
9.	est user of roubles outside Russia, have	**all but broken down**. On September 18th
10.	he system for settling trade payments has	**all but broken down**, and Czech and
11.	ly the South, where fundamentalists have	**all but chased** skinny-dippers out of
12.	come over Russia. Two years ago Russia	**all but collapsed**, in post-Soviet shock
13.	te old cronies. True, public works have	**all but come to a halt** in parts of the
14.	The work of the European Commission has	**all but come to a halt**. Its often
15.	ad . But another project, Euroquote, is	**all but dead**. Euroquote, a company owne
16.	ition government, but his party is being	**all but destroyed** by corruption scandals
17.	is to survive at all. The fisheries have	**all but died** in the face of western
18.	small threat to the chief executive has	**all but disappeared**. In effect,
19.	ldiers from the Republican Guard, it was	**all but empty**, with corpses and burnt-
20.	in . Initial opposition to such tests has	**all but evaporated**. Sceptics complained
21.	has lasted longer than most. She beats	**all but five** of her predecessors since
22.	tly to cameras being banned from courts.	**All but five** states now permit cameras in
23.	nce and more sustained attention: he has	**all but forgotten** his trumpeted domestic
24.	the finance ministry off. Investors had	**all but given up hope** that the government
25.	the insurance market has made insurance	**all but impossible** for small employers to
26.	ng plant, which makes crossing varieties	**all but impossible**. To get around this,
27.	legal takeover barriers, can make them	**all but impregnable**. A rare glimpse of
28.	With the final demise of the rouble zone	**all but inevitable**, the only question
29.	ticed. Outside rural areas, co-ops remain	**all but invisible** in the United
30.	emocracy. Under Mrs Thatcher, the curse	**all but killed it**. Glorying in her
31.	he Scots and Welsh now have devolution in	**all but name** and thus a freer hand to
32.	airliners. Boeing won 53 of the orders;	**all but one** of the rest went to Europe 's
33.	are about 500 such machines now in use.	**All but one** of the companies that build
34.	unemployment no fewer than 30 times ; and	**all but one** of those changes reduced the
35.	tario prosecutor withdrew charges against	**all but one**, a former public-works
36.	st is beaten to death by five policemen,	**all but one** of them white. How does the

37.	audio-conferencing systems have shut out	**all but one** voice and it often took
38.	to their lowest level since August. In	**all but one** of the previous 13 days the
39.	he average wage earner has been higher in	**all but one** of the Tories' 15 years in
40.	nt in Zagreb the struggle for Slovenia is	**all but over**. The Yugoslav army, having
41.	some divorces " later, the census is	**all but processed**. Mr Mosbacher's ruling
42.	After the new-issue market for junk bonds	**all but shut down** in 1990, American
43.	ilies left homeless by the earthquake has	**all but stopped**, thanks to a shortage of
44.	em traced to cow manure, that algae have	**all but suffocated it**. The sawgrass,
45.	centuries, its location was a secret to	**all but the initiated**, among whom he
46.	of terminology have been known to defeat	**all but the most intrepid** amateur
47.	homosexual explosion has frightened away	**all but the boldest** of starlings , house
48.	Boer republics, denying citizenship to	**all but the racially pure**. The latest
49.	le for the UN's Dollars 410 available to	**all but the most recent arrivals**, they
50.	gether, these restrictions in effect ban	**all but the narrowest** and most commercial
51.	4m . That is still much too expensive for	**all but the wealthiest** of gadget freaks .
52.	erage real return on Japanese shares. In	**all but three** countries, equities
53.	similar experiments had been reported.	**All but two** of them found the results
54.	`Me nar move. "His Labour Party won	**all but two** of the 17 seats at the last
55.	le , their competing policies make Russia	**all but ungovernable**. The only real

Appendix 2

Exercise on *all but* from the *Economist* and *WSJ* Corpus

Familiarise yourself with the grammatical and the communicative functions of *all but*.

All but introduces an exception which is either incorporated in or distinguished from the general statement. It has two matching syntactic roles: adverb and preposition.

This exercise practices recognition of the roles and functions. In each citation in the concordance, consider the word following *all but* and decide on its grammatical and communicative function:

- If it is a past participle or an adjective, then *all but* is adverbial; check that you can interpret the exception and you can understand it as incorporated in the general statement.

- If it is a numeral or *the* introducing a superlative, then *all but* is a preposition; check that you can interpret the exception as distinguished from the general statement.

E.g.:
1. *it was all but empty*
   empty is an adjective, so *all but* is an adverb. The meaning is 'almost, practically' and the exception is incorporated in the statement.

2. *it frightened away all but the boldest of starlings*
   the introduces a superlative, so *all but* is a preposition. The meaning is 'except' and the exception is distinguished from the statement.

Appendix 3

Exercise on *except that* from the *Economist* and the *WSJ* Corpus

Familiarise yourself with the communicative function of *except that*.

Here are some *except that* clauses, which can be used to make exceptions, either **contained by** or **invalidating** the general statement. Match each clause in group A with two of the statements that follow in Group B, in one case making a containable exception, and in the other case an invalidating exception.

E.g.: ... *except that* in this case the purchase had only been made a week before.

(a) containable: The two cases were similar ..
(b) invalidating: That was fine ..

Group A.
1. .. except that it hurts when you fall.
2. .. except that they are Labour MPs.
3. .. except that the matter is now out of their hands.
4. .. except that the exchange rate is fixed.
5. .. except that it uses a beam of protons instead of electrons.
6. .. except that it was rejected last year by the UN.

Group B.
1. The previous policy was rather similar ..
2. That is all fine by the Bundesbank ..
3. Snowboarding is more like surfing ..
4. That was a good idea ..
5. This deal is the same as the one above ..
6. The problem is the same as before ..
7. Nothing odd about them getting together ..
8. It's a great way of getting exercise ..
9. This delegation is identical to the last one ..
10. The nuclear microscope is similar to EPMA ..
11. It could be a good investment ..
12. It would have passed the safety test ..

Appendix 4

Concordance of *proper* (Attributive use) from the BBC corpus
55 out of a total 631 instances

1. Baghdad, **has not been given** full and **proper** access. Diplomats say the UN was
2. broke its own laws by **not** keeping **proper** accounts. There are also reports
3. feel that Japan **had still not** made a **proper** apology for occupying their
4. **pressure** on fellow employers to make **proper** assessments of their employees'
5. and he **urged** the government to pay **proper** attention to the findings of the
6. to go to war at all **you must be** a **proper** authority to use force, you must
7. **What we have to do** is look at a **proper** balance of the problem, set against
8. tactic or he really **wants** a **proper** border worked out and marked at
9. **rather than providing** what it calls **proper** child care facilities or decent
10. by private investment, for which the **proper** climate **is now to be created**. Mr
11. say this is because this snail under **proper** conditions **will** produce 250 young a
12. humanitarian gesture **would be given** **proper** consideration in future relations
13. he **believed it was only fair to give** **proper** consideration to the public's
14. the major industrial powers **without** **proper** consultation. The warning coincided
15. BBC has said that **it would exercise** **proper** discretion in reporting an
16. airlines who bring in people **without** **proper** documentation. Amnesty says that
17. was going to fine Egyptians **without** **proper** documents were also denied.
18. **wants to see** clean water supplies, **proper** drains; it wants less death among
19. price increases **without** giving any **proper** economic justification for them, or
20. and excise that they made all **proper** enquiries both to the company
21. **failure** of ministers to work out a **proper** financial strategy for higher
22. it was an unloaded airgun **without** a **proper** firing system. An invesigation into
23. I've even known people to go **without** **proper** food for themselves and their
24. which are **necessary** for the **proper** functioning of the organs. So
25. meeting, he too is **anxious to get** **proper** guarantees, as he sees it, that the
26. existence, but no newspapers, **no** **proper** hierarchy structure, no freedom to
27. of what is really **needed to provide** **proper** homes for homeless people. In
28. verification procedures to **ensure** **proper** implemtation of the agreement.
29. and beat up students - is **not** how a **proper** law-abiding government should
30. were just accused of **not holding** **proper** legal documents while almost two
31. arms through Greece **without** a **proper** license. Although Mr Ashwell has
32. more information is needed to **ensure** **proper** management and efficiency. One of
33. sought to **prevent or delay** the **proper** market response, nor insulated the
34. for allegedly **failing to provide** **proper** medical aid for the chief justice
35. prisons, including **lack of** food and **proper** medicine, interference with family
36. with the Germans, or **how can he have** **proper** meetings with the Commissioners,

37.	series of measures to **try and ensure**	**proper** monitoring, such as special flights
38.	which surround nerves. **Without**	**proper** myelin insulation, the signals
39.	and elsewhere who have **never** enjoyed	**proper** nation state status, and now want
40.	announcement **is no substitute for** a	**proper** national housing policy: We were
41.	irregularity was **the absence** of a	**proper** passenger list in Oslo, the port of
42.	she said, there was **no chance of**	**proper** peace. Without East Jerusalem, she
43.	**the quicker things were put in their**	**proper** place, **the better it would be** for
44.	children to be in **what he calls** the	**proper** place - the playground or the
45.	had happened **too quickly for**	**proper** planning to have been done. For his
46.	been performed had **not** followed the	**proper** procedures for staging it. But
47.	for five years **was adamant that**	**proper** procedures had been followed. He
48.	Bhatia, reports that **the lack of**	**proper** rescue equipment is hampering
49.	standards of **what the West sees as**	**proper** respect for human rights. But the
50.	have **a duty** to the taxpayer **to get** a	**proper** return from the same of the
51.	principle, as if the state had **no**	**proper** role at all in a democratic
52.	be a final solution, that is **not** a	**proper** solution. The Chinese can easily
53.	anxious to slow things down **so that**	**proper** stock can be taken of the
54.	games - **what Davies described as** a `	**proper** thrashing". The others to fall were
55.	imprisonment for staying **without**	**proper** travel documents. He was arrested a

Appendix 5

Concordance of *Andare incontro* from the Italian Corpus
49 instances in total

1. che venivano a trovarlo. **Andammo incontro alle signore**, una delle quali
2. uno dei miei parenti. **Andiamogli incontro.** La Regina, che era sempre pronta
3. metà la frase sui gravitoni. **Andò incontro a Gilda** nel giardino, disse sorridendo
4. tutto **l'incomodo a cui stava andando incontro**, prese la decisione di andare a
5. ate attività specifiche senza **andare incontro a fenomeni di radiolisi**. Altri ti
6. fantasia: e ciò proprio per **andare incontro alle sempre più variegate sfumature**
7. secondo il suo modello, **andare incontro al successo, oppure alla corruzione**
8. giovani per parte loro possono **andare incontro ad altri inconvenienti**, di natura
9. raddoppiare la probabilità di **andare incontro a un aborto spontaneo**. La notizia
10. ed il paziente rischia di **andare incontro ad effetti collaterali** indesiderat
11. anche le rimaste **non debbano andare incontro ad un analogo restauro**, con la lu
12. istenti, le altre dovrebbero **andare incontro a lisi**. Metodologie Produzione di
13. so tutta la notte . Non per **andargli incontro**, ma affinché la vedesse scappare
14. cora fuori. Lo so. **Voglio andargli incontro** per un pezzo di strada. Non ti sc
15. Ma anche ora i ricercatori **andarono incontro a una delusione**: le installazioni
16. arma . Ma era Hombre. **Si andarono incontro da amici**, da fratelli. Intanto s
17. edifici, che nel tempo **sono andati incontro a vicende tanto differenti**, conti
18. tuto prevedere **a cosa saremmo andati incontro**. Fra lo svolazzare delle gazze qu
19. non le apparteneva. **Le sono andato incontro** e la donna mi ha abbracciato."
20. ci assicura che non **sarebbe andato incontro a sofferenze peggiori**?". S'in
21. degli **insuccessi a cui Freud è andato incontro** ogni volta che ha cercato" di por
22. ano dimostrato **a quali rischi andava incontro** la monocoltura: soggetta alla osc
23. lui, **proprio perché diverso andava incontro**. L'avranno provata sì una bella
24. e **il tipo di reazioni cui andavano incontro**. La genetica affrontò invece, co
25. Mimì. **La perdizione a cui andiamo incontro**. Guarda lui, indicò Mimì: Sembr
26. almente". **A cosa pensa che andremo incontro in campo musicale**? "Secondo me,
27. Christine posò la valigia e **gli andò incontro**. "Tesoro. "Damon l'abbracciò
28. il segretario dc si alzò e **gli andò incontro**. "Allora la tua candidatura sarà
29. di aprir bocca. Si alzò e **le andò incontro** con le braccia tese. "Cara Matil
30. la nostra strada, **erano andate loro incontro** con le braccia cariche dei
31. lli d'animali. Giuseppe **andò loro incontro**, chiese ospitalità e se volevano
32. ucarioti l'm - RNA ottenuto **va ora incontro ad alcune modificazioni molecolari**
33. della tosse. I fumatori **vanno spesso incontro a una tosse cronica**, così come i
34. personal, occorre ricordare che **si va incontro a obsolescenza** a un ritmo assai più
35. regione del cromosoma Y che non **va incontro a ricombinazione meiotica**.
36. di ridurre **le modificazioni cui va incontro** il mezzo di coltura, e i tossici

37.	anno, meglio sapere **a cosa si va incontro**. Sarà un tipo generoso, spesso
38.	re di un personaggio centrale che **va incontro al fallimento** e all'autodistruzione
39.	**rifiuti cui il futurismo marinettiano va incontro**: anzi ne rappresenta una variante
40.	, che non si prepara, e che **va incontro alla probabile bocciatura**, né lo
41.	ne che corre e la Piulott che **gli va incontro** per strappargli di bocca l'anima
42.	ed è il caso più frequente) chi **va incontro a una bocciatura**. Ebbene, il
43.	ipendente e se decide di smettere **va incontro a una serie nutrita di sintomi** spi
44.	è tanto più notevole quanto più **va incontro a bisogni ancestrali dell'uomo**
45.	veri e propri ammortizzatori, **vada incontro ad un processo degenerativo**. Il
46.	tridimensionale cui le # hp - **vanno incontro**, nella varie condizioni sperimentali
47.	invece di subire la vita, **vanno incontro alle difficoltà** il divenire storico
48.	**la rapida disidratazione a cui vanno incontro**, e il ricovero in ospedale si impone
49.	le in fase di differenziamento **vanno incontro a significativi cambiamenti** morfol

Appendix 6

Concordance of *in the case of* **from the** *Birmingham Corpus*
50 instances out of a total 550

1. of subsidies can be illustrated **in the case of** Australia, where the est
2. equal rights for feminine emotion (or, **in the case of** Bhagwan followers,
3. fantasy in some cases than in others. **in the case of** Doris Lessing, at least
4. on shifts in values. As we shall see **in the case of** London's motorways, the
5. natives, friendly or otherwise. As **in the case of** Mars, however, writers
6. with any of Mao's henchmen, as he did **in the case of** Mikoyan, whom he had met
7. out it. It is possible to suggest that **in the case of** Mouldy you have saved a
8. of Britain are ground down, and how **in the case of** Mr Wodehouse, the
9. time she must spend with her husban; **in the case of** Mrs. White, this need
10. period is likely to be lengthier than **in the case of** Spain, because of the we
11. music that can be transmitted (50 %, **in the case of** ``independent'' stations
12. about the type of burial place. **In the case of** a reasonably well-to-do
13. hat of human beings, or whether, **in the case of** animals as young as Mij
14. , but may be as long as 50 years. **In the case of** asbestos, for example ,
15. at error elimination (EE); and as **in the case of** dialectic, this process
16. close to the one we obtained earlier **in the case of** elite succession among
17. throughout childhood. The answer **in the case of** evaporated milk. The
18. end in itself. This is especially so **in the case of** experiments which can
19. the situation is more complex than **in the case of** gases. The comparative
20. adult males and adult females, but **in the case of** hair-touching there is a
21. on the front and rear of the 2. **In the case of** motor cars or vans , the
22. development; and sometimes we need 1 **in the case of** my own music I know
23. aterials is also important. Generally **in the case of** non-renewable energies
24. York and tokyo do it for them. Except **in the case of** oil, and to some extent
25. circulation. A similar pattern emerges **in the case of** other leading radical
26. to have felt drawn from him, as **in the case of** our now-familiar woman
27. onto someone else (onto a doctor **in the case of** physical illness).
28. even a reasonable thing to assume; and **in the case of** relatively minor ills,
29. om others to complicate their illness. **In the case of** scarlet fever,
30. embody the single national interest. **In the case of** the NF this programme
31. Government might be involved, as **in the case of** the Groundnut Scheme,
32. were largely local authorities), **in the case of** the railways (which acco
33. believe still to exist did assemble. **In the case of** the Democrats it was
34. awakening of enlightened optimism **in the case of** the Liberals, and the
35. allowed myself to break this rule **in the case of** the USSR - the data
36. an expert witness on the truth drug **in the case of** the Boston strangler.

37.	trying out journalistic assignment.	**In the case of** the latter, you go with
38.	consider social and related factors:	**in the case of** the first canvas-sailed
39.	as the decisions might have been	**in the case of** the Comedie Francaise,
40.	children and primitive artists, but	**in the case of** the caricaturist the
41.	means of transforming their society.	**In the case of** the Americans the
42.	' The thing has a good hard grip and,	**in the case of** the child, distress
43.	without distinction - with some reason	**in the case of** the first film when it
44.	not be able to perform efficiently.	**In the case of** the distance runner
45.	which this ethis energy is used in.	**in the case of** the Sudan with its
46.	. It is not a sufficient answer that	**in the case of** the automobile one
47.	and then offer a few brief comments.	**In the case of** the first two
48.	cause and effect; and often, as	**in the case of** the 'social " motives
49.	lationary effects on the money supply.	**In the case of** the private sector,
50.	which people are prepared to accept	**in the case of** war or political unrest.

Appendix 7

Concordance of *nel caso di/del/della* etc. from the Italian Corpus
50 out of a total 319 instances

1. significato resta oscuro, come **nel caso degli** obelischi di Biblo (inizio
2. analogamente a quanto si verificava **nel caso degli** organismi viventi e dei
3. spersione del segnale risultante) **nel caso degli** algoritmi a massima potenz
4. peggiorativa, come, per esempio, **nel caso degli** "homines novi", uomini
5. ambienti simulanti l' acqua di mare **nel caso degli** acciai superferritici e le
6. supportare i nuovi software come **nel caso degli** elaboratori di terza
7. ambienti dell'industria alimentare **nel caso degli** acciai inox ferritici ELI
8. dell'effetto del rumore termico) **nel caso degli** algoritmi a minima
9. formaggio. Diverso è il discorso **nel caso dei** bambini. Poiché il loro
10. in passato, sulla Terra, **nel caso dei** giannizzeri: bambini che i
11. il contributo specifico, come **nel caso dei** volumi del Torcia - Santoli e
12. crescendo a trovare, tranne che **nel caso dei** comunisti, un terreno di
13. vanno tenute presenti soprattutto **nel caso dei** bambini. Una di queste è
14. fino a 0 @ grammi per litro **nel caso dei** vini passiti. Tannino, fino
15. introdurre al suo interno (come **nel caso dei** bagni). Lo spessore totale
16. ai suoi seguaci. A rafforzarla **nel caso dei** cristiani dovettero
17. di autenticazione; che è minore **nel caso del** narratore - personaggio o del
18. si riproduce, altre volte come **nel caso del** terzo sonetto vediamo
19. lano ogni tipo di discorso e che, **nel caso del** romanzo, finirebbero per
20. un argomento allora di attualità **nel caso del** l'arte "decadente", nel
21. anche ultimamente, se si vuole, **nel caso del** Banco Ambrosiano. Da ultimo
22. sono particolarmente importanti **nel caso del** glutatione, (GSH), per il
23. la collaborazione del paziente: **nel caso del** fumo, deve voler smettere.
24. mano in potenziali, per paura **nel caso del** pozzo, per vendetta in
25. non lo aveva consentito : come **nel caso del** sacerdote Pietro Roscitano,
26. essivo supporre un dividendo nullo **nel caso del** verificarsi di a i . Quando
27. tonalità semantica dei verbi, che **nel caso del** motto attribuiscono
28. Roma); altre volte invece, come **nel caso del** pregevole progetto di
29. dell' arte "decadente", **nel caso della** decadenza nobiliare)
30. l'approccio più diretto, almeno **nel caso del** carcinoma midollare della
31. rotetto penalmente; per esempio, **nel caso del** segreto di stato (su
32. intervento scientifico - tecnico **nel caso del** Mezzogiorno.
34. olidaristiche e corporative: come **nel caso del** "Lord Spleen" di Giovanni
35. truttura mitico - letteraria, che **nel caso del** romanzo di Bulgakov è data
36. del tempo quantico (per esempio, **nel caso dell'**analisi dell' ammortamento,
37. negli anni successivi. Anche **nel caso dell'**Iraq il petrolio è ormai

38.	solo, alcune sono armate, come	**nel caso dell'**inglese Ariel, che sul
39.	articolare essi hanno scoperto che	**nel caso dell'**amminoacido alanina questo
40.	influsso negativo anche sul corpo;	**nel caso dell'**ansiolitico si parte dalla
41.	rambe le eventualità si presentano	**nel caso dell'** Orlando furioso,
42.	terazione di metodologie EBL e SBL	**nel caso dell'**apprendimento incrementale.
43.	elati e così via ritroviamo, come	**nel caso della** zoppaggine, un' esperienza
44.	slavo le unità italiane e, come	**nel caso della** brigata Osoppo, non si
45.	risultati già ottenuti mostrano che	**nel caso della** "benzoilpiridina
46.	precisa, un fattore determinante	**nel caso della** trasmissione dati. La prima
47.	primitiva si nota particolarmente	**nel caso della** Cina, in cui l'opposizione
48.	informazioni di tipo diagnostico	**nel caso della** patologia neoplastica
49.	queste ed altre correlazioni anche	**nel caso della** DNA ligasi umana. Avendo
50.	uali DDC (dietilditiocarbammato)	**nel caso della** nitrito - riduttasi.

Appendix 8

Concordance of *in case of* from the Birmingham Corpus
45 out of a total 56 instances

1.	We were only on the first floor	**in case of a fire** happening. Lally said she
2.	recommended in case of emergency.	**In case of a burn**, phone the doctor for ins
3.	man being, and I wanted to be sure	**in case of a sudden emergency** that we gave
4.	always put him in the back seat	**in case of accident**.``Goodbye , goodbye ,
5.	ever. This will minimize your loss	**in case of accident or theft**. One pound
6.	torian lady embarrassingly exposed	**in case of accidents**, closed underpants wer
7.	ur later. It was understood that,	**in case of an urgent telegram**, Davis or him
8.	encircling Mardan to give warning	**in case of an attack**, but knowing the preci
9.	ust stay here. I've got to - just	**in case of anything** - and I must see Moses
10.	floor where the chiefs lived, but	**in case of attack** there were three others no
11.	of milk, a jar of pureed prunes	**in case of constipation**. Other tips.
12.	tropical sun and, perhaps, refuge	**in case of danger** from predators. Fresh wate
13.	groups who join in the lobby but	**in case of difficulty** contact one ofthe main
14.	and helmet. `I was only helping	**in case of distress**. I'll be in touch. Be
15.	contact the mother during the day	**in case of emergency**. The quality of care
16.	ahead of time what is recommended	**in case of emergency**. In case of a burn,
17.	with his headless department	**in case of emergency**. But, amazingly enoug
18.	mast and sail were constructed	**in case of engine failure**. There were Ort
19.	, 1 , . . . 9 , as a trial and,	**in case of error**, one of the remaining nine
20.	Location of means of escape	**in case of fire** 12. Location of water stop
21.	community just to replace a house	**in case of fire**. This is also thought to di
22.	the place up kept an eye on it	**in case of further vandalism** or moves from `
23.	sustain a paramilitary capability	**in case of general war**. These operations se
24.	muzzle-loader, already loaded,	**in case of immediate need**, powder-horn and
25.	it in polythene kitchen wrap	**in case of involuntary incontinence**, and at
26.	eparate from your cheques so that	**in case of loss** you will be able to give thi
27.	be there to pick up the pieces	**in case of massive calamity**. Such communitie
28.	er not. One of us should be here,	**in case of more Lady Alices**, don't you
29.	they had engaged to let him have	**in case of need** and requested them to send h
30.	essential, to have some support	**in case of overbalancing**. First, each le
31.	of assistance he could render	**in case of peering demons** and milkbottles of
32.	your waistband before the race	**in case of problems**! Prior to the race stay
33.	leopard, avoiding the milking shed	**in case of further questioning** but not
34.	would be a valuable stand-by	**in case of renewed difficulty** with Margaret
35.	the lads being keen to stock up	**in case of shortages** in either department on
36.	a sweater and a light raincoat	**in case of showers**. If you arrive during

37.	don't ," and closed her eyes	**in case of something terrible**. Nothing fata
38.	orders that had been given to him	**in case of the ultimate emergency**, he would
39.	the assistance of the police	**in case of resistance** to a civil commitment
40.	Under-ripe berries were preferred	**in case of transport hold-ups**, and were
41.	But they thought it just as well,	**in case of trouble**, that you believed . . .
42.	. It is a means of identification	**in case of trouble**, and when you sign on a
43.	that had been waiting nearby	**in case of trouble** saved the Indian police.
44.	the Second International, policy	**in case of war** had been exhaustively discuss
45.	his financial needs may be less	**in case of your death**, he could consider a

Appendix 9

Concordance of *in caso di* from the Italian Corpus
50 instances out of a total 83.

1.	rtamento della rete, di salvaguardarla	**in caso di afferrature** e di memorizzare
2.	Qui, al centro del canale di Sicilia,	**in caso di allarme** o di aumento della
3.	può porre difficoltà insuperabili	**in caso di baratto diretto o indiretto**
4.	grandi che erano caduti insieme, e che	**in caso di bisogno** ci sarebbero bastati
5.	che evita il bloccaggio delle ruote	**in caso di brusca frenata**. Un' altra
6.	inizio i molti tuffi fuori programma.	**In caso di caduta** un dispositivo
7.	sporre l'intervento dell'esercito.	**In caso di calamità naturali** dirige e
8.	un ciclo di # 0 @ massaggi soprattutto	**in caso di cellulite giovane**. Occhio al
9.	secondo un certo ordine e in modo che	**in caso di conflitto** (per esempio sulla
10.	diritto scritto (contra legem).Quindi	**in caso di contrasto** tra una norma consu
11.	ricordare alcune di queste regole:	**in caso di controversie** riguardanti la
12.	generale con un accurato check-up:	**in caso di debolezza organica**, i capelli
13.	rico; interrompe l'energia elettrica	**in caso di dispersione** o folgorazione.
14.	intesa fra loro e a rispettarla anche	**in caso di dissenso**. Il sindacato, per
15.	con me Trier dalle zampe storte, e	**in caso di disubbidienza** dei colpi di
16.	di interessi davanti alle Camere.	**In caso di dubbio**, la Corte decide di
17.	si erano impegnati alla reperibilità	**in caso di emergenze**". Ma perché questo
18.	di un cronogramma di attività.	**In caso di eruzione** si procederà ad un
19.	alto nel senso della circolazione. E	**in caso di esposizione ai primi raggi del sole**
20.	co e l'analisi degli effetti al suolo	**in caso di eventi significativi** nell'a
21.	reincrocio col genitore ricorrente o	**in caso di fenomeni di autoincompatibilità**
22.	comitato ne valuta la legittimità e,	**in caso di giudizio negativo**, li annulli
23.	questa castagna e non aprirla se non	**in caso di gran necessità**. Cammina camm
24.	prorogata se non per legge e soltanto	**in caso di guerra**. ART8. Le elezioni
25.	: riguarda l'arruolamento volontario	**in caso di guerra**. A sedici anni Giovan
26.	non può essere prorogata se non	**in caso di guerra**. Il motivo per cui la
27.	esercitate dal Presidente del Senato.	**In caso di impedimento permanente** o di m
28.	avrebbe preso e come le avrebbe usate	**in caso di incendio**. Accennava i movime
29.	ssero più pericolose di quelle grandi	**in caso di incidenti a catena** a velocità
30.	adeguati alle loro esigenze di vita	**in caso di infortunio**, malattia, invalidità
31.	Un po' di ciccia ci vuole, aiuta	**in caso di malattie**. Una fidanzata, ec
32.	cento nell'anno di espropriazione.	**In caso di mancato completamento** delle o
33.	pilessia che garantisce una copertura	**in caso di morte** o invalidità permanente
34.	essere giustamente scortati, aiutati	**in caso di necessità**, e tenuti
35.	cora ghiacciato, salvo lungo la riva;	**in caso di necessità** avrei potuto lavarm
36.	odologico, e cioè l'autorizzazione,	**in caso di necessità**, a convocare sussi

37.	retta fino al limitare del bosco dove	**in caso di necessità** sarei potuta sali
38.	grande specchio completa l'insieme.	**In caso di necessità** si può pensare a un
39.	dovrà essere garantito il suo arresto	**in caso di operazioni che esulano** dal pr
40.	protezione non può ovviamente agire	**in caso di panne** del cliente di Hallo se
41.	ova ricordare che il sistema bancario	**in caso di riduzione del personale**, non
42.	azione all'interno di una glove-box	**in caso di rilascio accidentale**. Verran
43.	io di sostanze inquinanti e nutrienti	**in caso di risospensione del sedimento** c
44.	ualcosa di reale e di osservabile? E	**in caso di risposta negativa**, a quale p
45.	aprile cadde presto in disuso giacché	**in caso di siccità** l'erogazione veniva
46.	diretto della compagnia assicuratrice	**in caso di sopravvenienza di malattia**
47.	principio è valido comunque, per cui,	**in caso di squilibrio**, il fluido elettr
48.	te nell' adulto ma che può riapparire	**in caso di stati neoplastici**. È riconos
49.	con Mitterrand alla presidenza poiché	**in caso di successo** non sarebbe" né ser
50.	meglio avere i capelli super-puliti.	**In caso di un invito ultimo - momento**,

INDEX

A
Aarts J.
    corpus definition 53
    intuition-based and observation-based grammars 69ff
    language use 52
    language variation 67
all but 25-29
anaphora resolution 70
andare incontro 113-116
annotation 71-74, 90
any 15-17, 65
artificiality 80-81
authenticity 55, 79
Atkins, S.
    corpus definition 53

B
bel 120-123
bello/bella 125ff
Berry R. 15, 66
Biber D.
    representativeness 57, 59ff
    sampling 59-62
    text-types 59-60
Bloomfield L. 170
    connotation 171
Bod R.
    statistical approach 58-59
    data-oriented parsing 70
Botley, S.
    anaphora 70
Bréal M. 166-167
broadly vs.largely 33-39
build up 113

C
carriera 126ff
changing roles (teaching) 43ff

Chomsky N. 173-175
    on corpus work 50, 51ff
Clear, J.
    corpus definition 53
    software 13
    stereotyping 101-102
Cobuild 85
co-selection 101, 106, 123, 128
collocation 5, 19, 89, 162
    and equivalence 150ff
collocational frameworks 105
colligation 5, 19, 89, 163
communicative grammar 29-33
competence vs. performance 68ff, 174
comparable corpora 6-7, 133-134
concordance
    KWICK 2-3, 13
    reading 3, 18, 41-42, 89, 98
connotation 171
    see also semantic prosody, Louw
context and co-text 87, 158-159
contextual theory of meaning 4-5, 14, 88ff, 157-164
contrastive linguistics 131-156
corpus
    definitions 2, 52ff
    vs. text 2-3, 116
    issues 47-64
        authenticity 55
        function 54
        representativeness 57-59, 78-79
        sampling 59-62
corpus-based approach 10-11, 17, 65-83,
corpus-driven approach 11, 17, 84-100,
    item/environment 101-130
    methodology 91
    word/lemma association 92-98
corpus-driven Linguistics 177-186
    categories 179

goals 177-178
  methodology 178-179
  standpoint 178
corpora
  monolingual
    Bank of English 12, 62, 90
    BBC corpus 12, 90
    Birmingham corpus 12
    BNC (British National Corpus) 54, 90,124
    Brown corpus 62
    corpus of contemporary Italian 12
    Economist corpus 12
    general purpose corpora 9
    ICE corpus 7-8, 62, 90
    learner corpora 9
    LOB corpus 62
    LSP corpora 8
    special corpora 8
    Survey of English Usage 52, 56, 62
    training corpus 72
    test corpus 72
    Wall Street Journal corpus 12
  multilingual 6-7
    comparable 6-7, 133-134
    free-translation 6-7
    parallel 6-7, 133
    translation 133, 134
    alignment 6, 7

D
data-driven learning 44
decline 92
delexicalisation 106, 116-123, 148, *see also* co-selection
delexical chunks 117
dichotomies
  competence/performance 68ff, 174
  langue/parole 98-99
disambiguation 25-29
discovery procedures 41ff
donna 125

E
educate 92-93
empirical approach 2ff
enrichment 72

equivalence
  and collocation 150ff
  functional equivalence 131,134, 150-151, 154
examples
  artificiality 80-81
  authenticity 55, 79
  feasibility 80
except that 29-33
extended units of meaning 18ff, 103-110
  definition 18-25
  disambiguation 25-29
  communicative grammar 29-33
  synonyms 33-39

F
facing/faced 93-96
false friends 33-39
fickle vs. flexible 18-25
Firth J.R. 4-5, 157-164
  context of situation 158-159
    see also collocation, colligation
  culture and ideology 123
  focal words 124, *see also* key words
  lexical and grammatical patterns 77
  selection of facts 85
  repeated events 88ff, 157
focusing adjectives 118ff, 148
form and meaning 99
Francis, N.
  corpus definition 53
Francis, G.
  artificiality of examples 80-81
  lexical grammar 105
  lexical phrases 102
  pattern grammar 77, 90
frequency of occurrence 89
function (of a corpus) 54-55
functionally-complete units of meaning 106, 110, 131ff, 154-155
functional equivalence 131, 134, 154
  and collocation 150

G
generalisability 78-79
genre 59
grammar

INDEX

communicative grammar 29-33
formal grammar 173-176
intuition-based and observation based grammars 69ff
lexis and grammar 76ff
lexical grammar 90, 105
lexicogrammar, *see* Halliday
pattern grammar 77, 90

H
Halliday M.A.K. 74-77
lexis and grammar 76ff
paradigmatic approach 74-75
probabilistic approach 74ff
functional equivalence 131
Harris, Z. 171-173
discourse 172
distributional analysis 172
Hunston, S.
pattern grammar 77, 90
lexical phrases 102
Hjelmslev J.
manifestable/manifested 78

I
in (the) case (of) 136-144
in (nel) caso di 136-144
ideology 123-128
inductive methodology 2, 14, 44, 91
internal criteria 61, 88
instantiation 74-77
insulation 68-71, 79
intuition 91
item/environment 101-130

J
Johns, T. 44

K
Kennedy G.
language description 86
keep 102, *see also* Clear
keywords 124-125
see also focal words, Firth, Stubbs

L
language teaching 14-46,

language use
empirical approach 2ff
the problem of 56, 78, *see also* Aarts
artificial examples of 81
langue/parole 98-99, 159, 167-169
largely
translation equivalence 151-154
vs. *broadly* 33-39
Leech G.
corpus annotation 71ff
corpus linguistics 52
methodology 47ff
representativeness 139
standardisation 71ff
test corpus 72
training corpus 72
lexical grammar,
see grammar, pattern grammar
lexical phrases 102
lexical syllabus 40-41
lexicogrammar, *see* Halliday
lexis
lexis and grammar 76ff
see also lexical grammar, lexicogrammar, pattern grammar, lexical syllabus
linguistic criteria
see internal criteria; corpus sampling
Louw, W.E.
collocation and genre 88
semantic prosody 111-113
insincerity 112
irony 112

M
May Fan
delexical chunks 117
McEnery, T.
corpus of abuse 54
anaphora 70
meaning
extended units of 18-39
historical landmarks 165-176
Mindt, D. 91

N
naked eye 104-106
new technologies 5-6

INDEX

O
observable data 51, 52, 69, 157

P
parole 86, 98-99, 159
pattern, definition 90
pattern grammar 77, 90
performance 70
paradigmatic approach 75
    paradigmatic vs syntagmatic 76
pivotal words
    see focal words, keywords, Firth
pretty 124
proper 106-110

Q
qualitative change 1, 48ff, 86, 91

R
real
    delexicalisation 118-120
    translation equivalence 144-149
reale
    translation equivalence 144-149
register 59ff
repeated events 88ff, 159-160
    formalisation of 89
    see also Firth; repetition
repetition 41-42, 88-89, 124, 159-160,
    see also Firth, Stubbs
report
    as distancing device 108
    in translation 132
representativeness 57-59, 78-79, 88, 139
Rissanen, M. 123

S
sampling 59-62
Sampson, G. 87
Saussure, F. de 167-170
sapere/saper 96-98
se per caso 142-144
selective adjectives 119ff
semantic preference 19ff, 105, 138
semantic prosody 19ff, 105, 111-116, 138-139
Sinclair J.
    annotation 73

Cobuild 85
corpus definition 53
corpus evidence 50
degeneralisation 135
delexicalisation 113ff
    see also co-selection
focusing/selective adjectives 119ff
    see also delexicalisation
form and meaning 99
idiom principle
    see phraseological tendency
naked eye 105
open choice principle,
    see terminological tendency
parallel corpora 133
phraseological tendency 104, 123
pre-corpus beliefs 86
semantic prosody 111
terminological tendency 104
translation equivalence 150-151
units of meaning 18ff, 103-106
word/lemma association 92-98
situational criteria,
    see internal criteria; corpus sampling
software 13
standardisation 71-74,
stereotyping 101-102, *see also* co-selection
structuralism
    European, *see* Saussure
    American, *see* Bloomfield, Zelig Harris
Stubbs, M.
    semantic prosody 112
    keywords 124-125
    repetition 124ff
Survey of English Usage 52, 56, 62
syllabus design 40-41
synonyms 33-39
systemic school *see* Halliday
Swales, J. 62

T
take a photograph 116,
    see also delexicalisation
take a decision 116,
    see also delexicalisation
text types 59ff,
    see also Biber, representativeness

Teubert, W. 124
Tognini Bonelli, E.
    functionally-complete units of meaning
        106, 110, 131ff
    translation 132-156
        equivalence 134ff
    translation corpora 133

U
unidirectionality 66
unit of currency 1, 18, 90-91, 128
unit of meaning 19, 101
    vs. unit of translation 133
    see also extended units of meaning, Sinclair
unit of translation 133

V
variation 6, 39, 43, 67,

W
Widdowson H.
    feasibility 80
whole texts 62
word/lemma association 92-98

In the series STUDIES IN CORPUS LINGUISTICS (SCL) the following titles have been published thus far:

1. PEARSON, Jennifer: *Terms in Context*. 1998.
2. PARTINGTON, Alan: *Patterns and Meanings. Using corpora for English language research and teaching*. 1998.
3. BOTLEY, Simon and Anthony Mark McENERY (eds.): *Corpus-based and Computational Approaches to Discourse Anaphora*. 2000.
4. HUNSTON, Susan and Gill FRANCIS: *Pattern Grammar. A corpus-driven approach to the lexical grammar of English*. 2000.
5. GHADESSY, Mohsen, Alex HENRY and Robert L. ROSEBERRY (eds.): *Small Corpus Studies and ELT. Theory and practice*. n.y.p.
6. TOGNINI-BONELLI, Elena: *Corpus Linguistics at Work*. 2001.